Radical Theologies and Philosophies

Series Editors
Michael Grimshaw
Department of Sociology
University of Canterbury
Christchurch, New Zealand

Michael Zbaraschuk
Pacific Lutheran University
Tacoma, WA, USA

Joshua Ramey
Grinnell College
Grinnell, IA, USA

Radical Theologies and Philosophies is a call for transformational theologies that break out of traditional locations and approaches. The rhizomic ethos of radical theologies enable the series to engage with an ever-expanding radical expression and critique of theologies that have entered or seek to enter the public sphere, arising from the continued turn to religion and especially radical theology in politics, social sciences, philosophy, theory, cultural, and literary studies. The post-theistic theology both driving and arising from these intersections is the focus of this series.

More information about this series at
http://www.palgrave.com/gp/series/14521

Bojan Koltaj

Žižek Reading Bonhoeffer

Towards a Radical Critical Theology

Bojan Koltaj
Canterbury Christ Church University
Canterbury, UK

Radical Theologies and Philosophies
ISBN 978-3-030-26093-4   ISBN 978-3-030-26094-1   (eBook)
https://doi.org/10.1007/978-3-030-26094-1

This Palgrave Macmillan imprint is published by the registered company Springer Nature
Switzerland AG
The registered company address is: Gewerbestrasse 11, 6330 Cham, Switzerland

To Mateja
Zelo, zelo…

PREFACE

Since my return to studies as a mature student, I have been reading the queen of sciences as the critical constant in pursuit of knowledge. Whether conspicuous or concealed, ostentatious or reserved, decisive or tentative, it unquestionably persists in reflection across a myriad of milieus. One of the many that drew my attention—and I do not purport to be a master of any—were its materialist incarnations full of daring and exciting contemplations. Originally my doctoral thesis, the book before the reader is an attempt to appropriate them in pursuit of a theology that wants to learn just as Aquinas wanted to learn from Arab philosophy. Its translation into a manuscript has in no small way been a journey of remembering the grounding and elan of my research into materialist theology.

Canterbury, UK   Bojan Koltaj
June 2019

ACKNOWLEDGEMENTS

I should like to thank a few people: Stephen N. Williams who first encouraged me to undertake this project, Ralph Norman who supervised the doctoral thesis, Ward Blanton and Andrew Hass, who advised me to turn it into a book, and the editorial team at Palgrave Macmillan who made it happen. Last but not least, Slavoj Žižek for his afterword—hvala!

Part of the introduction was first published in *International Journal of Theology and Philosophy* (January 2019), under the title, 'Critical Theology: Why Hegel Now?'. It is reprinted here with the permission of the journal, available here: https://doi.org/10.1080/21692327.2019.1 581654.

Contents

CHAPTER 1

Introduction

REFLECTION ON THEOLOGICAL THOUGHT

This book is concerned with reflection on (the act) content and implications of theological thought. Any activity of reflection upon thought, despite attempts to define it or at least deliberate its limits, is never undertaken in isolation but always in the company of its varied and challenging contemplative contexts. Any act of contemplation then, including theological, willingly or not, necessarily and ontologically, traverses the erected boundaries of its neighbours but also encounters its own. As 'thought takes on flesh' in each new environment, theological thought challenges that environment but also brings forth its own cultivation, enabling a deeper or further grasping of (previously considered) theological concepts. Rather than envisaging or understanding this process as a contestation and necessary correction of thought, it is to be viewed as an incarnation or deeper revelation of theological truth (in full flesh). It is thus in the new context, that a fuller understanding of theological thought emerges—a realisation of the magnitude or potential of theological concepts and how their revelation stretches our contextually conditioned understandings of them and the lim-

---

This chapter is derived in part from my article 'Critical Theology: Why Hegel Now?' published in the *International Journal of Philosophy and Theology* (February 2019), available online https://doi.org/10.1080/21692327.2019.1581654.

its that we have erected. This often unsettling but also liberating experience of the development of theological thought challenges our understanding thereof—our presuppositions of what it is to think theologically and our methods for carrying that out.

   This book attempts to do just that—tease out the assumptions of theological thought and their implications in engagement with its contemplative context. It will show how holding on to these presuppositions is problematic—they predetermine the outcome of reflection. Indeed, any such reflection upon thought, whatever the context in which it takes place, results only in their affirmation. As such, it does not allow for a truly critical engagement with its reflective context and is restricted to pitting of views against each other. Is it possible to think—engage in reflection upon theological thought—without presuppositions? I will argue it is.

CRITICAL THEOLOGY

Reflection upon and engagement with the context of theological thought is the focus or onus of the inquiry of (recent) critical theology, the touchstone of which can perhaps be located in Rudolf Bultmann's call for a theology of subjective existence taking into account the post-war reality and its implications and theology's critical responsibility.[1] This is presented in Jones' seminal *Critical Theology* (1995) which appropriated the term in pursuit of a theology reflective of its late twentieth-century context of modernity and addressing its concerns; A theology of an encounter, 'not only with God in Christ, but also with God in the everyday events of human life' (Ibid., p. 208). This encounter is also the onus of numerous contemporary theological thinkers, who have undertaken invaluable reflections upon theology's distinctly postmodern philosophical context. Of course, they do not carry out this reflection in a unified or uniform way, drawing the same conclusions (just as indeed the responses of theology of crisis varied). Thus, for example, Mark C. Taylor's 'a/theology', as a study of theology from

---

[1] Bultmann, 'Die Aufgabe der Theologie in der gegenwärtigen situation' (1933). Despite Bultmann not engaging in critical reflection of the political happenings in his wider corpus, as Gareth Jones points out in his *Bultmann* (1990), his Marburg address nonetheless represents a clarion call for the post-war modern theology's occupation with reflection upon its contextual 'existence'.

a post-structuralist perspective,[2] is in stark contrast to Graham Ward's[3] appropriation of Derrida in Barth's doctrine of analogy or Jean-Luc Marion's (1991) appropriation of Heidegger in discussion of the nature of God. In the work Marion proposes a phenomenological approach that preserves the divine in opposition to the 'death of God' of metaphysics; attempting to think of the concept of God 'outside of the doctrine of Being' (Ibid., p. xxiv).[4] Despite their arrival at different conclusions with regards to the understanding of theology in its postmodern philosophical context,[5] their common denominator is this critical reflection upon and engagement with their changing cultural context.

CRITICAL THEORY

The reflective position of critical theology not only transfigures and remodels but also challenges the understanding of theological thought, whatever its (disciplinary) neighbours. One particular contemporary challenge is in its engagement with critical theory. This interdisciplinary field or approach is distinguished from theory by going further than merely applying theoretical tools to the study of phenomena in order to increase our understanding of them.[6] Instead, it fosters debate between all the major social sciences, the arts and the humanities, examining the construction of knowledge in its social and historical context and demonstrating its assumptions and limitations, hoping to arrive at alternative accounts, interpretations and readings of phenomena which will produce tension within existing narratives. Critical theory's critique of knowledge construction and its assumptions is not merely external but first and foremost involves reflection upon the assumptions of its own inquiry, producing new perspectives in various contexts. This is also its challenge in engagement with theology.

Critical theory has since its beginning engaged or appropriated theological thought in its cultural criticism. In 1940 the German Marxist social critic and philosopher Walter Benjamin, in his *Theses on the Concept of History* (1968, p. 253), related the insight that theology itself is crucial in the

---

[2] Taylor, *Erring* (1984).

[3] Ward, *Barth, Derrida and the Language of Theology* (1995).

[4] See also his concise "Metaphysics and Phenomenology" (1997).

[5] See Ward (1997, pp. xl–xliii).

[6] See Horkheimer (2002, pp. 188–243).

development of the critical approach of historical materialism through the story of the Turk.[7] More recently, there has been a proliferation of Marxist-inspired thinkers, who explore theological resources, free of the preconceptions of orthodox Marxist thought, which refuses to countenance any tinkering with its basic philosophical categories. The list includes the work of Alain Badiou (2003), Giorgio Agamben (2005), Michael Hardt and Antonio Negri (2000, 2005), Terry Eagleton (2004, 2005, 2009) and indeed Slavoj Žižek who, in an attempt to demonstrate and critique the claims and failures of the current political system of liberal democracy, refer to classical theological sources, such as the letters of Saint Paul. In their work, theology acts as a conceptual pool facilitating and grounding critique, drawing attention to the assumptions and exclusions of social theories and ways to subvert them, while also charting ways towards organisation, maintenance or enhancement of social living. The Swedish theologian Ola Sigurdson argues that Marxism and theology have always shared an interest in what he calls hope—'a mutual expectation, beyond mere wishful thinking that something new is possible, a better society than the current alienated and social existence of humankind' (Sigurdson 2012, p. 5). In this philosophical sense, common to Sigurdson as a theologian and these thinkers, theology and critical theory could be understood as revealing the construction of knowledge and thereby enabling a glimpse into the socio-political reality with its faults and ways to overcome them. On one hand, then, critical theory's appropriation of theology has again drawn attention to the sociological potential of theological thought—in highlighting and challenging the 'existing' social theories.

EMERGENT CRITICAL THEOLOGY

Turning to how the understanding of critical theology is being developed or challenged in response to the specific context of critical theory, Graham Ward, in his formative *Theology and Contemporary Critical Theory* (2000), examined critical theory's employment of theological resources in the critique of modernity but also considered the implication of that for

---

[7] Yet it is important to note that Benjamin's consideration of the theological was not isolated, for an element of Marxist recognition or identification, if not appreciation, of a revolutionary dimension to Christianity has been present ever since Engels. See Collier's *Christianity and Marxism*. For a historical survey of attempts to connect the two traditions in European thought see Bentley's *Between Marx and Christ*.

theology as a discipline and called for a twofold response. Alongside a theo-logical assessment of critical theoretical thought, he advocated a discerning of its resources in the service of theology as a theoretical resource through which theological themes can find a contemporary expression. Yet while the first represents a pitting of views against each other and the second is an opportunity for theology to speak into the current socio-political context, neither of them allows for a challenging of theology's own understand-ing—its assumptions—or transfiguration of its thought. While there have been numerous undertakings of both to-date,[8] I wish to propose not only a discerning of the wide array of resources that critical theory has to offer, but foremost the appropriation of its approach that challenges assump-tions. The latter is the prerequisite to engage in a meaningful undertaking of both.

Outlines of such a reflection in critical theology are beginning to emerge in some recent attempts to appropriate critical theoretical resources in demonstration of theology's socio-political potential. An example of this is observed in Carl Raschke's ground-breaking *Critical Theology* (2016), which recognises the immense consequences of critical theory's appropria-tion of theology for theology itself and calls for naming the emerging genre 'critical theology', thus appropriating or developing the term in a certain way. Critical theology, Raschke argues, 'cannot serve as simply a brand marker for familiar ecclesiastical loyalties, or spiritualised varnish for what are hardscrabble ideological commitments, immune to challenge or revi-sion. A critical theology calls into question the very framework of conven-tional theological analysis and theory production' (Ibid., p. 10). Raschke's is the first work that directly attempts to trace the contours of this form of theological thinking by differentiating it from political theology. Con-comitantly, Jeffrey Robbins published his own thoughts in *Radical Theology* (2016), although avoiding the term critical theology and instead rehabil-itating the content and focus of radical theology beyond the confines of the death-of-God theology. By appropriating critical theory in exploration and demonstration of the socio-political potential of theology, these the-ological thinkers are taking tentative but ground-breaking steps towards

---

[8] Examples of both engagements will be presented in the next chapter through theolog-ical engagement with Žižek. Ward skilfully charts theological implications and responses at the end of each section considering what he identifies as the key critical theory emphases: representation, history, ethics and aesthetics.

appropriating the approach of critical theory in pursuit of a reflection on theological thought.

It is here, building upon these tentative first steps that venture beyond appropriation of critical theory in contemporary expression of theological topics or in demonstration of its socio-political potential, that I wish to further develop the understanding and scope of critical theology in reflection on the act, content, presuppositions and implications of theological thought. A furthering of the adjective 'critical' of wider theological thought, rather than a focus on specific disciplines or doctrines within it.

A SEARCH FOR TRUTH

Theology's critical character, observed in critical theory's appropriation of theological thought,[9] has always been one of challenging narratives and revealing exceptions in search for truth. Yet, this criticality is not only outward-facing or in relation to another but is the very condition and essence of theological thought, necessarily its root and essence. In his searching article on theology's engagement with critical social theory, Wayne Whitson Floyd (1991, p. 175) proposed: 'Theology is always a form of criticism, a search for truth against all its ideological competitors'. This thought can illustrate the radical understanding of theology's critical character, if we resist the temptation to fixate on the preposition 'against' too quickly. Failure to do so results in the determination of intent, where theology is understood as a search for truth against all its ideological competitors. However, if we leave the preposition to one side for a moment, theology in itself is revealed or understood as a (or perhaps the) search for truth (in the form of criticism). Floyd's sentence is then understood as: Insofar as theology is a constant critical search for truth, is it also a form of criticism against all its ideological competitors.[10] Turning to the New Testament, In the Sermon on the Mount Jesus said to the disciples, 'You are the salt of the earth; but if salt has lost its taste, how can its saltiness be restored? It is no longer good for anything, but is thrown out and trampled under foot' (Matthew 5:13). This is a call to preservation of distinct character in order that correcting or giving of flavour can be undertaken. The character

---

[9] Žižek's discussion of the implications of the book of Job 'Subtraction, Jewish and Christian' (2003, pp. 122–143) that will be discussed in this book is an example.

[10] I am not advocating the abandonment of the preposition in Floyd's thought, only the realisation of its foundation.

of theology is necessarily critical or, to appropriate Ward (2005, p. 266), 'a radicality inseparable from its orthodoxy'. In this way, not only do we live in the age of the critical, where theology must submit to it and be employed in its service, as Kant (1998, p. 100 [Axi]) would argue, but theology itself is and always was essentially critical.

I would like to propose that it is this critical character of theology, not only its potential for criticality towards its ideological competitors, which critical theory has discerned. It is also not only theology's hope that initiates or gives ground to critical theory's appropriation,[11] but rather theology as a search for truth through revelatory criticality, never allowing foreclosures but always challenging assumption, even its own.[12] Theology must remain true to this character, lest it loses its saltiness and becomes trapped in the magical circle of abstraction where, rather than constantly challenging the very framework of 'conventional theological analysis and theory production', as Raschke put it, theology surrenders its apocalyptic (i.e. revelatory) capacity and sempiternally validates what are 'hardscrabble ideological commitments' (Raschke 2016, p. 10). Any yielding under the objection that this sounds too opaque and fails to offer an unalterable and definitive body of thought, represents a compromise of its critical character and results in service to that which it is supposed to challenge. It is in application of this criticality in theological reflection, that I propose a furthering of the understanding, role and scope of critical theology.

In doing so, critical theology can further its remit to a critical reflection upon the framework of theological analysis and theory production in order to highlight and challenge the presuppositions that determine its content in any way and thereby—if I may be so bold—preserve its sanctity. Furthermore, by drawing attention to what theological thought presupposes, it also brings about a greater awareness of the historically or culturally embedded particularity of theology's own truth claims, thereby enabling theology to face up to its own assumptions and their inherent problems, and remove the automatism of perception in order to maintain an indeterminate understanding of theology.

[11] Cf. Sigurdson (2013, p. 5).

[12] Cf. Ward (1997, p. xlii): 'In our time, a space is being cleared and a time is being announced that only theological discourse can provide with a logic'. This is something to which Žižek is constantly drawing our attention—theological character as the excess or monstrous, transcendental, never submitting to an identity but rather blurring the hypostasized boundaries between them irrevocably. See Žižek (2006, pp. 68–123).

THE TASK: A CRITICAL READING

This book then engages theological thought with critical theory in order to highlight its presuppositions and allow it to face up to their inherent problems. I will do so in the example of a theological text that discusses the necessary social dimension of theology—Dietrich Bonhoeffer's *Sanctorum Communio*. This text will be read critically through the lens of a contemporary critical theorist Slavoj Žižek and his theological materialism. Žižek's 'struggling universality' of abandonment and its ethic of indifference challenging any notion of identity will be applied in consideration of Bonhoeffer's own social theology of a transcendental personalist 'community of saints' and its ethic of universal love. In this way, Bonhoeffer's theological arguments for true community and its form will be brought into their contemporary context, evaluating whether they are unassailable, and his conclusions are valid, particularly with regards to matters of ontology and identity. Finally, his thoughts on the social form of community will then be applied to and examined through contemporary struggles for social change.

THE OBJECT OF ANALYSIS: THE SOCIAL THEOLOGY OF DIETRICH BONHOEFFER

The thought of Dietrich Bonhoeffer is varied despite the brevity of his life (1906–1945). As a modern theologian[13] his contemplation of theological concepts was directed at their social and ethical dimension or application (3 August 1944 in DBWE 8: pp. 498–499). He carried out his intellectual reflection on faith in a modern world, in which humans operate autonomously, without sensing a need to refer to either the divine grace or truth. In the world-come-of-age, people no longer require God

---

[13] Modernity affected both the theological method and content, while, at the same time, theology critically evaluated and responded to modernity. Therefore, modern theology does not only denote a temporal category of theology, or indeed a theological character of modernity, but is also a term describing an engagement between theology and the modern. Insofar as it does not denote a mere persistence or reiteration of traditional theology in the modern era, nor an adaptation into the modern worldview, modern theology is rather to be considered as a particular example of the dialectical relationship between theology and its cultural context—the modern and theology. Likewise, Bonhoeffer's theological thought was influenced and to some extent shaped by modernity, which affected his theological method, as well as the content of his thought. At the same time, he critically evaluated and responded to modernity.

as a working hypothesis, whether in science, in human affairs in general, or increasingly even in religion (8 June 1944 in DBWE 8: p. 267ff.). The older view of God as God-of-the-Gaps was false and as man became more and more independent God was pushed out of increasingly larger dimensions of life, with theology retreating to the inner world of man. Bonhoeffer sought to provide a response to the world-come-of-age and called for Christians to understand it better than it understands itself (8 June 1944 in DBWE 8: p. 269ff.). This was a distinctly modern theology, attempting to come to terms with, orient and situate itself in a modern world, which seemed to operate without God's involvement, observed in the scientific approach, but also in the terrors of both World Wars. His interconnected ideas of Christ the vicarious representative, Christ existing as church-community, discipleship, cheap-grace and a call for a religionless interpretation of Christianity, continue to permeate theological academia and there have been numerous attempts to summarise his thought.[14] Yet all of those concepts, as Clifford J. Green (1999) convincingly argues, reflect Bonhoeffer as a theologian of sociality. The foundations of his theology with a distinct sociological orientation were laid during his theological education in Berlin and found their original expression in his first thesis, *Sanctorum Communio*. In this work, where Bonhoeffer employed social philosophy and sociology in the service of theology, he clearly expressed his conviction about 'the social intention of all fundamental Christian concepts' which appear 'fully understandable only in relation to sociality' (DBWE 1: p. 23[5]).[15] This book examines Bonhoeffer's sociological claims made in *Sanctorum Communio* that arguably made him into someone for whom theology 'was above all a form of *critical* theory, a style of thinking in the service of action' (Floyd 1991, p. 175).[16]

---

[14]Some examples: Bethge (1967), Dramm (2001), de Gruchy (1999), Feil (1991), Plant (2004), Dumas (1971), and Busch Nielsen et al. (2007).

[15]This is the reference for footnote 5 on page 23 of the first volume in the Dietrich Bonhoeffer Works collection (DBWE). According to Richard Roberts, this also qualifies *Sanctorum Communio* as a classic illuminating the relation between theology and the social sciences. See Roberts (2005, pp. 375–377).

[16]This quote is taken from Whitson Floyd's article discussing the sustained critical reflection of Bonhoeffer's thought.

THE ANALYST: THE THEOLOGICAL MATERIALISM OF SLAVOJ ŽIŽEK

Slavoj Žižek (1949–) is an internationally recognised Slovenian philosopher, theoretical psychoanalyst and critical theorist, and has been deemed 'one of the world's best known public intellectuals' (Gray 2012). His over eighty works and a multitude of articles have been translated into numerous languages, and he regularly speaks on various topics around the globe. Aided by examples from popular culture, Žižek uses Lacanian psychoanalysis, Hegelian philosophy and Marxist economic criticism to interpret social phenomena, including religion, and in particular Christianity. It is with regard to the latter that he considers himself a *Christian atheist* or *Christian materialist* (Žižek 2012, pp. 115–116).

Žižek agrees with the 'universalist' legacy of Christianity, which is best expressed in Galatians 3:28, where the Apostle Paul asserts that 'there is no longer Jew or Greek, there is no longer slave or free, there is no longer male and female; for all of you are one in Christ Jesus'. He identifies with the implication of this thought (at least as he perceives it) a complete egalitarianism of all people, and calls on Christianity to abandon its outer shell of religious form, manifested in institutional organisation and religious experience. Theology as post-metaphysical political thought, girded by universality for revolutionary thought and action, is the true legacy of Christianity. That is the reason why Žižek believes theology is indispensable and essential for any kind of socio-political engagement in the world, including the development of his own political thought and the outcome thereof—a radical universalism grounded in materialism which is distinctly theological in experience and form and continues to address core theological issues.[17] Thus even though his voice at times appears in discussion about the postsecular (e.g. Sigurdson 2010) and he shares with it the conviction that religion is socio-politically relevant, his philosophical context is rather post-Marxist critical theory that seeks to illuminate and dismantle the dualistic categories of religious and secular as perpetual mystifications

---

[17]This is seen in 'Building Blocks for a Materialist Theology' in *The Parallax View*, where Žižek not only carries forward the major conclusions concerning Christianity reached in his earlier works, but expresses new developments of ideological critique in theological terms (Žižek 2006, pp. 68–113).

of the capitalist political order.[18] Indeed, for Žižek, theology forms one of the most complex ways of speaking about radical political change.

It is thus through Bonhoeffer's and Žižek's mutual conviction about the sociological potential of theology that the point of contact for this interdisciplinary reflection is established.[19] In order to further clarify the interdisciplinary, critical theological conviction and nature of this work, I will refer to Bonhoeffer's own positioning in the foreword to the chosen text:

> In this study social philosophy and sociology are employed in the service of theology. Only through such an approach, it appears, can we gain a systematic understanding of the community-structure of the Christian church. This work belongs not to the discipline of sociology of religion, but to theology. The issue of a Christian social philosophy and sociology is a genuinely theological one, because it can be answered only on the basis of an understanding of the church. The more this investigation has considered the significance of the social category for theology, the more clearly has emerged the social intention of all the basic Christian concepts. 'Person', 'primal state', 'sin', and 'revelation' can be fully comprehended only in reference to sociality [Sozialität]. If genuinely theological concepts can only be recognised as established and fulfilled in a special social context, then it becomes evident that a sociological study of the church has a specifically theological character. (DBWE 1: p. 21)

In parallel to Bonhoeffer's employment of social philosophy in the service of theology, here it is critical theory that is employed in the service of theology's critical self-reflection. Only through such an approach, it appears, can we examine Bonhoeffer's conception of the church as a community structure and its sociological implications. This work then belongs not to a clear-cut discipline of theology or indeed sociology, but is perhaps to be understood as a critical theological theory which brings together concepts from various theoretical legacies and therefore transcends disciplinary

---

[18] In the section titled 'Postsecularism? No thanks!' of *Did Somebody Say Totalitarianism?* (2001, pp. 152–160), Žižek critiques Derrida and Habermas for reimagining religion as a politically compatible or servile philosophy which avoids challenging the current political or sociological makeup. Devoid of critical socio-political potential, its function is that of a fetish—to escape the uncomfortable dimensions of religion in favour of a mere thought experiment without any social consequences.

[19] As will become clear, another contact point between them is the impact of and engagement with the social philosophy of the German idealist Georg Hegel.

boundaries. The issue of the content of theological thought and its socio-logical potential is a genuinely critical one, because its full dimensionality can only be grasped from this interdisciplinary and critical perspective. The more this investigation has considered the significance of the social category for Bonhoeffer's theology on the one hand, and the significance of the theological category for Žižek's critical theory on the other, the more clearly the implications of their specific configurations have emerged.

AN ADMITTEDLY ODD READING

Given that we are nearing a hundred years since Bonhoeffer defended his doctoral dissertation in 1927, this raises the question of the relevance of *Sanctorum Communio* for today. Rather than a celebration of Bonhoeffer's thought or a dissection of what is still relevant and what is not, this book represents an attempt to think with Bonhoeffer as a contemporary (cf. Žižek et al. 2018, p. 3) in pursuit of a furthered or 'presuppositionless' critical theology; It is not just looking at the simple relevance of Bonhoeffer's text today but looking at what needs to be 'rethought' theologically. This sort of undertaking intentionally disrupts disciplinary borders and will perhaps be considered as a profanation but is necessary for it is in keeping with the constantly searching critical being of theology and a recognition of its context within which it continues to develop (rather than attempting to keep it as abstract). Bonhoeffer's thought continues to develop—not only during his lifetime but ever on and continually challenging its previous coordinates or constellations. With each new historical condition, it develops further and is manifest accordingly. What can we observe today by examining (the theory of) Bonhoeffer's theological concepts from the perspective of critical theory? This book will also not produce a comprehensive outline or understanding of Bonhoeffer or even only his first thesis (I will not delve into later parts of the text). It is intentionally partial or symptomatic in order to tease out the assumptions of the text's unconscious, rendering explicit what is implicit. Finally, the primary aim of this book is not to challenge the perhaps countless previous readings of Bonhoeffer, or even the fewer of *Sanctorum Communio*. For this would limit the engagement to an opposing of views. Instead, its aim is a creative reading that allows the emergence of something unexpected and new.

My reading, then, is a deliberately 'odd' reading that upsets the expected and familiar. It represents a sort of permutation that leads to the development of a new perspective or approach—towards a very specific understanding of reflection on and production of theological thought that changes the terrain of contemporary critical theology.

Bonhoeffer and Presuppositions?

In a collection of essays *Understanding Bonhoeffer* (2017), aimed at dissuading the contemporary reader from turning Bonhoeffer into something which he never was, Peter Frick's essay 'Understanding Bonhoeffer: from Default to Hermeneutic Reading' (2017, pp. 35–41) argues for the crucial awareness and challenging of the contemporary reader's presuppositions as we approach Bonhoeffer's texts. Despite acknowledging Bonhoeffer's own theological, ethical and homiletical presuppositions, Frick (ibid., pp. 12–21) does not challenge them or their implications. This book will do just that: through a critical reading, it will highlight the assumptions of Bonhoeffer's claims in *Sanctorum Communio* and examine their implications.

Frick's essay was first published in *Bonhoeffer and Interpretive Theory* (Frick 2013), which also aimed to clarify 'the assumptions that readers of Bonhoeffer bring to his texts and his life'… in order to meet the need for 'a sustained hermeneutical reflection for those who read Bonhoeffer and write about him' (p. 7). Yet that work also for the most part—or at least not with much conviction—does not consider Bonhoeffer's own presuppositions. The manifest exception is to be found in Lisa Dahill's contribution 'There's Some Contradiction Here' (2013, pp. 53–84), which draws attention to aspects of Bonhoeffer's 'almost entirely unexamined biases… [that] in the process reinforce structures of severe injustice in our world today' (p. 54). She contends that although Bonhoeffer grants the greatest hermeneutical privilege to the marginalised and excluded, his views on gender and hierarchy remain oppressive,[20] and argues that her undertaking of a gender-oriented reading of Bonhoeffer 'has the potential to provide for him as for any of us, the most liberating breakthroughs' (ibid., p. 58).[21] Dahill concludes with:

---

[20] Dahill also proposes her *Reading from the Underside of Selfhood: Bonhoeffer and the Spiritual Formation* (2009) as an example of the only (to her date) feminist reading of Bonhoeffer.

[21] Dahill points out that Bonhoeffer's androcentrism and gender essentiality was based on the order of creation, part 'of unexamined inheritance, rather than intentionally developed insight' (Dahill 2013, p. 65)—that is his. In the final part of her essay (pp. 77–83), she

Writing this essay has been hard, forcing me to face aspects of Bonhoeffer that threaten any idealization of him – that in fact oblige me to point out places I sense he was wrong. Yet it is also an incredible privilege to be providing glimpses of deep and as-yet-unresolved inner conflicts even in someone so great […] I rejoice in Bonhoeffer's life-long desire for liberation in Jesus Christ and in the ways these blind spots reveal the humanity of his journey of discipleship, a process for him – as for all of us – marked by ceaseless ascent into ever greater perfection but by confusion, missteps, humility, and ongoing probing, prayerful discernment. (Dahill 2013, p. 84)

I agree and propose that the Truth that is contained within the writings of Bonhoeffer, as well as the wider body of theological thought, only emerges and can be observed if we engage it in truly critical reading with the myriad of its contexts and do so without presuppositions. Only in this way do we not foreclose our thought and simply arrive at expected conclusions.

Outline

This chapter has positioned the book and serves as an introduction to its rationale. After introducing Žižek's conceptual framework of Hegel, Marx and Lacan who shape the general method of his critical analysis, the second chapter will provide an account of Žižek's engagement with theology, its importance for his political thought and the outcome thereof—a radical universalism grounded in the theology of dialectical materialism. It will also offer an admittedly cursory yet functional account of theological engagement with Žižek thus far in order to show the potential but also imperative for what is to follow—a Žižekian critical examination of Bonhoeffer's demonstration of the sociological potential of theology. Before that, chapter three will begin with a sort of necessary introduction to Bonhoeffer's own conceptual framework focusing on a selection of particular thinkers who, during his studies at the Friedrich Wilhelm University in Berlin, influenced Bonhoeffer's sustained engagement with social philosophical thinkers (such as Hegel): Ernst Toeltsch, Reinhold Seeberg, and Adolf von Harnack, and develop the social orientation of his theology. After this, Bonhoeffer's doctoral dissertation *Sanctorum Communio* will be read

proposes a Bonhoefferian understanding of gender which, she argues, might have developed in the right circumstances (if he did not move into the all-male world of Finkenwalde) but developed more his earlier rejection of all orders of creation.

from Žižek's perspective in order to examine: Bonhoeffer's understanding, criticism and development of Hegel, particularly his conception of universality based upon the subject–object relationship and the concept of objective spirit; his attempt to demonstrate the sociality of theological concepts of God, sin and the church; and his upholding of the latter as a model form of community. Finally, Bonhoeffer's thoughts on the social forms of society, mass and community will be examined through their application to contemporary struggles for social change—Occupy and Black Lives Matter. After a brief summary or evaluation of the lessons from this critical (symptomatic) reading, the conclusion will argue that this engagement is model for the development of a presuppositionless critical reflection upon theological thought—a radical critical theology.

References

Agamben, G. (2005). *The Time That Remains: A Commentary on the Letter to the Romans*. Translated by P. Dailey. Stanford: Stanford University Press.

Badiou, A. (2003). *Saint Paul: The Foundation of Universalism*. Translated by R. Brassier. Stanford: Stanford University Press.

Benjamin, W. (1968). *Illuminations*. Translated by H. Zohn. New York: Schocken Books.

Bethge, E. (1967). *Dietrich Bonhoeffer: Theologe – Christ – Zeitgenosse*. München: C. Kaiser Verlag.

Bultmann, R. (1933). 'Die Aufgabe der Theologie in der gegenwärtigen situation', *Theologische Blätter* XII, pp. 161–166.

Busch Nielsen, K., Nissen, U., and Tietz, C. (eds.). (2007). *Mysteries in the Theology of Dietrich Bonhoeffer*. Göttingen: Vandenhoeck & Ruprecht.

Dahill, L.E. (2009). *Reading from the Underside of Selfhood: Bonhoeffer and the Spiritual Formation*. Eugene, OR: Pickwick Publications.

Dahill, L.E. (2013). '"There's Some Contradiction Here": Gender and the Relation of *Above* and *Below* in Bonhoeffer', in Frick, P. (ed.) *Bonhoeffer and Interpretive Theory: Essays on Method and Understanding*. Frankfurt am Main: Peter Lang, pp. 53–84.

de Gruchy, J. (1999). *The Cambridge Companion to Dietrich Bonhoeffer*. Cambridge: Cambridge University Press.

Dramm, S. (2001). *Dietrich Bonhoeffer: Eine Einführung in sein Denken*. Gütersloh: C. Kaiser and Gütersloher Verlag. English: (2007) *Dietrich Bonhoeffer: An Introduction to his Thought*. Translated by T. Rice. Peabody: Hendrickson Publishers.

Dumas A. (1971). *Dietrich Bonhoeffer: Theologian of Reality*. London: SCM Press.

Eagleton, T. (2004). *After Theory*. London: Penguin Books.

Eagleton, T. (2005). *Holy Terror.* Oxford: Oxford University Press.

Eagleton, T. (2009). *Reason, Faith, and Revolution: Reflections on the God Debate.* New Haven and London: Yale University Press.

Feil, E. (1991). *Die Theologie Dietrich Bonhoeffers: Hermeneutik, Christologie, Weltverständnis.* München: C. Kaiser.

Floyd, W.W. (1991). 'The Search for an Ethical Sacrament: From Bonhoeffer to Critical Social Theory', *Modern Theology*, 7(2), pp. 175–193.

Frick, P. (ed.). (2013). *Bonhoeffer and Interpretive Theory: Essays on Method and Understanding.* Frankfurt am Main: Peter Lang.

Frick, P. (2017). *Understanding Bonhoeffer.* Tübingen: Mohr Siebeck.

Gray, J. (2012). 'The Violent Visions of Slavoj Žižek', *New York Review of Books*, 59(12). Available at http://www.nybooks.com/articles/archives/2012/jul/12/violent-visions-slavoj-zizek/. Accessed 20 September 2016.

Green, C.J. (1999). *Bonhoeffer: A Theology of Sociality.* Cambridge: Eerdmans.

Hardt, M. and Negri, A. (2000). *Empire.* Cambridge: Harvard University Press.

Hardt, M. and Negri, A. (2005). *Multitude: War and Democracy in the Age of Empire.* London: Hamish Hamilton.

Horkheimer M. (2002). 'Traditional and Critical Theory', in *Critical Theory: Selected Essays.* Translated by W.J. Greenstreet. New York: Continuum, pp. 188–243.

Jones, G. (1990). *Bultmann: Towards Critical Theology.* Cambridge: Polity Press.

Jones, G. (1995). *Critical Theology: Questions of Truth and Method.* Cambridge: Polity Press.

Kant, I. (1998). *The Critique of Pure Reason.* Translated by P. Guyer. Cambridge: Cambridge University Press.

Marion, J-.L. (1991). *God Without Being.* Translated by T.A. Carlson. Chicago: University of Chicago Press.

Plant, S. (2004). *Bonhoeffer.* London and New York: Continuum.

Raschke, C. (2016). *Critical Theology: Introducing an Agenda for an Age of Global Crisis.* Downers Grove: IVP Academic.

Robbins, J.W. (2016). *Radical Theology: A Vision for Change.* Bloomington: Indiana University Press.

Roberts, R.H. (2005). 'Theology and Social Sciences', in Ford, D.F. and Muers, R. (eds.) *The Modern Theologians.* Oxford: Blackwell, pp. 375–377.

Sigurdson, O. (2010). 'Beyond Secularism? Towards a Postsecular Political Theology', *Modern Theology*, 26(2), pp. 177–196.

Sigurdson, O. (2012). *Theology and Marxism in Eagleton and Žižek: A Conspiracy of Hope.* New York: Palgrave Macmillan.

Sigurdson, O. (2013). 'Slavoj Žižek, the Death of God, and Zombies: A Theological Account', *Modern Theology*, 29(3), pp. 361–380.

Taylor, M.C. (1984). *Erring: A Postmodern A/theology.* Chicago: University of Chicago Press.

Ward, G. (1995). *Barth, Derrida and the Language of Theology*. Cambridge: Cambridge University Press.

Ward, G. (1997). (ed). *The Postmodern God: A Theological Reader*. Oxford: Blackwell.

Ward, G. (2000). *Theology and the Contemporary Critical Theory*. London: Macmillan.

Ward, G. (2005). *Christ and Culture*. Malden: Blackwell.

Žižek, S. (2001). *Did Somebody Say Totalitarianism? Five Interventions in the (Mis)use of a Notion*. London and New York: Verso.

Žižek, S. (2003) *The Puppet and the Dwarf: The Perverse Core of Christianity*. London: The MIT Press.

Žižek, S. (2006). *The Parallax View*. London: The MIT Press.

Žižek, S. (2012). *Less Than Nothing: Hegel and the Shadow of Dialectical Materialism*. London: Verso.

Žižek, S., Ruda, F., and Hamza, A. (2018). *Reading Marx*. Cambridge: Polity Press.

CHAPTER 2

Žižek's Political Theology

Getting in the Mind of Žižek

As a critical theorist, Žižek's work draws on three main areas of influence: philosophy, politics and psychoanalysis.[1] Each of these areas is largely represented by the writings of a single individual: Georg Hegel for philosophy, Karl Marx for politics and Jacques Lacan for psychoanalysis. The ideas, methodologies and the general effect of each thinker overlaps in Žižek's work and together they furnish the conceptual framework with which he tackles the objects of his analysis, including theology. It is appropriate to devote some thought to observing this interplay, so we will be able to recognise it when we turn to Žižek's theological materialism and engage it with Bonhoeffer's social theology.

Looking for Contradictions with Hegel

In his considerations of the history of thought as it attempts to understand itself and its relation to the world ('The realisation of spirit in history' in Hegel 1998, pp. 44ff.), Hegel developed his understanding as dialectic—full of contradiction or negations that do not come from the outside, but are

---

[1] The synthesis of these three sources represents the scaffolding of the Frankfurt School and thus critical theory in general. While Herbert Marcuse (1955) introduced a combination of Hegel and Marx, Erich Fromm (1941) added his expertise on psychoanalysis.

© The Author(s) 2019
B. Koltaj, *Žižek Reading Bonhoeffer*,
Radical Theologies and Philosophies,
https://doi.org/10.1007/978-3-030-26094-1_2

inherent to thought and material reality itself and are as such the propulsion that drives thought and reality forward. He spoke of the dialectical relationship between the *Abstract*, the *Negative* and the *Concrete*—stages of thought that do not form distinct parts, nor are they sharply contrasted with each other. Instead, they are related to each other in the sense that the second stage is the negation of the first, and the third the negation of the second—the negation of the negation (Hegel 2010a, pp. 96f., 132f.; 2010b, p. 121). While the second element is the opposite of the first and the third element is in some sense the unity of these two opposites, it is not a simple, formal unity, but rather the unity of distinct determinations. Therefore, each element can be defined only in terms of the other—the contrast between them (2010a, pp. 361ff.). Accordingly, each element must always pass through the phase of the negative, and Hegel designates this movement with the word *Aufhebung*, translated into English as 'sublation', which carries connotations of both negation and elevation. For Hegel, the truth regarded as absolute must continually be *discarded*; but, in being discarded, it must at the same time be *taken up* afresh and *raised up* into a higher unity. It is this Hegel as a thinker whose focus is not on fixed, static meanings or structures, but on the *process* of conceptual transformation itself that is of interest to Žižek; as primarily a revolutionary spirit who opens up theoretical systems and for whom the moments of fracture that make critical thought possible are enduring dialectical points of impossibility.[2]

Following Hegel, Žižek's thought is itself based on the recognition that contradiction is the fundamental starting point of all philosophy, and indeed of all thought (Žižek 1989, p. 6).[3] Correspondingly, he points out how any idea about something is always disrupted by a discrepancy and the result is not absolute knowledge conceived as full and transparent, but a realisation that 'absolute knowledge itself is nothing but a name for the acknowledgment of a certain radical loss' (Žižek 1989, p. 7). In other words, the tension is never fully resolved.

---

[2] In this sense Žižek's reading of Hegel is not dissimilar to that of Gillian Rose, who argues that Hegel's *Phenomenology* is not a dominating absolute knowledge, but a gamble. See Rose's *Hegel Contra Sociology* (1981, p. 159). Žižek himself acknowledges Rose's interpretation of Hegel in *For They Know Not What They Do* (1991a, p. 103).

[3] For a good presentation of the Hegelian dialectics of contradiction in Žižek's thought, see Todd McGowan's 'The Necessity of an Absolute Misunderstanding' (2016, pp. 43–56).

An example to illustrate Žižek's dialectical thinking can be found in *The Puppet and the Dwarf*, in which Žižek attempts to explain his understanding of the doctrine of atonement, or the transformation of the condition through Christ. He lays out what he claims are two widely held positions:

> The first approach is legalistic: there is guilt to be paid for, and, by paying our debt for us, Christ redeemed us (and, of course, thereby forever indebted us); from the [second] participationist perspective, on the contrary, people are freed from sin not by Christ's death as such, but by sharing in Christ's death, by dying to sin, to the way of the flesh. (2003, p. 102)

These two perspectives, according to Žižek, are perhaps more familiar as the traditional (or conservative) view and the liberal view of the meaning of the Cross. The latter 'tends to deny the direct divine nature of Christ' (ibid., p. 103), presenting him as more of a model to follow. In an attempt to decide between the two, he states:

> In the abstract, of course, the participationist reading is the correct one, while the sacrificial reading 'misses the point' of Christ's gesture; the only way to the participationist reading, however, is through the sacrificial one, through its inherent overcoming. The sacrificial reading is the way Christ's gesture appears within the very horizon that Christ wanted to leave behind, within the horizon for which we die in identifying with Christ. (ibid.)[4]

Here Žižek is making one of his most characteristic dialectical moves, pointing out a 'mistake' that is nonetheless a necessary step in arriving at the correct position. In this specific case, the legalistic approach is clearly incorrect, and in fact Žižek argues that if we stay within its frame, 'Christ's death cannot but appear as the ultimate assertion of the law [...] which burdens us, its subjects, with guilt, and with a debt we will never be able to repay' (ibid.). However, if we attempt to skip directly to the other posi-

---

[4]Žižek's presentation of the historic understanding of atonement as crude dualism, whatever one makes of it, is not completely arbitrary, since what he describes here is essentially a recognition of the Christian approach to salvation, which, while complex, lies in two different areas. In the first place, salvation is understood to be grounded in the life, death and resurrection of Jesus Christ; in the second, the specific shape of salvation within the Christian tradition is itself formed by Christ—Jesus Christ provides a model or paradigm for the redeemed life.

tion, that position loses its punch.[5] The true meaning of Christ's death is not immediately the call for participation, but rather the break with the legalistic view, which opens up the space for participation in a new kind of social collective outside the logic of debt and repayment. In other words, the death of Christ on the Cross is considered as important as the call for participation. Indeed, the call for participation is not possible without the death of Christ on the Cross. Therefore, the participation perspective, properly conceived, is a kind of embodiment of the break with the legalistic perspective enacted by Christ's death on the Cross. It is this very negativity that provides the Cross its power.

This example perfectly illustrates Žižek's dialectical understanding, through which the concretization is found in the contradiction rather than the smoothing out of differences. This at-first-sight oxymoronic style of thinking is indicative of the whole approach to thinking that Žižek calls dialectical and which he employs when analysing everything, including Christian theology. This approach then helps to account for the surprising title with which he describes himself—a Christian atheist, or materialist Christian, and provides insight into such statements as the Christian tradition should be cherished by Marxism.[6] What this means is that the identification of Žižek's dialectical arguments is one of the most important ways to understand what he is saying, without which one is unable to follow his arguments.

Why We Gloss Over Them with Marx

In the preface to *The Žižek Reader*, Žižek professes himself as 'unabashedly Marxist' (Wright and Wright 1999, p. x), someone who is convinced about the truth and value of Marx's critique of capitalism and believes in the possibility of a better, alternative method of organising society. So, while Hegel's dialectic functions as the method of thought that Žižek practices, Marx's critique of capitalism presents the very grounds or motivation for why Žižek writes at all. Essentially then, his work can be understood as a contribution to the Marxist body of criticism, which attempts to subvert

---

[5] Here too Žižek recognises that the atonement is a very rich concept, and that it is impossible to adequately describe what happened or what happens in the atonement with one clear figure of speech or analogy.

[6] Indeed, this is the main thought behind *The Fragile Absolute* (Žižek 2000).

ideology—alter the way in which the world is understood in order that it might be changed for the better.

It was Louis Althusser (1918–1990) who sought to provide an explanation of how ideology functions. In his influential essay, 'Ideology and Ideological State Apparatuses' (Althusser 1971, pp. 121–173), he argued that ideology as a system of belief contains internal contradictions and requires a strategy of force to disguise them. It is therefore disseminated by the 'Ideological State Apparatuses' (such as the Churches, the education system, the family unit, the legal system, the political system, the media and culture) and maintained by the 'Repressive State Apparatus' (such as the police force and prisons). Ideology interpellates or hails us, we respond in reflex-like fashion, acting as required and remain captive. It is then a part of the relationship between the individual and society, where people respond consciously to ideology, but the latter is itself unconscious.[7]

It is exactly at this point that Žižek makes his most telling contribution to the Marxist tradition.[8] He agrees with Althusser that ideology is the way in which individuals understand their relationship to society, but provides a considerable supplement. The State Apparatuses, Žižek argues, are mechanisms that not only generate belief in a particular system, but do so before the subjects are even aware of it—they unconsciously pre-empt our belief and thereby habituate us to it.[9] He explicates this with the help of Pascal's Wager argument (Žižek 1989, pp. 36–40). If someone is struggling to believe, Pascal recommends simply acting like a Christian, i.e. engaging in Christian practices, for belief will follow soon enough. In the same way, the Ideological State Apparatuses work irrespective of whether individuals believe in them or not, simply by an individual's obedience. His treatise of subjects such as Hollywood, religious perversion, taboo topics and day-to-day activities, has brought about much interest in his assertion that our

---

[7] Insofar as it is how people relate to society, Gramsci argues, ideology will always exist, even in a classless society. This is contra Marx, who suggests that in such a society its appearance will be equal to its essence.

[8] Žižek's analysis of subjectivity as an ideological process is the main burden of *The Sublime Object of Ideology* (1989), which was published in the Laclau-Mouffe series of post-Marxist books reworking the Left project in terms of 'radical and plural democracy'.

[9] For a good presentation of Žižek's development of Althusser's thought, see Geoff Pfeifer's *The New Materialism* (2016).

acceptance of them as routine demonstrates our assent to the capitalist ideology.[10]

In this way the Slovenian cultural critic challenges the assumption that ideology is a 'conspiracy' by counter-proposing that we are all as individuals complicit in its operation (ibid., p. 29). The radical nature of Žižek's claim here should not be overlooked—we are all aware of the gaps and contradictions in our understanding of the world, but we turn a blind eye to them most of the time. Ideology then succeeds—not because it interpellates us and we react reflexively (as Althusser)—but because we want it to succeed. We want to believe that we live under a consistent system of belief, and therefore interpolate ourselves to make it seem so. It is therefore we who fill in the gaps and disguise the contradictions, not some political elite on our behalf. I will observe this challenge of Žižek in his engagement with theology where he aims to point out the parts of texts that highlight the gaps in our narrative of consistent belief that are perpetuated by our desire for it as such. For now, it suffices to say that while Hegel equips Žižek with the aim to uncover contradictions that drive the development of thought, Marx provides him with the understanding why we gloss over them.

Žižek found the theory of the instinctive and psychological processes that are the ground for why and how we do so in none other than the French psychoanalyst Jacques Lacan.

How We Do so with Lacan

The French psychoanalyst Jacques Lacan (1901–1981) is perhaps the most visible authority for Žižek—indeed, one of his main ambitions has been to provide a preliminary understanding of Lacan, to explain his theories.[11] He describes this ambition in an interview as follows:

> My most secret dream is to write an old-fashioned, multi-volume theological tract on Lacanian theory in the style of Aquinas. I would examine each of Lacan's theories in a completely dogmatic way, considering the arguments

---

[10]This is aptly illustrated in the documentary *The Pervert's Guide to Ideology* (2012), directed by Sophie Fiennes, in which Žižek appears in the scenes of various movies, pieces of music and day-to-day activities, exploring and exposing the ideological framework of our society.

[11]A prime example of this is certainly his explanation of Lacan's 'graph of desire' (Žižek 1989, pp. 100–124).

for and against each statement and then offering a commentary. I would be happiest if I could be a monk in my cell, with nothing to do but write my Summa Lacaniana. (Boyton 2001)

The task of explaining Lacan is complicated due to the latter's confusing style of writing, which is full of puns, Hegelian allusions and conceptual interplays, where theoretical divergences from psychoanalytic theory and philosophical theory occur.[12] Žižek has, in his tireless effort to clarify and elaborate Lacan's thought, manifested in the numerous works from *The Sublime Object of Ideology* onwards, brought about a popularity of Lacanian psychoanalysis, which is much broader and more ambitious than the traditional conception of psychoanalysis. In that narrow conception, psychoanalysis is a field of knowledge that comprises a method for treating neurotic patients and a set of theories about mental processes. As conceived by Lacan and extrapolated by Žižek, psychoanalysis has a distinctive view of symptoms, diagnosis and clinical structure, and as such has cosmic ambitions, as it engages with cognate fields of politics, philosophy, literature, science and religion to form an overarching theory that analyses every human endeavour.[13]

Lacanian psychoanalysis therefore serves as an illuminating and transformative spark for Žižek as he tackles theoretical examination and interpretation of a wide range of subjects.[14] This is particularly true of ideology, which Žižek addresses with reference to Lacan's three Orders as classify-

---

[12] For example, Stavrakakis expresses concerns about the 'intricacies of Lacan's discourse, his baroque and complicated style' (Stavrakakis 1999, p. 4). Lacan himself said 'I am not surprised that my discourse can cause a certain margin of misunderstanding', but this is done 'with an express intention, absolutely deliberate, that I pursue this discourse in a way that offers you the occasion of not completely understanding it' (Lacan cited in Samuels 1997, p. 16).

[13] These cosmic ambitions were grounded in Freud's ambition to give a psychoanalytic interpretation of human culture. It was in the 1950s that Lacan began to reread Freud's works in relation to contemporary philosophy, linguistics, ethnology, biology and topology.

[14] For a clear introduction to Lacan that is broadly in line with Žižek, see *The Lacanian Subject* (Fink 1995). The bulk of Žižek's references to Lacan are drawn from his seminars. Foremost among them are *Seminar XX* on feminine sexuality (Lacan 2000); *Seminar VII* (Lacan 1997) on ethics, which includes Lacan's reading of Romans 7; and *Seminar XI* (Lacan 1998), presenting the fundamental concepts of psychoanalysis.

ing all mental functioning: The Imaginary, The Symbolic and The Real.[15] While the Imaginary designates the process by which the *ego* is conceived, the Symbolic includes everything from language to the law, taking in all the social structures in between. This means that most of what is usually called reality is actually Symbolic, an impersonal framework of society within which human beings take their place. All-pervading, it considers and in some sense imprisons people even before they are born—by the use of names, familial ties, gender, race and so forth. From the description of the Imaginary and the Symbolic, it follows that the Real describes those areas of life which cannot be known, the things in themselves. In a way that means everything, for all knowledge of the world is mediated by language. If nothing is ever known directly, then the Real is the world before it is carved up by language (Lacan 2006, pp. 23–86). This means that what is Real avoids description, because by default words are used to identify each separate element of the world. Lacan therefore concludes that the Real resists Symbolisation (Lacan 1991, p. 164).

Žižek, who is sometimes called 'the philosopher of the Real' (Myers 2003, p. 29), traces a trajectory through Lacan's work revolving around the distinction between the Real and Symbolic in *Looking Awry* (1991b). While the realisation that we are condemned to living in the Symbolic might lead to the question of why any attention needs to be paid to the Real, Žižek, following Lacan, warns that the Symbolic and the Real are intimately bound up with each other (Lacan 1998, p. 37, cf. Žižek in Butler et al. 2000, p. 121). In *The Pervert's Guide to Cinema* (2006), Žižek explains this with the help of a scene from the film *The Matrix*, in which Morpheus, after showing Neo the actual state of the world run by machines, offers him the choice of two pills: one to remain in this reality, and the other to return to the virtual reality constructed by the machines. Žižek argues that Neo should have asked for a third pill, one which would enable Neo to see the virtual reality (Symbolic) but to be able to discern the Real elements

---

[15] Lacan's notion of the three interacting orders first appears in detail in what can be considered as the founding lengthy manifesto of Lacan's original thought, the 1953 *Écrit: The Function and Field of Speech and Language in Psychoanalysis* (2006), often referred to as the 'Rome Discourse'. It is important to stress the complexity of Lacan's thought and therefore what follows is not an attempt to summarise the meaning of his triad, but rather an attempt to provide an elementary outline of Žižek's employment of Lacan's *Orders* in his thought. For an illuminating article about the difficulties associated with summarising exactly the meaning of Lacan's triad, see Bowie (1979).

within it. Indeed, the Symbolic works upon the Real in that it cuts it up in myriad different ways. One of the ways in which the Real is recognised, Žižek argues, is by noting when something is indifferent to Symbolisation. Taking the example of human beings (Žižek 2001a, p. 104), one can see that some part of them is real by counting up the different ways in which we are symbolised, i.e. mammals, animals, the only extant members of the *hominin clade*, etc. Thus human beings enter the Symbolic Order when we are named or otherwise classified, but prior to that we are in the Real. The Real then comes after the Symbolic, in the sense that it is that which is left when the Symbolic is done slicing it up into articulate pieces (Žižek 1989, p. 49).[16] This will be observed with Žižek's contention that there is always a remainder that avoids the attempts to account for theological texts or events/acts, such as the death of Christ.

Another disclosure of the presence of the Real is anything that is interpreted differently. This will be observed in the suffering of Job, which in the story is interpreted in different ways by his friends. Yet their explanations revolve around the same brute fact of the suffering which carries on regardless of the reasons attributed to it. In other words, Job's suffering is an interruption of the Real. It is meaningless in itself and all these interpretations of it are mere attempts to Symbolise it (Lacan 1998, pp. 165–167).[17] Agreeing with Lacan, Žižek asserts that meaning and change can only be found within the reality of the Symbolic Order, whereas the Real is meaningless, senseless and does not change (Lacan 1991, pp. 219–220). We will observe how Žižek is constantly in pursuit of the traces of the Real in theological thought, for it alone is the arena of dialectic, wherein opposing terms can coincide (Žižek 1989, pp. 190–196; Žižek in Butler et al. 2000, pp. 120–122).[18] It is by utilising Lacan's Orders that Žižek lays out the

---

[16]Lacan also defines psychoanalytic *praxis* as a 'concerted human effort [...] which places man in a position to treat the Real by the Symbolic' (Lacan 1998, p. 6).

[17]Žižek also uses the example of AIDS (Žižek 1993, p. 44; 2012b, p. 4), which, so he argues, is interpreted by some people as a punishment for homosexuals, or a divine retribution for carrying on a non-Christian way of life. Others see it as part of a plot by the CIA to stem population growth in Africa, while other people consider it the result of humankind's interference in Nature. All these explanations revolve around the same brute fact of the disease which carries on regardless of the reasons attributed to it.

[18]It is only in the Imaginary that two terms can be reconciled in a harmonious synthesis, with the Symbolic functioning as the state where they are defined differentially. That is, where one is something because it is not something else.

instinctive and psychological processes that enable the ideological to function while also enable him to discern their contradictions. We will see next
specifically how theology will be added to provide an insight into the way
out of the ideological self-imprisonment.

Žižek's Creative Philosophy of Contradictions

We have briefly observed how the critical theoretical engagement of Hegel,
Marx and Lenin develops Žižek's thought as a philosopher of contradictions. Hegel equips Žižek with the aim to uncover contradictions that drive
the development of thought, Marx provides him with the understanding
of our complicity—why we gloss over them, and Lacan provides him with
the psychological processes that explain our desire to do so and enables
him to show their contradictions.

What has hopefully also become clear in this section is that Žižek does
not treat his sources as separate entities, but, in a creative way, instead
brings them together, expecting to reveal new insights and appropriations.
Indeed, his intellectual trajectory can be seen as a series of attempts to bring
them together in a coherent and compelling way and making them his own,
by demonstrating a disavowed but essential element of their thought.

In the introduction to the *The Sublime Object*, Žižek discloses his three-
fold aim: introduction of the fundamental concepts of Lacanian psychoanalysis, re-actualisation of the Hegelian dialectical method in philosophy
through a deployment of Lacan's key concepts, and development of the theory of ideology by clarifying the correlation between Marxism and Lacanian
psychoanalysis:

> It is my belief that these three aims are deeply connected: the only way to
> 'save Hegel' is through Lacan, and this Lacanian reading of Hegel and the
> Hegelian heritage opens up a new approach to ideology, allowing us to grasp
> contemporary ideological phenomena (cynicism, 'totalitarianism', the fragile
> status of democracy) without falling prey to any kind of 'postmodernist' traps
> (such as the illusion that we live in a 'post-ideological' condition). (Žižek
> 1989, p. 7)

Undeniably, Žižek's reading of Hegel, with its overwhelming emphasis
on negativity and loss (see, for example, Žižek 1989, pp. 161–162), is Lacanian in the sense that it fits with the general ethos of Lacan's writings about

a world structured around lacks, gaps and voids.[19] Likewise, well-known classic Marxist concepts, such as commodity fetishism (ibid., pp. 18–23), are read through the lens of Lacan's concepts, such as sublime object (ibid., pp. 74–77) and surplus enjoyment (ibid., pp. 50–55). However, it must be asserted that Žižek also elaborates Lacanian psychoanalytic theory in light of Hegel[20] and Marx; thus the relationship is reciprocal, rather than one-sided. The purpose of Žižek's inventive inter-reading is to develop a new and revolutionary way of analysing political life and culture for their contradictions. This will be explored next through Žižek's engagement with theology.

How It All Began?

When seeking to provide an account of Žižek's engagement with theology, the temptation is to speak of a 'theological turn'—that at a certain point in his philosophy he decided to engage theology. This is the case that Sharpe and Boucher make in *Žižek and Politics*, when they position it in the timeline of his engagement with Badiou from *The Fragile Absolute* (2000) onwards (Sharpe and Boucher 2010, pp. 194–195).[21] In parallel, Løland (2018, pp. 17–18) argues for the appearance of Paul in *For They Know Not* (1991a), while Skliris and Mitralexis (2019, p. 1) say that his engagement with theology 'begins mainly with the *Ticklish Subject*'(1989). However, Žižek's English-speaking readership misses the engagement with the theological dimension prior to his English publications. His *Znak, Označitelj, Pismo* (1976) is already an exposition of Hegelian ontotheology. Following

---

[19] However, that does not in any way mean that Žižek's reading of Hegel is Lacan's reading. The latter read Hegel in a more traditional way. Žižek is aware of this challenge and attempts to show that his own 'Lacanian' reading of Hegel is credible by demonstrating compatibility between Lacan's concepts and the basic structure of Hegel's thought. He argues that Lacan had a Hegelian style of thought even when he believed himself to be totally in opposition to Hegel (Žižek 1991a, p. 94).

[20] This strategy is particularly evident in *For They Know Not What They Do* (1991a), where Žižek provides an explanation of a concept from Lacan, such as the Real as the inconsistency of the symbolic register, then draws a parallel to Hegel's writings, such as the dialectical negation of negation, and then links it to Marx's understanding of ideological structure as void.

[21] In some way this is also true of Pound's brief introduction to Žižek's engagement with theological thought in Goodchild and Phelps' *Religion and European Philosophy* (2017, pp. 479–491—particularly page 482) for the author himself relies upon Sharpe and Boucher (among others).

that, his first analysis of historical shifts between far right and left totalitarianism of the last two centuries *Zgodovina in Nezavedno* (1982) contains an advance insight into his 'theological materialism' (see pp. 102–115). His later veneration of the questioning Job can be compared to his account of Abner's conversion in *Atalia* (pp. 29–31) in *Birokratija I Uživanje* (1984). The same work also contains Žižek's analysis of the sovereign as cross stitch with the help of Kierkegaard (pp. 46–47). Žižek's materialism has always to some extent featured or referred to the theological.

It can be said, however, that it is only in his encounter with Badiou that Žižek begins to develop further his own distinctive understanding of the origin of Christianity and its relationship to Judaism and paganism.[22] Prepared in *The Ticklish Subject*, it is developed in three books, which he published in quick succession: *The Fragile Absolute* (2000), *On Belief* (2001a) and *The Puppet and the Dwarf* (2003). These books should be read together in order to gain a sense of the constant revision and development that Žižek's thinking undergoes in order to arrive at its present form, as observed in works like *The Parallax View* (2006), *Paul's New Moment* (Žižek 2010b, pp. 92–99), *The Monstrosity of Christ* (Žižek and Milbank 2009), *God in Pain* (Žižek and Gunjević 2012) and *Less Than Nothing* (2012a), and also in other recent works, such as *Living in the End Times* (Žižek 2010c, pp. 80–134) and *Absolute Recoil* (Žižek 2014, pp. 245–282), which include chapters or large sections on theology.

Rather than accepting talk of a theological turn, it is more appropriate to speak, as Roland Boer does (2009, pp. 335–390),[23] of theology as playing an important part in Žižek's development as a distinct political thinker. In *Contingency, Hegemony, Universality* (2000), Judith Butler criticises Žižek on the grounds that while his psychoanalysis provides an important contribution to how ideology works at an individual level, it does not provide a solution or a way out (Butler in Butler et al. 2000, pp. 28–29). It rather insists on the notion of constitutive exception, which simultaneously enables and hobbles every effort at emancipation, thereby subverting it:

---

[22] Kotsko (2008, pp. 6–7) is thus correct in his inference that that theology merely comes to play an increased role in Žižek's later thought.

[23] Even though he still speaks of a theological turn in Žižek's thought or 'conversion', Roland Boer offers a valuable account of Žižek's development as a political thinker and the role of theology in that process.

We think we have found a point of opposition to domination, and then realize that that very point of opposition is the instrument through which domination works, and that we have unwittingly enforced the powers of domination through our participation in its opposition. (ibid., p. 28)

Since Žižek's psychoanalytic thought cannot enact change and is therefore impotent, it cannot provide the basis for a viable politics, Butler argues.[24] So, rather than speaking of a theological turn, it is exactly in a response to or development of his political thought that theology plays a crucial role. By engaging further with Christian theology, first Paul and then Jesus, Žižek escapes from the closed-circuit of Lacan's psychoanalysis and emerges as a distinct political thinker.

BADIOU AND PAUL'S TRUTH-EVENT

After the challenge of Butler, Žižek engages with Alain Badiou's similar charge in *The Ticklish Subject* (1999) that psychoanalysis cannot give us any political position.[25] This is or could be considered as Žižek's first effort at a militantly political book (ibid., p. 4), in which he sets about engaging and critically examining Badiou's notion of the truth-event in *Saint Paul* (2003). Thus the point of contact between Žižek and Badiou is not the latter's use of Paul, but his concern with truth, an account of universality. This interest in truth shows Žižek in stark contrast to postmodern philosophy, which refuses to deal with the notion. While he agrees with the postmodern assertion that there is no going back to some premodern understanding of truth, Žižek nevertheless argues for the necessity of a new concept of truth (Žižek 1993, pp. 3–4). This is the point of contact with Badiou, who agrees and proposes that truth or its nature, rather than being a positive body, is something that *happens*, i.e. an *event*.[26] In other words, it does

---

[24]Likewise, Laclau argues that Žižek's political thought is not advanced and 'remains fixed in very traditional categories'. In other words, it is underdeveloped and is merely juxtaposing Marx and Lacan (Laclau in Butler et al. 2000, pp. 206, 209).

[25]Žižek engages or refers to Badiou at various points in his earlier works, but proper engagement comes only in *The Ticklish Subject*. See Žižek (1991a, pp. 188, 270), Žižek (1997, pp. 26, 59, 92), and Žižek (1993, p. 4).

[26]I am here following Žižek's presentation of Badiou's theory in Chapter 3: 'The Politics of Truth, or, Alain Badiou as a Reader of St. Paul' of *The Ticklish Subject* (1999, pp. 127–170). Badiou's Pauline application of event is developed from his seminal *Being and Event* (2006),

not concern the state of things (*being*), but is rather an *event* of location of the political act and subject. The place where that event comes from is the marginalised. Each truth-event corresponds to a given situation, in which all elements are present, but not all are represented. For example, a country contains people who live there without being officially recognised as citizens or legal residents. Žižek agrees with Badiou's conceptualisation of universalism that it is those very excluded, with no place in the order or system, that embody the true universality and represent the whole or entirety in contrast to others, which only represent their particular interests (Žižek 2003, p. 112). It is therefore exactly this excluded element which is the site from which a truth-event erupts. When it does so, only those who embrace the truth-event are *subjects* in the proper sense of the word, and their attempt to follow the consequence of it is called a truth-process. Žižek and Badiou agree that universalism is always the result of a great process of struggle of the excluded that opens with an event.

Badiou then uses Paul as an utmost example of a subject naming the truth-event (Badiou 2003, p. 2).[27] The resurrection of Christ as an unexpected event seizes Paul, causing him to dedicate his life to spreading the gospel. The Pauline category of death or living in the flesh marks the realm of *being*—not being aware of the event—while life or living in the Spirit

which is built in reliance upon Heidegger's *Being and Time* (1962). For a good discussion of Badiou and Žižek's radical act, see Pfeifer's *New Materialism* (2016).

[27]This reading of Paul without the presupposition of any specifically Christian belief or commitment is perhaps pioneered by Jacques Lacan, who, in his seminar on the *Ethics of Psychoanalysis* in 1959, as the lecture draws to a conclusion, uses Romans 7 and paraphrases it to discuss desire (Lacan 1992, p. 83). Lacan explains his use of Paul and the religious text in the following manner: 'We analysts [...] do not have to believe in these religious truths in any way, given that such belief may extend as far as what is called faith, in order to be interested in what is articulated in its own terms in religious experience – in the terms of the conflict between freedom and grace, for example [...]. There is a certain paradox involved in practically excluding from debate and from analysis things, terms and doctrines that have been articulated in the field of faith, on the pretext that they belong to a domain that is reserved for believers' (Lacan 1992, pp. 170–171).

Similarly, Badiou writes in his preface to *St Paul*: 'I care nothing for the Good News he declares, or the cult dedicated to him. But he is a subjective figure of primary importance'. Like Lacan, he emphasises that it is possible and indeed legitimate to read Paul: 'we may draw upon [him] freely, without devotion or repulsion' (Badiou 2003, p. 1). For Badiou, Paul is taken to be exemplary of a kind of commitment that he believes to be necessary for contemporary politics.

marks the realm of living in light of the *truth-event*.[28] Therefore the resurrection is to Badiou the key to Paul's truth-event and his death is merely another indication that God became a human being. Certainly, the resurrection is for Badiou a fable, but he understands that as the very condition for universality—it is not tied to any element of the life of Jesus and enables Paul to structure a subject, which is 'devoid of identity and suspended to an event whose only "proof" lies precisely in its having been declared by a subject' (ibid., p. 5).[29] The differences in this world have thus become indifferent in light of the new event and are materialised in the Pauline conception of church.[30]

Žižek concurs with Badiou's subject without identity and expresses it psychoanalytically as the 'intrusion of the traumatic Real that shatters the predominant symbolic texture' (Žižek 1999, p. 142), a reminder that the subject is not only its Symbolic representation. However, he disagrees with Badiou in two ways: first, the religious example is not only an example but is actually an implicit paradigm for the theory of the truth-event. Second, it is not the resurrection of Christ which seizes Paul, but actually his death on the Cross (ibid., pp. 145–147).[31] He delivers his critique with the help of the Freudian notion of the death drive as that which persists beyond life and death.[32] This negative gesture of detaching oneself from

[28] Žižek on the other hand contrasts *being* and *truth-event* as between law and love. The order of being is the domain of law, whereas the truth-event and fidelity to it belongs to the way of love—what he calls 'the properly Christian way of Love [*agape*]' (Žižek 1999, p. 47). This construction seems theologically odd, since in Pauline theology the contrast is between law and grace, and this is also emphasised by Badiou. See Badiou (2003, pp. 63, 66–67, 74–85). This is picked up by Boer, who argues that Žižek realised his mistake and moved onto grace in *On Belief* (Boer 2009, pp. 337, 349–351). However, Žižek seems to be highlighting the importance of fidelity to the truth-event here. He does say later that the life in 'love is accessible to all of us through grace' (Žižek 1999, p. 147).

[29] Interestingly, while Badiou does not require a historical Jesus, he does on the other hand desire a historical Paul. See 'Who is Paul?' in Badiou (2003, pp. 16–30).

[30] In *Being and Event*, Badiou describes the church precisely as the post-evental 'operator of faithful connection to the Christ-event' (Badiou 2006, p. 392).

[31] Reading the crucifixion as key is also evident in Taubes' *Die politische Theologie des Paulus*, where he insists that it is precisely the message concerning the crucified Messiah which subverts Imperial authority. Indeed, he regards Romans as a declaration of war on the Roman Empire (Taubes 1993, p. 16).

[32] For an interesting theological examination of Žižek's use of Paul, see O. J. Løland (2018) who discerns Žižek's 'introspective' Paul (pp. 113–148) and then considers its application in

a given situation, Žižek argues, is absolutely necessary if something new is to emerge. In Badiou's reading, the death of Christ, as he puts it, has no inherent meaning whatsoever, for it merely prepares the site for the event. However, Žižek argues, in order that his universal message might matter more than his person, Christ had to die (Žižek 1999, p. 157), for it is only through the 'murder of particularity' that universality follows (Žižek 2003, p. 17f.).[33] Only by this negativity can the subject be established. As such, Žižek's criticism is that by ignoring Christ's death on the Cross and merely talking about the resurrection, Badiou understands the truth-event as just a radically new beginning and as such a pseudo-event.

The same criticism continues on to Badiou's reading of Romans 7 (Žižek 1999, pp. 147–149, cf. Badiou 2003, pp. 75–85),[34] in which Paul grapples with something akin to the notion of the *inherent transgression*. The very emergence of a certain 'value' serving as a point of ideological identification relies on its transgression, on some mode of taking a distance from it:

> What shall we say, then? Is the law sinful? Certainly not! Nevertheless, I would not have known what sin was had it not been for the law. For I would not have known what coveting really was, if the law had not said, 'You shall not covet.' But sin, seizing the opportunity afforded by the commandment, produced in me every kind of coveting. For apart from the law, sin was dead. Once I was alive apart from the law; but when the commandment came, sin sprang to life and I died. I found that the very commandment that was intended to bring life actually brought death. For sin, seizing the opportunity afforded by the commandment, deceived me, and through the commandment put me to death. (Romans 7:7–11)

By both Žižek and Badiou, Paul is here understood as the prime example of someone who is starting to become conscious of the contradictory char-

---

Žižek's political thought. Løland challenges it and advocates Nancy Fraser's political theory (pp. 149–196). What is most interesting is Løland's endeavour to show Žižek's presuppositions in his reading of 1 Corinthians (see "Rewriting the Apostle Against Wisdom in 1 Corinthians", pp. 87–112). However, this hermeneutical piece misses the point of Žižek's interpretative endeavour or anti-hermeneutic.

[33] See also Žižek (2018, pp. 36–43).

[34] For a shorter but precise summary of Žižek's engagement with Badiou's reading of Romans 7, read Žižek's 'Paul and the Truth Event' in Davis et al. (2010, pp. 92–99). For a more thorough theological discussion, see Løland's 'Badiou's Truth-Event: Paul Enters the Scene' (2018, pp. 43–51).

acter of the Symbolic Order.[35] They also both agree that the only way out is by identifying with some truth-event. However, whereas Badiou argues for a direct identification with the resurrection in order to escape Law as the obscene superego supplement, Žižek argues that the only solution is that one must die to the law:

> What 'death' stands for is at its most radical, not merely the passing of earthly life but the 'night of the world,'[36] the self-withdrawal, the absolute contraction of subjectivity, the severing of links with 'reality' – this is the 'wiping of the slate clean' that opens up the domain of the symbolic New Beginning. (1999, pp. 154)[37]

The only way to escape the contradictory Symbolic Order, in this case the Law, is by symbolically dying to it, rather than merely enacting a new beginning within it. According to Žižek, that is what marks a real, subjective truth-event.

Therefore, in the process of engaging Badiou's philosophical account of universality, the latter's reading of Paul as the founder of Christianity leads Žižek directly to his own reading of Paul and Christianity.[38] His critique is not developed in purely theoretical terms, but finds Žižek arguing that there is an inner necessity to this turn to theology as 'only Christianity opens up the space for thinking the inexistence of the big Other, insofar as it is the religion of a God who dies' (Žižek 2013b, p. 176). The question of what exactly this means is the subject matter to which I turn my attention

---

[35]Their reading of Romans 7 here essentially follows Lacan's reading of the Law as Symbolic in 'On the Moral Law' (Lacan 1997, p. 83).

[36]Hegel's phrase 'night of the world' is employed by Žižek frequently (1992, pp. 50–52; 1994, p. 145; 1996, p. 78; 1997, pp. 8–10; 2006, p. 44). It is used to express the radical negativity of the subject, the overwhelming excess at the moment of doubt, which is the origin of the Cartesian subject. In 'PART 1: Spirit according to its Concept' of the Jena lectures on the Philosophy of Spirit, Hegel writes that 'the human being is this night, this empty nothing, which contains everything in its simplicity – an unending wealth of many representations, images, of which none belongs to him – or which are not present. This night, the interior of nature, that exists here – pure self [...]. One catches sight of this night when one looks human beings in the eye – into a night that becomes awful' (Hegel 1983).

[37]See also p. 159.

[38]However, while Žižek clearly connects Paul's universalist legacy to Christianity, Badiou places it in the transhistorical revolutionary/communist context. Thus, in *Del'ideology*, Badiou and his co-author François Balmès regard Paul as a 'communist invariant', together with Thomas Müntzer and the German peasant revolt (Badiou and Balmès 1976, pp. 60–75).

next. For now, however, the following observation is in order: Through this engagement with Badiou, Žižek begins to develop his own reading of Christian theology and its import for his own political thought. As we shall see, the latter is thought out through the former (and vice versa).

CHRISTIANITY'S PERVERSE CORE

The engagement with Badiou's reading of Paul and the truth-event leads Žižek to conclude that 'what we need today is the gesture that would undermine capitalist globalisation [with particularisation] from the standpoint of universal Truth, just as Pauline Christianity did to the Roman global Empire' (Žižek 1999, p. 211). Just as the global Empire, which was held together by a non-substantial link to the Roman legal order, was undermined by Pauline Christianity from the standpoint of universal Truth, the same standpoint is needed in the struggle against capitalist globalisation. In a sense, all of Žižek's books on Christianity represent an attempt to grapple with the full implications of this statement. In all of them, after calling for a Pauline-style intervention, he turns to an analysis of what it is about the contemporary situation that makes a Pauline gesture possible and necessary.

Žižek's own understanding of contemporary society is that it is increasingly characterised by perversion.[39] This comes from the fact, already observed in Žižek's discussion of the postsecular, that modernity has permanently undercut the big Other of society.[40] Whereas before God was the privileged name for the big Other, ordering everything and everyone's place in society, once that was no longer the case, the subjects were left in a double bind. Building on Lacan's premise, Žižek argues that the role of the big Other was to prohibit and thereby shield the subjects from harmful pleasures, while at the same time providing a small amount of pleasure through the law's inherent transgression. This means that in modernity, without the law, pleasure threatens to overwhelm the subject, while on

[39]The term is here by Žižek perceived in a broader sense, applied beyond its usual sexual context primarily to political situations—thus for instance describing Stalinism and Nazism as utterly perverse political ideologies (e.g. 1993, p. 195; 1997, p. 69; 2001a, p. 139; 2007, p. 227). It marks a conservative 'solution' to the problem of the decline of the big Other, which reveals a belief in its existence. In that sense, 'perversion is not subversion' (1999, p. 247).

[40]See also Chapter 1: 'On the One' of Žižek (1991a, pp. 7–60).

the other hand, the breakdown of law also threatens to deprive the sub-ject of the small amount of pleasure derived from transgressing the law. According to Žižek (2003, p. 53), any way to counteract the nonexistence of the big Other through an attempt to instal the law artificially or codify its transgression is *Perversion*, and reveals the desperate desire and belief for its existence.[41]

What, then, is the way to avoid perversion, and what does Christianity have to do with that? This is developed and clarified in *The Puppet and the Dwarf*, in which, by again focusing on the problem of *perversion* in Romans 7 as presented by Lacan, Žižek clarifies the connection between the contemporary situation and Pauline intervention. Given that Žižek presents Paul's argument as geared toward escaping perversion, does he propose that the only option is a straightforward turn to the Christian position? Not at all. In Chapter 2 of *The Puppet and the Dwarf*, entitled 'The Thrilling Romance of Orthodoxy' (2003, pp. 34–57), Žižek uses G. K. Chesterton's (1874–1936) *Orthodoxy* (1996) and injects his insights into contemporary debates that show a certain perverse logic,[42] while arguing that perversion is actually the key strategy of existing Christianity (Žižek 2003, p. 53). The Christian system of prohibition and self-denial 'is the only frame within which we can enjoy pagan pleasures: the feeling of guilt is a fake enabling us to give ourselves over to pleasures' (ibid., p. 57). It exhibits the installation of the law artificially and at the same codify its transgression—what he calls a 'fake sacrifice' (ibid., pp. 49–50[43]).

In fact, Žižek goes so far as to wonder if the Christian God is himself a pervert, in that he seems to need the Fall to occur in order to be able

---

[41] As an example, Žižek goes on to mention the imposition of 'traditional values' by the Christian fundamentalists in the United States. While on the surface this imposition represents an attempt to suppress destructive pleasures, the Christian fundamentalist position is at the same time sustained by an 'ambiguous attitude of horror/envy with regard to the unspeakable pleasures in which sinners engage' (Žižek 2003, p. 68).

[42] For example, upholding democratic values through torture (Žižek 2003, p. 37).

[43] While otherwise following Chesterton, Žižek here critiques him for his 'doctrine of conditional joy'—joy that depends on what is forbidden (Chesterton 1996, p. 40). By insisting that there is a constitutive exception (you may have joy, if you…), Žižek argues, Chesterton remains within perversion.

to redeem humanity.[44] He needs Judas to commit the despicable act of betraying Jesus in order to carry out his plan of redemption. It is this very moment of perversion, where God himself seems to operate according to the principle 'let us do evil that good may result' (Romans 8:3), that is the perverse core of Christianity to which the subtitle of *The Puppet and the Dwarf* refers. Therefore, the Christianity of today cannot be the cure for perversion, since it is itself perverted. What is required is to dispose of this perverted core and recover the true, authentic Christian message with its revolutionary potential embodied in its founding gesture. To this we turn next.

THE STORY OF JOB

The first necessary step in removing Christianity's perverse core, Žižek argues, is to fully grasp the distinctiveness of the Jewish context within which Pauline Christianity arose. Just what Žižek means when he talks about the Jewish context is again a project that he develops throughout his books pertaining to Christianity.

In *the Fragile Absolute* and *On Belief*, Žižek attempts to ground his understanding of Judaism in Freud's *Der Mann Moses und die monothe-istische Religion* (1939). In this alternative account of the emergence of Jewish Monotheism, Freud presents Moses as an Egyptian who adhered to the worship of Aton, the first recorded monotheism. When the Pharaoh who had imposed Aton-worship was deposed, Moses turned to the Jewish slaves and led them out of Egypt in the hope of perpetuating the religion of Aton. Moses proved to be a harsh leader, which eventually led to a rebellion against him. The Jews killed him and did away with Aton worship. However, just as the murdered primaeval father in *Totem und Tabu* (1913) was transformed into a domineering internalised authority by his guilty sons, the murdered Moses returned in a more fearsome and powerful form as Yahweh. Freud argues that Paul's creation of Christianity based on the death of Christ was an attempt to move beyond this primal crime and the inherent guilt. Whereas the Jews and other religions are forever haunted by guilt for their act because they do not admit to committing it, Žižek

[44] This draws on Žižek's previous discussions of the philosopher Malebranche as proposing that God incited Adam and Eve to sin in order to be able to redeem them (Žižek 1999, pp. 116–119 at p. 118).

concludes, Christians achieve a kind of purification, or are at peace, because they openly admit to it (Žižek 2000, p. 90).

It is in *The Puppet and the Dwarf* ('Subtraction, Jewish and Christian' 2003, pp. 122–143) that Žižek for the first time develops his own account of Jewish origins, which becomes the basis for his most systematic stance on Christianity. Abandoning Freud's account, he instead focuses on the (unusual) figure of Job as the founder of the Jewish religion.[45] The choice of this Old Testament figure is due to his representation of doubt or questioning of the symbolic Order, which, Žižek argues, is the absolutely necessary first step toward revolutionary change:

> What makes the Book of Job so provocative is not simply the presence of multiple perspectives without a clear resolution (the fact that Job's suffering involves a different perspective than that of religious reliance on God); Job's perplexity stems from the fact that he experiences God as an impenetrable Thing; he is uncertain what He wants from him in inflicting the ordeals to which he is submitted, and, consequently, he – Job – is unable to ascertain how he fits in the overall divine order, unable to recognise his place in it. (Žižek 2003, p. 124)

Žižek's understanding of Job is adopted from G. K. Chesterton's philosophical essay *The Book of Job: An Introduction* (1916), with particular interest in the commentary's emphasis that the *Book of Job* does not provide a satisfactory answer to why Job suffers, why God tests Job or why God refuses to explain His design. It is with reference to the latter that Chesterton remarks, 'The refusal of God to explain His design is itself a burning hint of His design. The riddles of God are more satisfying than the solutions of man' (ibid.). In Žižek's words, God 'comes to share Job's astonishment at the chaotic madness of the created universe' (Žižek 2009a, p. 48). What occurs is a Hegelian transposing of epistemological limitation into an ontological fault (cf. Žižek 2003, p. 55): God himself is astonished. It is through this dialectical transition that God or the big Other as the constitutive exception, Chesterton's or actually existing Christianity's perversion of conditional joy, is overcome:

---

[45] See also Žižek's 'A Meditation on Michelangelo's *Christ on the Cross*' in Davis et al. (2010a, pp. 176–179).

God is here no longer the miraculous exception that guarantees the normality of the universe, the unexplainable X who enables us to explain everything else; he is, on the contrary, himself overwhelmed by the overflowing miracle of his Creation. Upon a closer look, there is nothing normal in our universe — everything, every small thing that is, is a miraculous exception; viewed from a proper perspective, every normal thing is a monstrosity. (Žižek and Milbank 2009, p. 50)

Cf. with Chesterton:

To startle man, God becomes for an instant a blasphemer; one might almost say that God becomes for an instant an atheist. He unrolls before Job a long panorama of created things, the horse, the eagle, the raven, the wild ass, the peacock, the ostrich, the crocodile. He so describes each of them that it sounds like a monster walking in the sun. The whole is a sort of psalm or rhapsody of the sense of wonder. The maker of all things is astonished at the things he has Himself made. (Chesterton 1916, p. xxiii)

When God appears at the end of the book, Žižek argues, he doesn't provide an answer to Job's questions, but 'acts like someone caught in a moment of impotence – or at the very least, weakness – and tries to escape his predicament by empty boasting' (Žižek 2003, p. 125). It was Job, the revolutionary ideal, who brought God to this point of confusion and seeming bewilderment by His own creation, with his relentless questioning. He is the archetypal figure of someone resisting meaning. Certainly, this is very different to the traditional understanding of Job as a patient sufferer with a firm belief in God. Nonetheless, Žižek argues that the book is an exemplary case of the critique of ideology in human history. The book dismisses any attempt of legitimising suffering, represented by Job's 'comforting' friends,[46] against whom God himself takes Job's side (Job 42:7–9). Žižek goes on to point out that what is most interesting is Job's silence after God

[46]Žižek compares the three friends and their insistence on inscription of meaning to the three doctors in Freud's account of a dream in which he examines his patient Irma's throat (Žižek 2009a, p. 53).

speaks.[47] He does not continue with an open declaration that God has failed him, but remains silent. According to Žižek, this is

> neither because he was crushed by God's overwhelming presence, nor because he wanted thereby to indicate his continuous resistance, that is, the fact that God avoided answering Job's question, but because in a gesture of silent solidarity, he perceived the divine impotence. God is neither just nor unjust, simply impotent. What Job suddenly understood was that it was not him, but God himself, who was actually on trial in Job's calamities, and He failed the test miserably. (2003, pp. 126–127)

In a way, Žižek argues, Job's silence also indicates that the Jewish community still persists with something analogous to the superego structure. Even though God's omnipotence is discredited, Jews still continue to engage in ritual practices as if nothing happened, in order to conceal God's impotence (ibid., p. 129). More importantly, along the line of Marx, it is not only ritual practices but the observation of the Jewish Law, with its dimension of divine justice, which legitimises any temporary injustices. The Jewish Law stands as the prime example of the ideological fantasy. In fact, this is what leads Žižek to contend in *The Parallax View* that 'the proclamation of the Decalogue is not the normal case of ideological interpolation: The Decalogue is precisely a law *deprived* of the obscene fantasmatic support' (Žižek 2006, p. 427). It is therefore imperative that any attempt to escape from the perverse logic of the obscene superego supplement start here.

CHRIST ESCAPES THE CYCLE

Only with an understanding of its Jewish context, Žižek argues, can Paul's revolutionary gesture be properly understood. Actually, in opposition to Nietzsche, who understands Paul as power-hungry and filled with hatred and desire for revenge against the Jewish Law (Nietzsche 1964, pp. 39–42),

---

[47] Žižek simply ignores Job's response to God in 42:1–6, where Job admits that he was wrong and God was right. No doubt, he could argue that Job's reply is in a sense part of Job's subsequent decision to keep the status quo. Still, he is quick to notice verses 7–9 regarding Job's friends. Chesterton certainly doesn't understand God as silent, but as rebuking not only Job's comforters, but also Job—the accuser: 'God rebukes alike the man who accused and the men who defended Him'. See Chesterton, *The Book of Job*, http://www.chesterton.org/introduction-to-job/.

Žižek understands Paul as a Jew, rather than a convert.[48] From this perspective, Paul did not abandon the Jewish position, but did something with and within the Jewish position itself. What Paul did was to bring about a subversive new understanding of the Law, which was otherwise an obstacle to the Gentiles (Žižek 2003, pp. 92–121). In explaining how Paul manages to do this, Žižek echoes Freud's basic scheme of the relationship between Judaism and Christianity, namely, his contention that Paul founds Christianity by revealing what Judaism kept hidden. Yet where Freud views Christ as a repetition of Moses, Žižek views him as a repetition of Job.

However, Christ's repetition of Job is not just a simple repetition, but a radicalisation. In other words, Christ brings the act of Job to its conclusion. Job, who out of solidarity chooses to remain silent upon discovering God's impotence, in this way maintains the logic of the subject supposed to believe, keeping up appearances for the sake of the big Other. This big Other is no longer God, but the human public in general. Christ, however, breaks this cycle of the subject supposed to believe through his cry of dereliction on the Cross (Matthew 27:45–46), which, because he is the Incarnation of God, represents more than just a cry of anguish and pain, as Žižek explains: 'Christ's words on the Cross "Father,[49] why have you forsaken me?" — in this moment of total abandonment, the subject experiences and fully assumes the inexistence of the big Other' (2002b, p. 180). Because Christ himself is God, this is rather a proclamation of judgement: where there is supposed to be God, there is nothing. There is no objective meaning in history and no big Other who guar-antees the happy outcome of our lives and deeds. What is more, 'the impotent God who failed in creation' is the split Absolute subject: 'the traumatic experience *of* God is also the enigma *for* God himself – our failure to comprehend God is what Hegel called a "reflexive determination" of the divine self-limitation' (Žižek

<hr/>

[48]Judaism is thus in a dialectical relationship to Christianity: Without Judaism first identifying and remaining faithful to the fantasmatic kernel, Christianity would not have been able to identify with it and show it to be empty. Without the Jewish community constituted as an ethnic remainder, Paul would not have been able to claim that the whole of humanity is a remainder.

[49]In his quotation of Christ's cry of dereliction in Matthew 27:45–46, Žižek replaces 'eloi – God' with 'Father', thus bringing it into a smoother compatibility with Lacan and Freud's role of the father in psychoanalysis. Pound contends that in this way Žižek conflates two distinct events: Christ's forsakenness by 'God' in Matthew and his committal to the 'Father' in Luke 23:46. The result is of course that abandonment has the last word. See Pound (2008, pp. 48–49). Thus Žižek's 'error' is indeed intentional, like his selectivity.

2001a, pp. 132–133). By borrowing Chesterton's words, Žižek claims that on the Cross, 'God seemed for an instant to be an atheist' (Žižek 2003, p. 14).

Theologically speaking, Žižek's understanding of the death of God himself on the Cross is along the lines of Philippians 2:7—Christ empties himself in a kenotic way, and in this way enables or brings about a gap (Žižek 2003, p. 26; 2010c, p. 118). In this sense, the Christian God of kenosis is the actualised difference in that he himself is the very person who provokes the question of whether he is still God.[50] This kenosis in its radicality as self-sacrifice of God is enabled by the fact that Christ is God. While the God of the Old Testament is still 'the real thing of beyond', the divine dimension of Christ is 'just a tiny grimace, an imperceptible shade, which differentiates him from other (ordinary) humans'. In that sense Christ is '"the Thing itself", or, more accurately, "the Thing itself" is nothing but the rupture/gap that makes Christ not fully human' (Žižek 2001b, p. 101).

According to Žižek, this theme of the death of God still constitutes a challenge today, and for reasons which are indeed consistent with the critique of the perverse core of the actually existing Christianity that he presents in *The Puppet and the Dwarf* (2003). As he sees it, the very concept of Trinity or the triune God leads not only to monotheism, but also ultimately to atheism. The importance of the belief that God himself dies on the Cross is displayed in the early church history, with Tertullian, who held that the true Christian belief is that God himself died and yet lives eternally, and also during the Aryan controversy and against Apollinarian circles, when Athanasius insisted that it was God himself who was crucified (Tertullian's *Adversus Marcionem* cited in Jüngel, 1977, p. 85).[51] However, any discussion of or reference to the crucified God loses the edge where Athanasius claims that Christ did not suffer in his divinity, but in his flesh for us (Athanasius' *Contra Arianos*, cited in Jüngel, 1977, p. 86). Afterwards the theological discussion of the death of God subsides and only re-emerges in the late nineteenth and twentieth century. As a result, Žižek argues, it remains an enigma (Žižek 2009a, p. 39). Žižek's understanding

---

[50]Žižek probably derives this understanding of kenosis from Chesterton. The concept appears also in Gianni Vattimo's integration of the concept of the death of God in 'the God who is Dead' (Vattimo 2002, pp. 11–24).

[51]The examples of Tertullian and Athanasius are here mentioned only to illustrate the extent or importance which a theoretical understanding of the Cross in Christianity has occupied.

of the Cross here is fully Hegelian in that the infinite pain of the loss or death of God is sublimated in God himself, 'as a moment of the supreme Idea':

> God himself is dead [...], purely as a moment of the supreme Idea, the pure concept must give philosophical existence to what used to be either the moral precept that we must sacrifice the empirical Being, or the concept of formal abstraction, to re-establish the idea of absolute freedom and along with it the absolute passion (as in suffering), the speculative Good Friday in place of the historic Good Friday, to speculatively re-establish Good Friday in the whole truth and harshness of its godlessness. (Hegel 1977, pp. 190–191)

This re-establishment of the Good Friday in its 'whole truth and harshness of its godlessness', Žižek argues, is the potential (if read properly) of Chesterton's non-perverse reading of the death of God. Indeed, Žižek's claim is even that it was 'Chesterton, who thought through the notion of the "death of God" to its radical conclusion: only in Christianity God himself has to go through atheism' (Žižek 2009a, p. 39). The fact that God in Chesterton's reading is a suffering God means first of all that God is involved with his creation, indeed involved in the suffering (Žižek 2009a, pp. 47–48). Since it is God himself who dies on the Cross, this reading of the event prevents any attempt at resurrection of God as the big Other, perversion. In contrast to the standard form of atheism, where 'God dies for men who stop believing in him; in Christianity, God dies for himself' (Žižek 2003, p. 15). Since God did not die for us, but for himself, this precludes a sacrificial reading of his death.

This non-perverse God who dies for himself is a God who refuses to guarantee the meaning of our reality, a God who is no longer above or beyond, but engaged in this reality, as in his answer to Job and in Christ's cry on the Cross. In a long comment on Job in one of his conversations with Glyn Daly, Žižek gives the following elaboration: '[T]he moment you accept suffering as something that doesn't have a deeper meaning, it means that we can change it; fight against it. This is the zero level of critique of ideology – when you don't read meaning into it' (Žižek and Daly 2004, p. 161). Žižek is quick to reply to any objection under the umbrella of the inscrutability of God's ways by recalling Job's lesson:

> The legacy of Job precludes such a gesture of taking a refuge in the standard transcendent figure of God as a secret Master who knows the meaning of what

appears to us to be a meaningless catastrophe, the God who sees the entire picture in which what we perceive as a stain contributes to global harmony. [...] Christ's death on the Cross thus means that we should immediately ditch the notion of God as a transcendent caretaker who guarantees the happy outcome of our acts, the guarantee of historical teleology – Christ's death on the Cross is the death of this God, it repeats Job's stance, it refuses any 'deeper meaning' that obfuscates the brutal reality of historical catastrophes. (Žižek and Milbank 2009, pp. 54–55)

If God is dead not just for us but for himself, then what does Žižek do with the biblical account of the resurrection? Does he ignore it or dismiss it in order to avoid resurrecting God as absolute? As explained in *The Monstrosity of Christ* he reads it in a Hegelian way, insisting that 'Crucifixion and Resurrection [...] should be perceived not as two consecutive events, but as *a purely formal parallax shift on one and the same event*: Crucifixion *is* Resurrection – to see this, one has only to include oneself in the picture' (ibid., p. 291). He goes further by saying that this is not a Hegelian reading, but Pauline, since it was the Apostle who reread the death of Christ as a triumph, thus sublating crucifixion as already resurrection (1991a, p. 78).

A Theological Materialism

This proclamation of God's impotence in Christ's cry of dereliction, Žižek argues, marks the emergence of materialism and explains his insistence at the (previously mentioned) start of *The Puppet and the Dwarf* that in order to become a dialectical materialist one should go through the Christian experience (Žižek 2003, p. 6). The Christ-event reveals not only the nonexistence of the big Other, but opens up the space for thinking about its implications (Žižek and Milbank 2009, p. 287), that is the inconsistency and contingency of reality itself (2006, p. 79).[52] The event not only reveals that there is nothing but material reality, but also that this material reality is itself inconsistent and incomplete. Without this experience, for example, the religious core survives in humanism, even up to Stalinism with its belief in history as the big Other that decides on the objective meaning of our deeds. In a 2008 Lecture at Vanderbilt University entitled 'Between Fear and Trembling: On Why Only Atheists Can Believe' (Žižek 2008a),

[52] For a good presentation of this, see Pfeifer's 'Žižek and the Materialism of the Immaterial, or Why Hegel Is Not an Idealist' (2016, pp. 93–113).

Žižek gives the example of many communist cadres who committed sui-
cide when Stalinism was renounced in Russia. The reason for that, Žižek
argues, was not that they were unaware of the atrocities that were committed (quite the opposite), but the fact that there was now no historical big
Other to justify it. Without the Christian experience the big Other remains.
Žižek's description of a true dialectical materialist as one who necessarily
goes through the Christian experience, indicates clearly that the Christian
experience itself is not dispensable. In other words, only Christianity has
the ability to become genuinely materialistic.

This was again confirmed at *The Actuality of the Theologico-Political Con-
ference* at the Birkbeck Institute, hosted by Žižek himself, who, to Eric
Santner's question of why the persistent turning to Christianity, replied
that without the theological, critique of ideology fails. 'The old syntagm,
the "theologico-political", acquires new relevance here: it is not only that
every politics is grounded in a 'theological' view of reality, it is also that
every theology is inherently political, an ideology of a new collective space'
(Žižek 2010c, p. 119).

Žižek claims that genuine materialism and Christian theology mutually
presuppose each other; therefore the role of theology in his work cannot
be reduced to the status of an illustration or a passing fad, and neither can
it be dismissed as a purely negative concern. The latter seems to be the
understanding of Žižek's engagement with theology by John D. Caputo.
In his review of *The Monstrosity of Christ*, he expresses doubts about Žižek's
sincerity and guesses that his true intent is to undermine Christian belief
in God:

> We all know that Žižek can very well make his main case with no mention
> of Christ at all, that he can use the seminars of Lacan, the films of Alfred
> Hitchcock or the novels of Stephen King just as well. His whole point, as
> he says elsewhere, is subversive: to build a Trojan-horse theology, to slip the
> nose of a more radical materialism under the Pauline tent of theology in order
> to announce the death of God […]. He discusses Christian doctrines like the
> Trinity, the Incarnation and the Crucifixion, the way an analyst talks with a
> patient who thinks there is a snake under his bed, trying patiently to heal the
> patient by going along with the patient's illusions until the patient is led to
> see the illusion. (Caputo 2009)

However, Caputo's understanding of Žižek acting like an analyst showing that God is dead is incorrect by not being radical enough, since for

Žižek God himself is the analyst showing that he is dead. Far from Žižek insincerely subverting belief, he rather sincerely engages the essence of Christian belief: a God who suffers and dies.

Schelling's *Die Weltalter* (1946) is for Žižek the founding text of dialectical materialism, not despite its theological content, but precisely because of it:

> The point is not to reject what is not true in Schelling, the false ('obscurantist,' 'theosophico-mythological') shell of his system, in order to attain its kernel of truth; its truth, rather, is inextricably linked to what, from our contemporary perspective, cannot but appear as blatantly 'not true,' so that every attempt to discard the part or aspect considered 'not true' inevitably entails the loss of the truth itself [...]. (Žižek 1996, p. 7)

Indeed, Christianity is the prerequisite of the critique of ideology. This critique is inherently Christian in and of its experience and is itself articulated in theological terms and continues to address core theological issues. This is seen in *The Parallax View*, in which Žižek not only carries forward the major conclusions concerning Christianity reached in his earlier works, but expresses new developments of ideological critique in theological terms (2006, pp. 68–123). It is through explicit discussions of theological terms that notions such as the reality of human freedom are introduced. Such notions, which possess a symbolic authority, are then grounded in the material, the physical. He does this by engaging with the sciences, such as cognitive science, quantum mechanics and evolutionary theory.[53] In this way, Žižek does not end up affirming the metaphysical concept of God, but replaces an outdated and instinctive metaphysical system with a materialistic model, which can make sense of the latest science and simultaneously does justice to the experience of human freedom. Dialectical materialism is thus a non-reductive type of materialism, which does not claim that 'everything is matter', but instead confers upon 'immaterial phenomena a specific positive nonbeing' (2006, p. 168).

---

[53] See his recent 'Marx Reads Object-Oriented Ontology' (Žižek 2018, pp. 23–31), where quantum physics provides an insight into immateriality of materialism. See also Žižek (1996, p. 230), where Žižek uses quantum physics to provide a scientific grounding for the idea that the realm of deterministic physical law is 'non-all'. Thus human subjectivity emerges out of the order of determinism in a dialectic manner.

At the same time, this type of materialism is not simply non-reductive, i.e. it does not merely posit non-material beings. Instead it is truly dialectically sublated (One is only defined in relation to the other and incorporates the other into itself.) in that the autonomous symbolic level of reality is necessarily grounded in the contradictory material level (Žižek 1996, p. 74). In his treatment of the understanding of the death of Christ described above, Žižek therefore proposes that the proper understanding is only that which grounds the symbolic in the material—the understanding that exposes the human subject as self-legislating, without a divine master. God thus functions as the ultimate ethical agency putting the burden on humanity to organise itself. In *Paul's New Moment*, Žižek thus concludes: 'This is why I – precisely as a radical leftist – think that Christianity is far too precious a thing to leave to conservative fundamentalists. We should fight for it. Our message should not be, "You can have it," but "No, it's ours. You are kidnapping it"' (Žižek 2010a, p. 181). Therefore, Žižek's dialectical materialism is properly theological materialism.

A Theological Overcoming of the Constitutive Exception

In *On Belief* (2001a), Žižek fully spells out the import of Christianity's overcoming of the constitutive exception for his political thought, which takes on the form of Leninism, and by this providing a full reply to Butler's accusation of the political impotency of his psychoanalytic thought. On the last pages of the book, Žižek is clear:

> Here enters the 'good news' of Christianity: the miracle of faith is that it IS possible to traverse the fantasy, to undo this founding decision, to start one's life all over again, from the zero point – in short, to change Eternity itself (what we 'always–already are'). Ultimately, the 'rebirth' of which Christianity speaks (when one joins the community of believers, one is born again) is the name for such a new Beginning. (ibid., p. 148)

It is important to observe the change of language that occurs away from Lacanian terminology in this passage. Instead, it leans heavily on theological terminology, which enables a political act.[54] At the end of the book Lacan subsides and we instead find references to Søren Kierkegaard, Karl Marx, Evelyn Waugh, Berthold Brecht, Friedrich Wilhelm Joseph von Schelling and Vladimir Lenin. It is Lenin, with his absolute commitment to the revolutionary cause and the suspension of ethics in its name, who is a repetition of the paradigmatic Christ-event, and who changed the coordinates of the liberal-capitalist world order (ibid., p. 114).[55] Lenin's advocation of actual freedom, representing the ability to step outside or transcend the particular context in question, as opposed to formal freedom, where the freedom is only apparent and its boundaries are in fact set by a certain situation, is thus the choice to change the very coordinates of that situation. Lenin's actual vs. formal freedom is thus of the same order as Christianity's possibility of a thoroughly new beginning, and Roland Boer is certainly right when he extrapolates that Žižek's deliberation of Lenin's actual vs. formal freedom is a Leninist formulation not only of Badiou's Being and the event, but first and foremost of law and grace in Paul's theology (Boer 2009, p. 112). While there are frequent references to Lacan in *On Belief*, the main points of Christian theology are no longer interpreted by means of his categories, but by Lenin, in the company of whom theology articulates key political points.

[54] A little earlier Žižek actually invokes the term 'miracle', quoting Lenin's contention that 'in some respects, a revolution is a miracle' (Žižek 2001a, p. 84).

[55] Žižek actually compares Lenin as a revolutionary figure to Paul and Christ to Marx, although he is not the first to do so—Badiou does so as well. See Badiou (2003, p. 2), cf. Žižek (2000, p. 2). Of course, Žižek's Lenin is the Lenin of the revolutionary moment from April to October 1917 (not the earlier or later one). He is presented as the purest historical example of an evental subject who has had the courage to act without the sanction of the big Other. Boucher and Sharpe critique Žižek that this image of Lenin is not actual, complete or true. See 'Repeating Lenin, an Infantile Disorder?' in Sharpe and Boucher (2010, pp. 225–228). Of course Žižek is well aware that there are more controversial aspects to Lenin, but he refuses to reduce the potentiality of Lenin to that contentious figure. This is also his reply to accusations of supersessionism on account of his re-appropriation of Hegel's problematic model of religion (see Hart 2002, pp. 553–557). Žižek is more than aware of Hegelian narrative as ideological legitimization of Western colonialism, but argues that it is wrong to stop there and overlook Hegel's philosophy as providing the 'ultimate subversive intellectual tools that allow us to discern and question the very Eurocentric colonialist bias' (ibid., p. 580). By doing so, Hart reduces Hegel to a mere racist ideologue of capitalist colonialism.

Militant Politics of External and Contingent Grace

One such example is Žižek's theological articulation that Lenin's actual freedom, or Badiou's event, or Christianity's act of a thoroughly new beginning, is only a possibility of something new; it is not ensured. This point is very important and deserving a quote from Žižek:

> By taking upon himself all the Sins and then, through his death, paying for them, Christ opens up the way for the redemption of humanity – however, by his death, people are not directly redeemed, but given the POSSIBILITY of redemption, of getting rid of the excess. This distinction is crucial: Christ does NOT do our work for us, he does not pay our debt, he 'merely' GIVES US A CHANCE – with his death, he asserts OUR freedom and responsibility, i.e. he 'merely' opens up the possibility, for us, to redeem ourselves through the 'leap into faith,' i.e. by way of choosing to 'live in Christ' – in imitatio Christi, we REPEAT Christ's gesture of freely assuming the excess of Life, instead of projecting/displacing it onto some figure of the Other. (2001a, p. 105)

As already noted, *On Belief* is saturated with theological language, but in relation to this quote one term is deserving of special mention: 'grace' (ibid., pp. 1–5). Žižek understands grace as the unexpected, unpredictable revolutionary moment, which arrives from the outside. Theologically speaking, grace concerns salvation, which cannot be earned or deserved, but is rather given by God as a pure externality and contingency, to use Žižek's terminology.

While God is an entirely different matter for Žižek, he does stress the analogous impossibility of predicting revolution, thus maintaining the externality of grace. Even if one assesses the social and political situation, it is impossible to predict how, when, or even why the revolution will occur.[56] In this context of Žižek, God stands for the radically unexpected. Thus we see Žižek developing a materialist theology of grace as external, unexpected and beyond human agency, which appears as fore-ordained only after it was received, all in order to explain that a suspension of political coordinates appears as leading up to it and inevitable only after it occurs. When Paul announces the Messiah and thereby brings about a revolution against the

---

[56]Thus for example the Arab Spring, a surge of collective action throughout North Africa and the Middle East, was unpredictable and indeed unpredicted.

existing symbolic order of Judaism and Hellenism, this is not an externalisation of an internal event, but an event whose Truth only becomes evident or revealed afterwards. Žižek's theory of a political act seeks to promote or give courage to the promotion of political alternatives. These, however, are unimaginable or we can say no more about them, but as soon we enter the domain of this political act, it becomes cognitively accessible and allows us to experience a truly new communality.

For Žižek, it seems, theology forms one of the most complex ways of speaking about radical political change. Moreover, as Boer points out, his militant politic 'is an inescapably radical and revolutionary *theological* doctrine' (Boer 2009, p. 376). Theology is political and the political is theological; therefore, political theology is not only possible, but necessary (Žižek 2010c, pp. 118–119). The attempt to think politically, without religious categories, was a failure, Žižek argues, and contends that today's political thought has been turned into an ethics and a legal philosophy that promotes moral values and ethical policies. Seeking change in this way, Žižek argues, is a closed loop where every attempt to transgress the law, insofar as it is carried out in within its framework, actually affirms it.[57] Theology can help to revive the political, to re-politicise politics, by constructing new political subjects who break out of the ethico-legal entanglement and ground a new collective space. Žižek concludes: 'Paraphrasing Kierkegaard, one can say that what we need today is a *theologico-political* suspension of the ethico-legal' (ibid., p. 119). It is to Žižek's appropriation of Kierkegaard that we now turn.

Žižek's Atonement: An Act of Madness That Suspends the Law

Žižek's doctrine of atonement is in stark contrast to the four dominant traditional atonement models. In *Did Somebody Say Totalitarianism?* (2001c, pp. 45–59), he dismisses all four of them and instead argues that:

> Christ's sacrifice, with its paradoxical structure (it is the very person against whom we humans have sinned, whose trust we have betrayed, who atones and pays the prices for our sins), suspends the logic of sin and punishment, of

---

[57] Following this, see Vladimir Safatle's attempt in his 'Politics of Negativity in Slavoj Žižek' (2016, pp. 69–84) to think institutions of 'negativity' that would 'de-identificate subjects'.

legal or ethical retribution, of 'settling accounts,' by bringing it to the point of self-relating. (ibid., pp. 49–50)

Christ is the self-willed victim who, despite Peter's protestations, freely gives himself over to the chief priests. His death thus performs a psychoanalytic cut, by introducing a moment of madness and suspending the Law or social convention. Far from mediation between God and the world in the traditional sense, Christ is the *vanishing mediator*, whose death is the death of God as the big Other or the constitutive exception (Žižek 2010a). The atonement is thus best understood as a break, a cut or trauma, in the sense that Christ traumatises the Jewish Law and the systems of retributive justice by committing a senseless act not circumscribed by social convention.[58] It is in *The Fragile Absolute* that Žižek begins to spell out Christianity's breaking out of the logic of constitutive exception, of the vicious cycle of law and sin (2000, pp. 99–100, 133, 135, 143). This is the 'Christian experience' to which Žižek refers as necessary in order to become a true dialectical materialist, the recognition or realisation that Christ stands for a break with all totalities and cosmic schemes. Instead of the indiscriminate, postmodern talk about differences, Christ divides between good and bad in accordance with the Gospel, saying: 'Do you suppose that I came to bring peace on earth? I tell you, no, but rather division' (Luke 12:51).

God's self-abandonment on the Cross is already upheld in *For They Know Not* as the ultimate example of a dialectical negation of negation, a change in perspective that transforms an apparent defeat into victory (1991a, p. 29). Using theological language, Žižek calls this triumph the resurrection, but interprets it in a non-traditional way.[59] His interpretation is in line with Hegel, for whom the death of God in Christ represents the giving over of God's self to the world, whereas his resurrection was and is in the community.[60] It is identical with the advent of the Holy Spirit,

---

[58] Žižek therefore sees Christ as an example of the death drive—bringing into focus the desire for death in his relentless pursuit of Calvary. It is this desire for death that upsets the socio-symbolic (Žižek 2001a, pp. 107–110).

[59] For how this non-literal resurrection functions, see 'Paul and the Truth Event' (Žižek in Davis et al. 2010b, pp. 87–92).

[60] The move from religion to politics by the Young Hegelians that was to follow, and that was in a way more obviously critical of religion, was thus traced out already by Hegel. Such is the case of *Das Leben Jesu* (1864), in which David Strauss examined the representation of Jesus's life in terms of an elaborate understanding of myth, in which the incarnation of the

as the bond of the new community founded on Christ's revelation on the Cross. Thereby, in a dialectical reasoning, the Holy Spirit is the immediate consequence of the crucifixion, or the public revelation that the big Other does not exist.[61] Žižek states that 'from the Christian standpoint, praising Christ *is* the act of accusing God-the-Father' (Žižek 2010c, p. 115). In other words, it is an embodiment of the negativity of the Cross. Žižek describes this with reference to Matthew 18:20, 'For where two or three gather in my name, there am I with them', but departs from the original by interpreting it as 'When there will be love between two of you, I will be there' (Žižek 2013b, p. 177). The Christian community is thus, like the Jewish community, bound together by solidarity with the impotence of God as the big Other. What distinguishes the Christian community is its dispensing with the Jewish secret:

> The secret to which the Jews remain faithful is the horror of the divine impotence – and it is this secret that is revealed in Christianity. This is why Christianity could only occur after Judaism: it reveals the horror first confronted by the Jews. (2003, p. 129)

Žižek considers Christianity's subjective destitution as an act or even model of traversing the political order (Žižek 1989, p. 161). The death of God allows a breaking free from the existing normative order. Only in such a consideration is one able to act outside the existing socio-political order.

THE HOLY SPIRIT COMMUNITY

This community of the Holy Spirit is a new form of sociality, which is formed and held together through the revelation of the big Other's impotence, but also replaces him in his abdication (Žižek 2010c, pp. 371–375; 2014, p. 274). This new community is thus established and organised upon the remainder, that which is left and could not be killed on the Cross (Žižek

Logos was not solely limited to Jesus, but was through him distributed among the multiplicity of individuals.

[61] In an interview, 'Žižek and Dupuy: Religion, Secularism, and Political Belonging', given together with Jean-Pierre Dupuy, Žižek, after delivering an account of his understating of the resurrection, explains or rather defends it by saying: 'Maybe my reading of the resurrection is too simplistic, but it is my reading!' (Žižek and Dupuy 2014, 1t 44:20).

2013a, p. 173).[62] The experienced state of destitution thus becomes a catalyst for change:

> Paradoxically, the fall of this big Other [...] is not the same as the disappearance of belief – in a way, it opens up the space of an authentic belief which sustains an act, a belief which is no longer transposed onto, sustained, or covered by some figure of the big Other. In taking the risk of an act, I fully assume the belief in myself, accepting that there is no Other to believe for me, in my place. This is the properly Christian belief, the message of God's death: the Christian community of believers is alone with its belief, freely assuming full responsibility for it, no longer relying on a transcendental authority that would guarantee it. (Žižek 2010c, p. 134)

While destitution is here understood by Žižek as having a dimension of the terrifying, in that it represents a realisation that man is utterly alone without the ideological support of the big Other, it is at the same time a realisation of freedom. Forsakenness thus enables a new form of community which is significantly characterised by two things: It is a sociality that is truly *universal*, in that everyone can participate in it, and the participation is *direct*, irrespective of their social status and position (ibid., p. 120). In the words of Paul: 'There is neither Jew nor Greek, there is neither slave nor free, there is no male and female, for you are all one in Christ Jesus' (Galatians 3:28). It is also the first form of sociality without any hidden agendas, Žižek claims, for it is truly revealing of the nothingness behind it (2000, p. 139).

Because of that, it is a community which truly embraces differences. The death of Christ, or God's self-undermining, opens up the possibility of a collective of subjects who are directly confronted with each other apart from the symbolic fiction imposed by the big Other. This kind of love, founded on the Real of the subject (2009b, p. 105; 2003, p. 130), is the opposite of sentimental love which idealises the other subject, in that it directly identifies with its finitude and weakness. In other words, it is not simply a form of liberal tolerance, which abstracts from differences, such as race, religion or gender, and accords everyone a generic set of human

---

[62]Žižek is here using Eagleton's exposition of the sacrament of the Eucharist (Eagleton 2008, p. 272).

rights. Christian love,[63] Žižek argues, goes beyond that by loving people not in spite of their differences, or despite their weaknesses, but loving them exactly for those traits. In this way it is an event or moment of caring for people as they truly are.[64] The maxim 'God is love' (1 John 4:8) should thus be read alongside 'No one has ever seen God; but if we love one another, God lives in us and his love is made complete in us' (1 John 4:12):

> And here love enters: the most radical moment of love is not the belief of others which sustains the subject in its existence, but the subject's own counter-gesture, the terrifyingly daring act of fully accepting that its very existence depends on others, that – to put it in somewhat inappropriate poetic terms – I am nothing but a figure in the dreamspace of an inconsistent other. (Žižek 2014, pp. 274–275)

In order to elaborate the radical character of this Christian love, Žižek turns to the words of Jesus from Luke 14:26: 'If anyone comes to me and does not hate his father and his mother, his wife and his children, his brothers and sisters – yes, even his own life – he cannot be my disciple'. For Žižek this verse embodies the ethical suspension achieved by the Cross (1999, p. 115),[65] whereby the substance of social life is renounced, in order for it to exist as such. Thus the verse is not read as a constitutive exception of the social order, but the very means of breaking from it. Here 'love

---

[63] Žižek is diverging from trend here by focusing on Christ, for it is usually Paul's emphasis on love, which becomes especially important for materialist readings. Beginning perhaps with Jacob Taubes' (1993, pp. 52–53) warning that Paul's love is not to be understood as in any way sentimental, but as ingredient to a rather clear-eyed political project. With reference to Romans 13:8–10, Taubes supposes that it is Paul rather than Jesus who is the decisive inventor of a love ethic and notes that where Jesus is said to have reduced the commandments to two—love of God and of neighbour—Paul dispenses with the first and emphasises only the latter. Of course, Žižek does uphold Paul to Christ as a Lenin to Marx, but it is important to note the engagement of Žižek with Christ and his teachings as a theological figure (just as Paul), rather than a militant figure.

[64] For an interesting read, see Tupinamba's 'Concrete Universality' (2019, pp. 104–116), where the author reads Žižek's Holy Spirit community against Jean-Claude Milner's 'paradoxical community'.

[65] Of course, Žižek puts a political spin on this verse by explaining that it is about respect and obedience towards superiors, while the original context is not so much about superiors but about familial ties. Nevertheless, the basic logic of argumentation can stand. This is another example of Žižek's symptomatic attitude, where the text and theology do not necessarily match, as we have seen in his exegesis of Job and of Christ's last words.

itself enjoins us to "unplug" from the organic community into which we were born' (Žižek 2014, p. 121). It is in the light of this love that Žižek reads Galatians 3:28 as a call for a general universalism indifferent to social divisions.

Žižek's Kierkegaardian Suspension of the Ethical

The work of this love is that which suspends the ethical. In Chapter 2 of *The Parallax View* (2006, pp. 68–123), Žižek develops this suspension of the ethical through a critical reading of Søren Kierkegaard's interpretation of the story of Abraham's sacrifice of Isaac in *Fear and Trembling* (2005). In the very moment when the ethical becomes a temptation, Kierkegaard reflects, Abraham overcomes his own ethical convictions and only by faith alone, outside worldly coordination, by telling no one about this. In that very moment he assumes an almost higher position than God himself—Abraham stands in an absolute relation to the Absolute, where 'the ethical is reduced to the relative' (Kierkegaard 2005, pp. 82–83). His behaviour appears absurd—he is willing to murder his own son, whom he treasures more than anything else. Certainly, Kierkegaard is not concerned with putting the ethical in general under question, but the scene presents an antagonism which cannot be overcome. Suddenly the man of God and a murderer of a child appear in the same person. It is this very antagonism, as presented by Kierkegaard, which for Žižek demonstrates the tension of the Christ-event and the subsequent truth-events.

Thus the radical and individualistic position observed by Kierkegaard in Abraham's inhumane and yet God-fearing belief becomes for Žižek an argumentative vehicle which enables the thinking of a politically militant subject. Žižek reads the compelling of a higher necessity to betray the very ethical substance of one's being as the revolutionary compelling the subject (2001c, p. 14), introducing a gap into the very order of being (2003, p. 37). This subject is faithful to a truth-event, which is not legitimised by the symbolic order. Abraham's acceptance of the incomprehensible will of God sets about to destroy the symbolically imposed picture of the loving and caring father, the patriarch. For Žižek it is exactly his ability to sacrifice that which gives meaning to his life or world, which delivers the subject in a certain sense to freedom and thereby true subjectivity. This is also exactly the aspect that he sees in the death of Christ on the Cross—the self-emptying.

Therefore, the real paradox of Kierkegaard's faith lies for Žižek in the seeking after the meaning of life in reference to God, wherein the gap between God and man cannot be overcome. The believer risks everything *for nothing* (Žižek 2006, p. 97). It is only after Kierkegaard's 'infinite resignation', the realisation that there is no guarantee that the absolute dedication will be compensated, that Kierkegaard's radicality of the leap of faith is reached. In Kierkegaard's own words:

> But the understanding comes to a standstill at the absolute. The contradiction is to require of a person that he make the greatest possible sacrifice, dedicate his whole life to being sacrificed – and why? Well, there is no why. (Kierkegaard 1991, p. 120)

He continues in his journal: 'At first sight the understanding says that this is madness. The understanding asks: What's in it for me? The answer is: nothing' (Kierkegaard 1970, p. 186).[66]

Žižek concludes that there is but a fundamental practico-ethical decision about what kind of life one wants to commit oneself to. Thus the new community is called upon to repeat this fundamental shift in coordinates, the primordial choice made by Christ, for itself (Žižek 2001a, pp. 148–149).

Indeed, as Žižek's engagement with theology develops it becomes ever more reliant on Kierkegaard. When discussing crucial questions such as the Law and transgression, love, the religious suspension of the ethical, the fundamental Christian break, he defers to Kierkegaard. For example, Žižek quotes from *Works of Love*: 'We do not applaud the son who said "No", but we endeavour to learn from the Gospel how dangerous it is to say, "Sir, I will"' (Kierkegaard 1962, p. 102, cf. Žižek 2000, p. 148). Kierkegaard's comment here refers to Matthew 21:28–31, which he understands as the radical demand that requires one to give up everything in order to follow Christ. Žižek employs this thought when it comes to Luke 14:26 as a suggestion that one should in fact '*hate the beloved* out of love and in love' (Kierkegaard 1962, p. 114, cf. Žižek 2000, p. 126). According to him, this is the work of love, comparable to Che Guevara's or Lenin's revolutionary violence (Žižek 2003, p. 30)—not only love, but Christian

---

[66]This is my own translation of the German: 'Auf den ersten Blick sagt der Verstand, daß dies Wahnsinn ist. Der Verstand fragt: Was springt für mich dabei heraus? Die Antwort lautet: nichts'.

love. Luke 14:26 then is to be read in the context of the following account in Matthew to highlight its intent of breaking down ideological constraints:

> While Jesus was still talking to the crowd, his mother and brothers stood out-side, wanting to speak to him. Someone told him, 'Your mother and brothers are standing outside, wanting to speak to you.' He replied to him, 'Who is my mother, and who are my brothers?' Pointing to his disciples, he said, 'Here are my mother and my brothers. For whoever does the will of my Father in heaven is my brother and sister and mother'. (Matthew 12:46-5-)

When Jesus speaks of 'hating' one's parents, he means in so far as they stand for the social hierarchy or system with its ideological structure, which the community of the Holy Spirit bypasses. It is with regards to the ideo-logical constraints that the Christian love brings division rather than unity; it uncouples from the given ethnic and political identities and is redefined as a position of active engagement, a struggle.[67]

The Other of the Neighbour

The radicality of Galatians 3:28 is of course an implication or elaboration of Romans 13:8, wherein Paul writes that 'he who loves his neighbour has fulfilled the law'. The theological injunction to love one's neighbour originates from the covenant at Sinai in the Old Testament: 'Do not seek revenge or bear a grudge against anyone among your people, but love your neighbour as yourself' (Leviticus 19:18). In the New Testament, how-ever, the meaning of the concept of 'neighbour' has been universally trans-formed, based on Christ's teaching in the parable of the Good Samaritan (Luke 10:25–37), where it is indifferent to social divisions and includes everyone.

In his contribution to *The Neighbour* (Žižek 2013a, pp. 134–190), Žižek ponders what this call to love the neighbour as yourself reveals about sub-jectivity and argues that it stands as a challenge to the so-called ethical turn in contemporary thought, a turn often linked to the thought of Emmanuel Levinas (Žižek 2007, pp. 164–166). Žižek's main target is what he char-

---

[67] According to Žižek, this is also how one is to read the imperative to 'turn the other cheek', found in Matthew 5:38–40, as a subversive gesture which destabilises, rather than an act of obedience of either doing nothing or striking back. Again, the latter is really a constitutive exception.

acterises as an ethics of the paradigmatic citizen of contemporary Western civilizations, who in his search for happiness without stress exhibits a fear of an excessive intensity of life that might disturb it. For Žižek, a whole series of contemporary commodities and phenomena embody this anxiety and vulnerability apropos of excess: coffee without caffeine, beer without alcohol, up to the desire to prosecute wars without casualties (Žižek 2002a, p. 10). Žižek proposes that this fear of excess reveals not only that there is something more to the subject, but that this itself is the subject, and that this dimension is missed in the ethical turn in contemporary thought in general, and in the work of Levinas in particular (Žižek 2013a, pp. 159–169). Insisting upon it reveals the properly political potential of the Christian love of the neighbour.

The attempt to account for oneself is always conducted within a certain intersubjective context and reveals our constitutive exposure to the Other (Žižek 2008b, p. 45). That also means that the Other is not or ought not to be recognised in an absolute manner, but to recognise its impenetrability. It is this exposure that grounds our ethical status, a solidarity of the vulnerable: 'what makes an individual human and thus something for which we are responsible, toward whom we have a duty to help, is his/her very finitude and vulnerability' (Žižek 2013a, p. 138).

Any type of the big Other, as the symbolic order, seeks to mediate and regulate our coexistence, but the excess or the Real cannot be gentrified and with it, reciprocal exchange is impossible (ibid., p. 143). In other words, our intersubjectivity depends on the Symbolic order. The challenge posed by Christian love, Žižek argues, is to resist this gentrification of the neighbour, and instead accept its radical impenetrability. Thus a collective emerges, which no longer relies on an ethnic identity, but is instead struggling (ibid., p. 154). This love, as encapsulated in Galatians 3:28, is thus not against the background of universal hatred, but of universal indifference, where one is indifferent toward all and in this way loves the individual.

CAN SUCH A COMMUNITY PULL ITS WEIGHT?

Given that the ultimate concern of Žižek is political, that might seem utopian or at best an idealistic hope for the political future, but Žižek argues that such a non-ideological social bond has been experienced after Apostle Paul as well. Examples include the Ancient Greek democracy, Lenin's Bolshevik revolution, Eastern Europe's undermining of Communism in the eighties, or indeed the recent Occupy movement against Capitalism (Christ is their precursor, a mythic form of something that reaches its true form in the logic of the emancipatory political collective).

Žižek's theoretical reasoning or argumentation itself is logically stronger than it might first appear. First, this kind of community is not maintained by the big Other, and therefore it does not parallel the contemporary fundamentalist perversions. Those are a mere mirror image and reaction against the current condition that has made them what they are, but still remain caught in the mirror.[68] Second, following on from Žižek's insistence upon the contingency of materialist grace described above, he is clear that this new sociality is therefore capable of, but does not guarantee, a truly ethical or political act, outside of its ethico-legal entanglement. It represents only a possibility of something new; it is not ensured. Third, this form of sociality is also not united by the lack or absence of the big Other, as in that being the only thing that holds the community together.[69] The dismantling of the big Other only marks the catalyst for a community which then develops, or is able to develop—a community of deference. In that sense it is not a negative community.[70] Fourth, Žižek is quick to admit and deliver a warning that this form of social collective is inherently fragile. In the case of Lenin's revolution, it led to the perverse ideology of Stalinism; likewise, the communality of the Arab Spring was taken over by religious fundamentalists[71]. Christianity also declined into perversion, when it transformed Christ's sacrifice into an insurmountable debt and thus bound the subject, rather than setting him/her free (Žižek 2003, p. 110). The big Other was thus resurrected and Christianity became a new kind of law, hiding the impotence of the big Other. Without the proper stance in

[68] A horrific example of this is illustrated in the brutal act of execution of the Jordanian pilot by ISIS in early February 2015. Upon capturing the pilot, ISIS supporters launched a Twitter campaign (global neoliberalism?) calling for brutal execution suggestions, prompting numerous ideas, including the actual execution. Thus they used a 'democratic' method of deciding the pilot's fate, which, however, with its determined outcome, was far from democratic, but merely an act of formal, rather than actual freedom.

[69] I.e. the only thing we have in common is the missing other.

[70] The Arab Spring protests were not merely negative in that they represented a reaction to the corruption and abuse by their government, but included an attempt towards or experiment in communality.

[71] The student and academic protesters were then proclaimed as the enemies of the movement by the religious fundamentalists, whose dream was religiously fundamental and intolerant of any other vision.

relation to its founding act, this unique form of universal love in various contexts collapsed in on itself.

However, recognising Žižek's argumentations—that this kind of community is not held together by the big Other and is at the same time not negative, and qualifications of fragility and contingency—, the question remains whether such a community can be anything else than an event? It is well to point out its fragility; however, is it not more important to ask whether such a community of radical love can exist without the ideological support of the big Other? Even for the absence of the big Other, its existence is essential in the first place. In Žižek's case, the death of God event is necessary and cannot be excluded since otherwise we would remain trapped in the system of debt—without God there is no death of God. If the Symbolic is just about everything that we call 'reality', will not the subject be eternally resurrecting the big Other—an arbitrary and changing chain of signifiers—be they God or 'History' or 'development' or something else? Following Žižek's argument, was this not the case with Christianity and the Bolshevik revolution? After all, if we again follow Žižek, the subject exists on the borders of the Real and the Symbolic. The question then is: Do we need ideological support to 'be'? It seems Žižek does not aim to present us with a sustainable and resilient alternative, but rather a possibility of a break or radical change, which we have to continually repeat as a series of unplugging. What he proposes is not so much a thought of revolution, but 'revolutions'—as in the final instalment of the Matrix trilogy. To the earlier question Žižek would respond that with ideological support authentic being is perverted.

This is the challenge of Geoffrey Holsclaw's *Transcending Subjects* (2016), where the latter accuses Žižek of being stuck in critiquing the normative order but unable to offer a stable and as such viable alternative social theory. Holsclaw puts the failure down to Žižek's Hegelian understanding of freedom and social change or his 'self-transcending immanence' to which he opposes Augustine's 'self-imanenting transcendence'. In other words, rather than destroying freedom, 'transcendence is the only means to freedom' (Holsclaw 2014, p. 8)—a freedom that is stable and thus a viable alternative.

The crux of Holsclaw's argument about stability is where the change comes from. He argues that due to man's sinfulness, change must have an external source (Holsclaw 2014, p. 176); an Augustinian conversion of putting on the will of Christ and relinquishing one's own is required

(Holsclaw 2014, p. 168). The maintenance of Christ as the external and transcendent creator and sustainer of a new pilgrim identity, he argues, is the absolutely necessary critical distance that enables the critique of the current or any political setup—an exchange between two realities, rather than being caught in one. Only change of the subject from the citizen of the earthly city to the pilgrim on the journey towards the heavenly, enables a true change of the human society (Holsclaw 2014, pp. 219–221) and only the transcendent brings the change about.

Yet, two questions emerge to Holsclaw's argument as to the pilgrim social form and insistence that change only emerges from the transcendent. With regards to the social form, Holsclaw argues that Žižek's inability to provide a viable alternative is ultimately due to his acceptance of Hegel's duality of subject and society, while he ought to heed Augustine's duality of societies (Holsclaw 2014, pp. 233–234). However, Holsclaw's critique of Žižek is built on a misunderstanding. Rather than inferring two natures of the subject and two societies as separate from each other, Žižek (1999, p. 24) proposes an unfinished and contingent understanding of the materiality of both the subject and the community (Subject=not-all, the historical reality=not-all), wherein the subject is not only the cause for and sustainer of the current setup, they are also the possibility of change. As Pfeifer (2016, p. 115) notes, the subject's own split nature thus does not create a separation from the society but, upon realisation of the unfinished reality and thus its relation to the community, presents the possibility of change without the need for a transcendental agent. Furthermore, is Augustine's or Holsclaw's proposal not rather the creation of a new society of abstraction? A dichotomy where one identity is created against or in contrast to the other and as such separates the subject from society? Not only does the subject not see themselves in the existing coordinates but does so from new coordinates that obfuscate the Real of the subject.

Second, the insistence that change is possible only if it comes from the transcendental (and external) leaves us in a state of despair. While perhaps a tenet of orthodox Christianity, this is sociologically a very problematic claim that lends itself to a sort of colonial dichotomy where 'the other' is in constant need of 'redemption' from the outside which is necessarily 'transcendent' and as such dispenses with it (redemption). Instead, Žižek proposes that true change can only emerge from within by realising that the current setup is the not-all and a change is possible. Only by abandoning longing for an Absolute that is finished, consistent and stable, by realising that what seemed as complete and total is not and is instead contingent and unfinished, does it not yield its potential to reliance upon the external or transcendent. Instead, by realising that '…there is no transcendental 'big Other', there are no criteria that we can apply to historical phenomena themselves' (Žižek 2012a, p. 387), society exercises its freedom as an agent of change. If reality itself is contingent and unfinished, then constant change is the only stability and the challenge is to '… *repeat the beginning again and again*' (Žižek 2010c, p. 210). Only in this way also, does the subject view themselves as part of the universal, rather than an abstracted and therefore alienated particular.

Therefore, while Holsclaw is in pursuit of a stable alternative, his pilgrim identity alienates the subject and the society from each other and themselves and his insistence that change is not possible lest it come from an external transcendent agent cripples the human spirit.

Now that I have explored Žižek's theological materialism and the resulting community of abandonment, it is time to turn to Bonhoeffer's social theology and its community of saints.

THEOLOGICAL ENGAGEMENT WITH ŽIŽEK THUS FAR

Before engaging in the critical reading, it is necessary to give a brief analysis of theological engagement with Žižek thus far and in this way demonstrate why such an approach is necessary. Rather than attempting to provide an extensive or exhaustive account of various responses and propose an alternative, I want to show why such a presuppositionless approach is crucial for any and all.

'We Need to Talk'—Evaluating Žižek's Materialist Theology

Theological engagement with Žižek's thought coincides with his rise to international acclaim after his first English publication *The Sublime Object of Ideology* in 1989 and loosely fits within Ward's (2000b) double response to critical theory observed in the introduction. Among the very first theologians who have responded to Žižek's work were members of the radical orthodoxy movement. This school of theology originated in the United Kingdom and is named after its first edited volume, *Radical Orthodoxy* (Milbank et al. 1999), which brought together its leading lights in commitment to Augustine and Aquinas with a harsh criticism of modern and secular thought from a postmodern perspective. Their utmost concern is the issue of ontology, or the underlying metaphysical framework of reality. They find an alternative to the modern ontology, which they regard as nihilistic, in *analogia entis*—the analogy of being, a synthesis of Neo-Platonism and Christianity which was achieved by Augustine and further developed by Thomas Aquinas. Only this analogy of being can allow for a genuinely meaningful worldview, in which God is the fullness of being and all created beings participate in it analogically. The radical orthodox thus maintain that unless every discipline is framed by a theological perspective, it defines a zone apart from God and thus without grounding. Radical theology's response to Žižek is thus not primarily due to his turn to theology, but due to his ontological philosophy, which they consider as unjustified. That said, however, their engagement seeks to address and respond to a philosophy of a materialism which, even if not grounded in the divine transcendence, is theological.

It is the movement's foremost figure John Milbank who has engaged Žižek most often and most directly.[72] We can gain good insight into the engagement by focusing on two works: first, *Theology and the Political* (Davis et al. 2005), which includes Milbank's contribution under the title 'Materialism and Transcendence' (Milbank 2005) and second, *The Monstrosity of Christ* (Žižek and Milbank 2009), a work that can be considered as the outcome of a developing dialogue between them. In both of these Milbank is recognising Žižek's engagement with theology but more importantly pointing out that he does so incorrectly. It is as if Milbank were saying: 'this is not how one thinks theologically'.

In *Theology and the Political*, Milbank begins by demonstrating that due to Marx's reductive materialism, post-war Marxist thinkers sought a non-reductive form of materialism, and in doing so borrowed from Platonic, Aristotelian, Idealist and even theological thought (Milbank 2005, pp. 393–398). This initial demonstration enables an understanding of the context, form and essence of, among others, Žižek's appropriation of theology and his thought in general as Hegelian. Accordingly, Milbank is correct in recognising that Žižek is practicing a Hegelian death-of-God theology resulting in universality (ibid., p. 422). In his navigation through the con-

---

[72] It was Graham Ward, however, who first engaged with Žižek in *Cities of God* (2000a) and then later added a section on him to the conclusion of the second edition (2000b) of *Theology and the Contemporary Critical Theory* (1996).

tours of Žižek's thought, Milbank also upholds Christianity's universality through the particular (ibid., p. 404), but—as already observed with the more recent challenge of Holsclaw—argues that Žižek's atheistic universality of struggle or tension functions only as an ontology of revolution, rather than sociality: 'if universalism springs from an event, then to lose mythos and history is to lose the event, and so to lose the universal' (ibid., p. 411). This nihilism, Milbank argues, is due to his inability to consider analogy, which mediates between the universal and particular, grounding engagement with others in a shared analogy of being, as pointing beyond themselves to God. Thus, while Milbank agrees with Žižek that Christianity is aligned with materialism and that the true form of universalism or sociality is Christian, he rejects his theological materialism as nihilist and ontologically incorrect. Milbank's engagement with Žižek in *Theology and the Political* presents the parameters for their further engagement: while they both pursue a radical content of Christian theology and its sociological potential, they do so on a different grounding—one upon an orthodox ontology of *analogia entis* and the other upon an atheist ontology of *verlassenheit* [abandonment].

The Monstrosity of Christ (2009) is based on a premise that Žižek and Milbank both agree on—that Enlightenment reason has run its course. The question then, which they both answer differently, is what becomes of theology after secular Enlightenment reason has run its course? Žižek argues that secular reason is sublated by the dialectic of theological materialism, whereas, building on his criticism in *Theology and the Political*, Milbank argues that it is replaced by paradox or analogy.

One of Milbank's main criticisms in the book is that, in following Hegel, Žižek is adopting a Protestant metanarrative and neglecting the Catholic tradition (Žižek and Milbank 2009, p. 112). Milbank argues that Žižek's treatment of Catholics such as Chesterton, Kierkegaard[73] or Eckhart is done through a Protestant lens and is therefore inaccurate.[74] Indeed,

---

[73] Milbank here insists on his consideration of the Lutheran theologian Søren Kierkegaard as a Catholic. He argues that Kierkegaard's linking of faith with reason restored a basically Catholic perspective and further mentions Kierkegaard's Catholic critique of Luther for exalting faith at the expense of works.

[74] An example of this is Žižek's re-appropriation of the words of Chesterton's detective Father Brown: 'he was made man' (Chesterton 2006, pp. 394–395). Chesterton used these words to portray how Western culture's retreat into spiritualism and its willingness to believe in anything must be read as an inability to sustain the traumatic reality of the incarnated

Žižek's claim that atheist Christianity is the true Christianity is only possible because he accepts a dialectical (that is, a truly Protestant) version of Christian doctrine as the most coherent (ibid., p. 117). As an alternative to Žižek's nihilistic interpretation, Milbank's proposed analogy is variously found in the same sources that Žižek uses but has interpreted differently, such as Eckhart, Kierkegaard, Chesterton and Henri De Lubac. Such Catholic perspective, so Milbank, affirms a kind of materialism that is quite positive in that it affirms a mediating link between matter and spirit—the Holy Spirit (ibid., p. 125). Milbank points out Žižek's problematic theological method and the ensuing 'strange' interpretation of Christianity.[75]

Žižek, on the other hand, refuses to engage with Milbank's paradox as it is not truly materialist, since it still maintains an ideological structure of the big Other. The metanarrative that Žižek uses—Protestant (Hegelian) dialectic—is the only one that he will use, for it alone has, according to him, a truly materialistic essence and potential. This results in an impasse, which is perhaps best summed up by Žižek's final contribution to the work (ibid., pp. 235–306), in which he observes that the exchange with Milbank has been reduced to each man reiterating his respective notions and has therefore exhausted its potentials (ibid., p. 235).

God. For Žižek, however, these words mean, along the lines of Hegel, that the external or transcendent God is now a contingent fact of human freedom itself. See Delpech-Ramey (2010, pp. 122–123). However, this criticism of Žižek, as right as it may be, can also be made of Milbank, who compares Kierkegaard to Eckhart and Chesteron. See Harris (2011, pp. 35–41 at p. 38).

[75] That is, 'strange' in the sense that Žižek's resulting interpretation of Christianity is something completely alien to the traditional conception. Indeed, Žižek's materialistic interpretation of theology appears odd to the classical theological reader, insofar as it lacks a serious consideration of the wider traditional or current biblical scholarship, or engagement with the multifaceted theological scholarship. For example, in Žižek's presentation of the weakness of the legalistic reading of the atonement (2003, pp. 102–103), he simply ignores the response to that in the form of Anselm's *Cur Deus Homo* (1898) in the eleventh century. He also rarely refers to any contemporary New Testament scholars or contemporary theologians in general. There are few exceptions, such as when in his description of God as perverted he refers to the English edition of Rudolf Bultmann's *New Testament Theology* (Žižek 2003, p. 118), or when using John Howard Yoder's rejection of the 'Constantinian shift' as an illustration of a non-reconciled political standpoint (Žižek 2010c, pp. 129–130).

Why Does Žižek Refuse to Play by the Rules?
Milbank's is but one call of many theologians[76] to consider or engage with the wider body of theological scholarship and read them in the accustomed or orthodox way—to respond as a theologian. More recently, there has been another significant contribution to this theological endeavour of assessing Žižek's thought in the form of an edited volume *Slavoj Žižek and Christianity* (2019). As much as the volume offers a good presentation of Žižek's 'theological' thought and its dimensionality,[77] it remains within the coordinates of (broadly defined) theologians[78] and the 'decaffeinated' theologian—as the editors of the volume describe Žižek (ibid., p. 15). Yet, Žižek is not a theologian. His approach is rather that of a theoretical psychoanalyst who examines theological thought for the break with its orthodox understanding—something that interrupts the narrative of an accepted meaning. Rather than a Gadamerian hermeneutic of desire for a correct reading, as Løland notes (2018, pp. 57–61), Žižek's approach is that of a psychoanalyst interpreter showing us what the thinkers themselves weren't even aware of communicating and—for that matter—what we as their contemporary hearers are not as we interpret them. The emphasis then is not so much what the author of the theological text meant but rather how it speaks into our subjective experience or to use Žižek's own words: 'situated in its structural conditions of possibility' (Žižek 2002b, p. 317). Rather than enquiring about what the thinker really wanted to say, Žižek's is the endeavour of uncovering the sometimes faintest of glimmers that upsets our understanding and, in this way, reveals our attempts to cope with the Real conditions of our existence and their problems.

---

[76] Among these are Frederik Depoortere (2008), Marcus Pound (2008), and Roland Boer (2009, pp. 275–390).

[77] Particularly the chapter by its editors 'The Slovenian and the Cross', pp. 1–45.

[78] Such as Brian Becker's 'From psychoanalysis to metamorphosis', pp. 67–85, Chase Padusniak's 'No wonder, then, that love itself disappears', pp. 86–103, and Jack Louis Pappas' 'Rethinking universality: Badiou and Žižek on Pauline theology', pp. 154–166. The exceptions are Grimshaw, Ventis and Hamza. Grimshaw argues that Žižek should have considered the potential of radical (Death-of-God) theology ('Žižek and the Dwarf: a short-circuit radical theology', pp. 199–2180). Ventis' challenge from a liberal perspective argues that Žižek's (and indeed wider Christianity's and Marxist) truth-claims are deeply ideological and as such vice, rather than virtue ('Pacifist pluralism versus militant truth: Christianity at the service of revolution in the work of Slavoj Žižek', pp. 117–153).

Therefore, it is important to remember this in attempting to understand his refusal to engage as an endeavour which is doomed to sempiternal repetition and instead looks at texts or thought with materialist potential for critical insight for epistemological advancement—subversion of the existing coordinates. To further enlighten this politics of refusal from another perspective, one could consider Walter Benjamin's essay 'Zur Kritik der Gewalt' (Benjamin, 1920–1921, pp. 179–204). In it Benjamin argues that challenges to, or violations of, the law always threaten to turn full circle and become a law-making violence of their own. This is a cycle bound to endless repetition, like that of the mythical punishment of Prometheus (ibid., pp. 196–197). In the light of this problem Benjamin proposes that the only *revolutionary* form of violence that does not reinstate the violence of the law are proletarian strikes. Rather than extorting concessions from the bosses, the general strike makes no demands other than the complete transformation of social relations and of work itself. This type of strike is a pure means and therefore not violent because its ends are radically senseless, unreasonable and extravagant according to capitalist logic. The strike's only intention is non-participation in the logic of ends and means and a refusal of mythical imperatives in which transgression of the law meets with punishment. It is along these lines that Žižek argues in his conclusion to *The Parallax View* (Žižek 2006, pp. 381–385) that sometimes the best way to fight against ideology is to do nothing. He illustrates his politics of refusal by using the enigmatic title character of Herman Melville's story *Bartleby the Scrivener* (2009), who answers every request with the phrase: 'I would prefer not to'. Žižek explains that in order to radically refuse the ideological system, he must sometimes also radically refuse the devices by which he distances himself from it, and in this way convince himself that he is not part of the problem. This, he argues, like God's self-abandonment on the Cross, is another example of a dialectical negation of negation, a change in perspective that transforms an apparent defeat into victory. Perhaps, then, Žižek would respond to the request to engage with theological scholarship similarly, by responding: 'I would prefer not to!'

In this manner, theological engagement with Žižek seems to take the form of merely accentuating the unreconcilable differences between traditional theological perspectives and Žižek's atheist materialist metanarrative. Is the limit of this engagement then to assess and differentiate? If so, then the question presents itself whether it is meaningful to keep engaging him? Milbank certainly seems to think it is not, as demonstrated in an interview for *The Immanent Frame* (Schneider 2010) shortly after the co-authored volume. To a question about the prospects for a philosophical encounter with theology that does not assent to a transcendent deity, Milbank responds: 'I think that, in the end, the prospects are non-existent' (ibid.).

'Pull Up a Chair'—Demonstrating the Sociological Import of Theology

The other response that Ward (2000b) suggests for theology is that of discerning critical theory's resources in the service of theology as a theoretical resource through which theological themes can find a contemporary expression—to engage in 'Cross-cultural conversation; not where we are the key players, but where we have a contribution to make' (ibid., viii). That 'confrontational, not simply analytical' (Ward 2005, p. 266) contribution is the demonstration of the socio-political potential of theology.[79]

Today, Žižek is perhaps one of the most well-known contemporary philosophers and cultural critics and speaks to socio-political issues around the globe, often in the company of other prominent contemporary philosophers. Be it at the 'Occupy' movement protesting in Wall Street against the moral bankruptcy of Western Capitalism (Žižek 2011), or speaking to the (then) Greek 'new left' party Siriza to seek a way out of the ever-deepening Greek economic crisis (Žižek 2012c), or expressing support for the 2010 UK student protests against spending cuts to further education and an increase of the cap on tuition fees, or encouraging the critical thinking of students in South America disillusioned by the corrupt leadership of their countries, or discussing problems arising from the 'Arab Spring' revolution, Žižek's speeches on radical change are highly sought after, noted and analysed for import. Given that Žižek appropriates theological thought in service of his critical theoretical interventions, it represents an opportunity for theology to speak into the socio-political issues of the twenty-first century adroitly, effectively, responsibly and in a self-reflexive manner in pursuit

---

[79] See also Frick's thoughts on the confrontational method of critical theology in (2017, pp. 217–219).

of a distinct sociological conviction. After all, this is what Žižek calls for in *The Monstrosity of Christ*—for theological partners in this endeavour.[80]

One instance where this can be observed is in the engagement of the Croatian Lutheran theologian Boris Gunjević. In *God in Pain* (Žižek and Gunjević 2012), Gunjević welcomes Žižek's challenge and goes about demonstrating that there are many hidden treasures in the history of Christianity (including its revolutionary potential), which lie buried and undiscovered for perhaps hundreds or even thousands of years (pp. 1–26). Indeed, it is theology's responsibility to uncover these treasures that at times might have been considered rejects or obsoletes. He goes on to claim that:

> Inasmuch as theology is a deliberation on ecclesial practice in the light of God's word, then this practice must be shaped by the theological virtues of faith, hope, and charity, ever ready to communicate liberty, equality, and fraternity. (ibid., p. 26)

This quote clearly shows that Gunjević has not simply taken Žižek's side, for he still considers theology to be the only fitting thought which can offer incarnational resources and incarnational tools for changing the world. Gunjević, however, recognises that to challenge Žižek over his meta-narrative and his theological method is unproductive. Instead, throughout the chapters of the book Gunjević discusses the incarnational tools and ecclesial practices that Christianity offers.

In the second chapter (ibid., pp. 73–102) Gunjević gives the example of Augustine's response to the accusation that the fall of Rome was Christianity's fault *City of God* (1950–1954), which can serve both as a contrast to or rebuke of the current global capitalist politics, and as constructive instruction for the alternative way ahead.[81] He mentions Augustine's observation that the Empire did not become vast and powerful because of its political allies or its military might but because, after subjugating other nations, the

---

[80] However, Milbank does not proceed any further from critiquing Žižek's nihilism and the Hegelian metanarrative. This has already been observed about the debate in *Theology and the Political* (Kotsko 2009, p. 117).

[81] Interestingly, this is also what Gustavo Gutierrez says in his *Theology of Liberation* (which, it can be said, is a manifesto of Liberation Theology in some ways), in which he praises Augustine's *City of God* as the classic correct method of theological approach, because the Word of God is being brought to bear on the present historical situation (Gutierrez 1974, p. 5).

Romans brought them into the common Roman state (Žižek and Gunjević 2012, pp. 88–90). In other words, they were all granted equal rights and privileges in the community of Rome. It was exactly the guidance of the one true God with its ideal of the heavenly city which helped the Romans in this. Furthermore, the Romans attained their glory and supremacy because of the orderly guidance for desire, as it is only that which builds proper community (ibid., pp. 95–96). Augustine critiqued the virtues of the Empire which always sought to increase capital and legitimise various forms of terror. He suggested that the only way to strip away the supports for this is to engage in ecclesiastical practices, and in this way counter these Empire virtues by not participating in them. This no doubt resonates with Žižek's politics of refusal ('I would prefer not to!'). This instruction that Gunjević observes in Augustine functions as a subversive counter-parable to the imperial metanarrative (ibid., p. 100). What Gunjević, in the tradition of Augustine, calls 'nomadism' or ascetic exercise, and Žižek calls 'politics of refusal', becomes 'the fundamental coordinates that help ground the political subject' (ibid., p. 102). In this they both agree. Gunjević does not attempt to convince Žižek of the need either to abstain from Empire virtues or to engage in ecclesial practices, for indeed that would be to bring the engagement to its end yet again.

Gunjević engages Žižek as a critical theorist analysing the daily socio-political realities and their ruptures, rather than as a theologian. As such he acts exactly in the way Žižek does and no doubt expects the same of his potential theological sparring partners—in other words, by radically refusing the devices by which he might distance himself from such atheistic interpretations. In this Gunjević resists the temptation of convincing himself that he is not part of the problem that is Žižek's heterodox interpretation of Christianity. Through this 'negation of negation', an apparent defeat (the failure to engage with Žižek's atheistic elements) is transformed into victory. It is as if Gunjević himself is simply saying, 'I would prefer not to!'[82]

This sort of theological engagement with Žižek—what Ward calls response—brings about a greater awareness of the historically embedded

---

[82]Yet another example expressing the indispensable contribution of theology's socio-political import is Løland's work that wishes to demonstrate how Žižek's philosophy, with all its cultural and political analyses, serves theology to broaden its view of what is existentially at stake in our time' (Løland 2018, p 11).

particularity of theology's own truth claims, shows their further dimensionality and potentially removes everyday theological texts from the automatism of perception and makes them appear in a new light. This is what is observed with the Swedish theologian Ola Sigurdson who, in *Slavoj Žižek, The Death of God, and Zombies* (2013), argues that Žižek's psychoanalytically inspired notion of the undead is structurally similar to Augustine's understanding of human subjectivity in *Confessions* (1961)—they both reject any superficial and transparent understanding of self. Žižek's psychoanalytic discussion of concepts makes theological sense, Sigurdson argues.

'Where Next?'—Towards a Meaningful Critical Engagement

While appreciative of both—Milbank's attempt to respond critically to Žižek's theological materialism and Gunjević's engagement in Žižek's consideration of theology as the ultimate political act through a discussion of the incarnational tools and ecclesial practices that Christianity offers—I am proposing that in order for this sort of engagement to be truly critical, going beyond reproduction of the same knowledge or repeating of the same viewpoints, it needs to be carried out without pressupositions. Unfortunately, neither of these two approaches in itself allows Žižek's materialist interpretation to challenge theology's self-understanding, allowing it to examine theological assumptions. While Gunjević goes further from Milbank's pitting of his views against Žižek, it is still not an open or full engagement in the form of a self-critical reflection upon insights of Žižek's thought and is instead an example of what Bonhoeffer calls 'wills willing beside each other'.

As pointed out in the introduction, the effectiveness and meaningfulness of both ways of responding to critical theoretical thought depends upon their approach for the manner in which they are carried out predetermines their result. If the theological approach is guarded with stipulations that do not allow a challenge of its claims, theology subscribes to a position and narrows its critical potential. Likewise, only through a critical reflection upon theological assumptions, brought to light in engagement with its contextual partners, can the sociological potential of theology as never submitting and not yielding to a position be demonstrated. It is the approach that can bring both of Ward's responses to critical theory together in a full engagement.

Therefore, I suggest that the potential of engagement with Žižek lies in the challenge that his materialistic interpretation poses to theology's self-understanding. Not unlike Freud's own reconstruction in *Moses and Monotheism* of the story of Moses and his death in an attempt to uncover this violent and guilt-ridden core in Judaism, Žižek proposes an unacknowledged and phantasmal core which emerges through the gaps and cracks of the actually existing Christianity. What if we were to take seriously Žižek's perceptions of the cracks of the narrative of theological thought and allow them to critically examine its body or rather our perception thereof? Accordingly, the next chapter engages Žižek's materialist theology in a critical reading of Bonhoeffer's theology of *Sanctorum Communio* in a specific way: appropriating Žižek as a critical theorist in reflection on the content, its presuppositions or assumptions and implications of Bonhoeffer's social theology, without predetermining the expectation or outcome of the debate or even what is off limits within it.

Thus, the rationale of the critical reading that follows is along the lines of the 'political criticism' of the French Marxist literary critic Pierre Macherey, who, in *A Theory of Literary Production*, observes that:

> The speech of a book comes from a certain silence, a matter which it endows with form, a ground on which it traces a figure. Thus, the book is not self-sufficient; it is necessarily accompanied by a certain absence, without which it would not exist. A knowledge of the book must include a consideration of this absence. (Macherey 1978, p. 85)

This, he argues, establishes the usefulness and legitimacy of asking of every production what it tacitly implies, but does not say. The challenge of critical reading is therefore to get beneath the surface of a text's ideological assumptions by asking of it what it does not say, to expose its silences and evasions. According to Macherey, literary texts have a particular ability to reveal ideological contradictions, which turns a literary study into a politically subversive act. No doubt it is absolutely legitimate to ask of theological texts what they tacitly imply, what they do not say. When read in this way, they reveal the ideological narratives inscribing or creating meaning and thereby the veiled presence of the Real—the critical core of theology. This, I am certain, will be shared by many as of utmost importance when discussing the sociological potential of theology.

REFERENCES

Althusser, L. (1971). *Lenin and Philosophy and Other Essays*. Translated by B. Brewster. London: New Left Books.

Anselm. (1898). *Cur Deus Homo?* London: Griffith Farrar.

Augustine. (1961). *The Confessions of St. Augustine*. Translated by R.S. Pine-Coffin. Middlesex: Penguin Books.

Badiou, A. (2003). *Saint Paul: The Foundation of Universalism*. Translated by R. Brassier. Stanford: Stanford University Press.

Badiou, A. (2006). *Being and Event*. Translated by O. Feltham. London: Continuum.

Badiou, A. and Balmès, F. (1976). *De l'ideology*. Paris: Francois Maspero.

Becker, B.W. (2019). 'From Psychoanalysis to Metamorphosis: The Lacanian Limits of Žižek's Theology', in Mitralexis, S. and Skliris, D. (eds.) *Slavoj Žižek and Christianity*. New York: Routledge, pp. 67–85.

Benjamin, W. (1920–1921). 'Zur Kritik der Gewalt', in Benjamin, W. *Walter Benjamin Gesammelte Schriften. Band II. 1*. Frankfurt am Main: Suhrkamp, pp. 179–204.

Boer, R. (2009). *Criticism of Heaven: On Marxism and Theology*. Chicago: Haymarket Books.

Bowie M. (1979). 'Jacques Lacan', in Sturrock, J. (ed.) *Structuralism and Since*. Oxford: Oxford University Press, pp. 116–153.

Boyton, R. (2001). 'Enjoy Your Žižek: An Excitable Slovenian Philosopher Examines the Obscene Practices of Everyday Life, Including His Own,' *Linguafranca*, 26 (March 2001). Available at http://linguafranca.mirror.theinfo.org/9810/zizek.html. Accessed 20 September 2016.

Butler, J., Laclau, E., and Žižek, S. (2000). *Contingency, Hegemony, Universality: Contemporary Dialogues on the Left*. London and New York: Verso.

Caputo, J.D. (2009). 'The Monstrosity of Christ: Paradox or Dialectic?'. Review of *Monstrosity of Christ*, by S. Žižek and J. Milbank. *Notre Dame Philosophical Reviews* [Online]. Available at http://ndpr.nd.edu/review.cfm?id=17605 Accessed 20 September 2016.

Chesterton, G.K. (1916). *The Book of Job*. London: C. Palmer & Hayword.

Chesterton, G.K. (1996). *Orthodoxy*. New York: Doubleday.

Chesterton, G.K. (2006). *The Complete Father Brown Stories*. Ware: Wordsworth Editions.

Davis, C., Milbank, J., and Žižek, S. (eds.). (2005). *Theology and the Political: The New Debate*. Durham: Duke University Press.

Davis, C., Milbank, J., and Žižek, S. (eds.). (2010). *Paul's New Moment: Continental Philosophy and the Future of Christian Theology*. Grand Rapids: Brazos Press.

Delpech-Ramey, J. (2010). 'Supernatural Capital: A Note on the Žižek-Milbank Debate', *Political Theology*, 11(1), pp. 122–123.

Depoortere, F. (2008). *Christ in Postmodern Philosophy: Gianni Vattimo, René Girard and Slavoj Žižek*. London and New York: T&T Clark.

Eagleton, T. (2008). *Trouble with Strangers: A Study of Ethics*. Oxford: Wiley-Blackwell.

Fink, B. (1995). *The Lacanian Subject: Between Language and Jouissance*. Princeton: Princeton University Press.

Freud, S. (1939). *Der Mann Moses und die monotheistische Religion*. Amsterdam: A. de Lange.

Frick, P. (2017). *Understanding Bonhoeffer*. Tübingen: Mohr Siebeck.

Fromm, E. (1941). *Escape from Freedom*. New York: Farrar & Rinehart.

Gutierrez, G. (1974). *A Theology of Liberation: History, Politics and Salvation*. Translated by I. Caridad and J. Eagleson. London: SCM Press.

Harris, M.M. (2011). 'The Meaning of Christ and the Meaning of Hegel: Slavoj Žižek and John Milbank's (A)symmetrical Response to Capitalist Nihilism', *Reviews in Cultural Theory*, 2(2), pp. 35–41.

Hart, W.D. (2002), 'Slavoj Žižek and the Imperial/Colonial Model of Religion', *Nepantla: Views from South*, 3(3), pp. 553–578.

Hegel, G.W.F. (1977). *Faith and Knowledge*. Translated by W. Cerf and H.S. Harris. Albany: SUNY Press.

Hegel, G.W.F. (1983). *Hegel and the Human Spirit*. Translated by L. Rauch. Detroit: Wayne State University Press. Available at https://www.marxists.org/reference/archive/hegel/works/jl/ch01a.htm. Accessed 20 September 2016.

Hegel, G.W.F. (1998). *Lectures on the Philosophy of World History*. Translated by H.B. Nisbet. Cambridge: Cambridge University Press.

Hegel, G.W.F. (2010a). *The Science of Logic*. Translated by G. di Giovanni. Cambridge: Cambridge University Press.

Hegel, G.W.F. (2010b) *The Science of Logic*. Translated by G. di Giovanni. Cambridge: Cambridge University Press.

Holsclaw, G. (2014). *Transcending Subjects: Augustine, Hegel, and Theology*. Chirchester: Wiley-Blackwell.

Kierkegaard, S. (1962). *Works of Love*. Translated by H.V. Hong and E.H. Hong. New York: Harper & Row.

Kierkegaard, S. (1970). *Tagebücher. Band 4*. Düsseldorf and Köln: Diedrichs.

Kierkegaard, S. (1991) *Practice in Christianity*. Translated by H.V. and E.H. Hong. Princeton: Princeton University Press.

Kierkegaard, S. (2005). *Fear and Trembling*. Translated by A. Hannay. London: Penguin Books.

Kotsko, A. (2008). *Žižek and Theology*. London and New York: T&T Clark.

Kotsko, A. (2009). 'That They Might Have Ontology', *Political Theology*, 10(1), pp. 115–124.

Lacan, J. (1991). *The Seminar of Jacques Lacan: Book II: The Ego in Freud's Theory and in the Technique of Psychoanalysis 1954–1955.* Translated by S.W.W. Tomaselli. New York: W.W. Norton.

Lacan, J. (1992). *The Seminar of Jacques Lacan Book VII: Ethics of Psychoanalysis.* Translated by D. Porter. New York: W.W. Norton.

Lacan, J. (1997). *The Seminar of Jacques Lacan: The Ethics of Psychoanalysis.* Translated by D. Porter. London: W.W. Norton.

Lacan, J. (1998). *The Seminar of Jacques Lacan: The Four Fundamental Concepts of Psychoanalysis.* Translated by A. Sheridan. London: W.W. Norton.

Lacan, J. (2000). *The Seminar of Jacques Lacan: On Feminine Sexuality, the Limits of Love and Knowledge.* Translated by B. Fink. London: W.W. Norton.

Lacan, J. (2006). 'The Function and Field of Speech in Language in Psychoanalysis', in *Écrits: The First Complete Edition in English.* Translated by B. and H. Fink. London: W.W. Norton, pp. 197–268.

Løland, O.J. (2018). *The Reception of Paul the Apostle in the Works of Slavoj Žižek.* New York: Palgrave Macmillan.

Macherey, P. (1978). *A Theory of Literary Production.* Translated by G. Wall. London: Routledge & Kegan Paul.

Marcuse, H. (1955). *Reason and Revolution: Hegel and the Rise of Social Theory.* London: Routledge & Kegan Paul.

McGowan, T. (2016). 'The Necessity of an Absolute Misunderstanding', in Hamza, A. and Ruda, F. (eds.) *Slavoj Žižek and Dialectical Materialism.* New York: Palgrave Macmillan, pp. 43–56.

Melville, H. (2009). *Bartleby the Scrivener: A Story of Wall Street.* New York: Melville House Publishing.

Milbank, J. (2005). 'Materialism and Transcendence', in Davis, C., Milbank, J., and Žižek, S. (eds.) *Theology and the Political: The New Debate.* Durham: Duke University Press, pp. 393–428.

Milbank, J., Pickstock, C., and Ward, G. (eds.). (1999). *Radical Orthodoxy: A New Theology.* New York: Routledge.

Mitralexis, S. and Skliris, D. (eds.). (2019). *Slavoj Žižek and Christianity.* New York: Routledge.

Myers, T. (2003). *Slavoj Žižek.* London: Routledge.

Nietzsche, F. (1964). *Morgenröte, Gedanken über die moralischen Vorurteile.* Stuttgart: Kröner.

Pfeifer, G. (2016). *The New Materialism: Althusser, Badiou and Žižek.* New York: Routledge.

Pound, M. (2008). *Žižek: A (Very) Critical Introduction.* Grand Rapids and Cambridge: Eerdmans.

Pound, M. (2017). 'Slavoj Žižek (1949–)', in Goodchild, P. and Phelps, H. (eds.) *Religion and European Philosophy: Key Thinkers from Kant to Žižek.* Oxford: Routledge, pp. 479–491.

Rose, G. (1981). *Hegel Contra Sociology*. London: Athlone Press.

Schelling, F.W.J. (1946). *Die Weltalter: Fragmente in den Urfassungen von 1811 und 1813*. München: Biederstein & Leibniz.

Schneider, N. (2010). 'Orthodox Paradox: An Interview with John Milbank', *The Immanent Frame*, 17 March. Available at http://blogs.ssrc.org/tif/2010/03/17/orthodox-paradox-an-interview-with-john-milbank/. Accessed 20 September 2016.

Sharpe, M. and Boucher, G. (2010). *Žižek and Politics: A Critical Introduction*. Edinburgh: Edinburgh University Press.

Sigurdson, O. (2013). 'Slavoj Žižek, the Death of God, and Zombies: A Theological Account', *Modern Theology*, 29(3), pp. 361–380.

Stavrakakis, Y. (1999). *Lacan and the Political*. London: Routledge.

Strauss, D.F. (1864). *Das Leben Jesu*. Leipzig: F.A. Brockhaus.

Taubes, J. (1993). *Die politische Theologie des Paulus: Vorträge, gehalten an der Forschungsstätte der evangelischen Studiengemeinschaft in Heidelberg, 23–27. February 1987*. München: Wilhelm Fink.

The Pervert's Guide to Cinema. (2006). Directed by S. Fiennes [DVD]. Charlottesville and Wien: Amoeba Films and Mischief Films.

Tupinamba, G. (2019). 'Concrete Universality: Only That Which Is Non-All Is for All', in Mitralexis, S. and Skliris, D. (eds.) *Slavoj Žižek and Christianity*. New York: Routledge, pp. 104–116.

Vattimo, G. (2002). *After Christianity*. Translated by L. D'Isanto. New York: Columbia University Press.

Ward, G. (2000a). *Cities of God*. New York: Routledge.

Ward, G. (2000b). *Theology and the Contemporary Critical Theory*. London: Macmillan.

Ward, G. (2005). *Christ and Culture*. Malden: Blackwell.

Wright, E. and Wright, E. (eds.). (1999). *The Žižek Reader*. Oxford: Blackwell.

Žižek, S. (1976). *Znak, Označitelj, Pismo*. Beograd: Mladost.

Žižek, S. (1982). *Zgodovina in Nezavedno*. Ljubljana: Cankarjeva Založba.

Žižek, S. (1984). *Birokratija I Uživanje*. Beograd: Studentski Izdavački Centar.

Žižek, S. (1989). *The Sublime Object of Ideology*. London: Verso.

Žižek, S. (1991a). *For They Know Not What They Do: Enjoyment as a Political Factor*. London: Verso.

Žižek, S. (1991b). *Looking Awry: An Introduction to Jacques Lacan Through Popular Culture*. Cambridge: The MIT Press.

Žižek, S. (1992). *Enjoy Your Symptom! Jacques Lacan in Hollywood and Out*. New York and London: Routledge.

Žižek, S. (1993). *Tarrying with the Negative: Kant, Hegel and the Critique of Ideology*. Durham: Duke University Press.

Žižek, S. (1994). *The Metastases of Enjoyment: Six Essays on Women and Causality*. London: Verso.

Žižek, S. (1996). *The Indivisible Remainder: An Essay on Schelling and Related Matters*. London: Verso.

Žižek, S. (1997). *The Plague of Fantasies*. London and New York: Verso.

Žižek, S. (1999). *The Ticklish Subject: The Absent Centre of Political Ontology*. London: Verso.

Žižek, S. (2000). *The Fragile Absolute: Or, Why Is the Christian Legacy Worth Fighting for?* London and New York: Verso.

Žižek, S. (2001a). *On Belief*. London: Routledge.

Žižek, S. (2001b). 'The Rhetorics of Power', *Diacritics*, 31(1), pp. 91–104.

Žižek, S. (2001c). *Did Somebody Say Totalitarianism? Five Interventions in the (Mis)use of a Notion*. London and New York: Verso.

Žižek, S. (2002a). *Welcome to the Desert of the Real! Five Essays on September 11 and Related Dates*. London: Verso.

Žižek, S. (2002b). *Revolution at the Gates: Selected Writings of Lenin from 1917*. London and New York: Verso.

Žižek, S. (2003). *The Puppet and the Dwarf: The Perverse Core of Christianity*. London: The MIT Press.

Žižek, S. (2006). *The Parallax View*. London: The MIT Press.

Žižek, S. (2007). *In Defence of Lost Causes*. London: Verso.

Žižek, S. (2008a). 'Between Fear and Trembling: On Why Only Atheists Can Believe,' 8 November, mp3 file, 2:11:58, Stevenson Centre Lecture Hall, Vanderbilt University. Available at http://discoverarchive.vanderbilt.edu/handle/1803/501. Accessed 20 September 2016.

Žižek, S. (2008b). *On Violence*. London: Picador.

Žižek, S. (2009a). 'From Job to Christ: A Paulinian Reading of Chesterton', in Caputo, J.D. and Alcoff, L.M. (eds.) *Paul Among the Philosophers*. Bloomington: Indiana University Press, pp. 39–58.

Žižek, S. (2009b). *First as Tragedy, Then as Far as Farce*. London and New York: Verso.

Žižek, S. (2010a). 'A Meditation on Michelangelo's Christ on the Cross', in Davis, C., Milbank, J., and Žižek, S. (eds.) *Paul's New Moment: Continental Philosophy and the Future of Christian Theology*. Grand Rapids: Brazos Press, pp. 176–179.

Žižek, S. (2010b). 'Paul and the Truth Event', in Davis, C., Milbank, J., and Žižek, S. (eds.) *Paul's New Moment: Continental Philosophy and the Future of Christian Theology*. Grand Rapids: Brazos Press, pp. 92–99.

Žižek, S. (2010c). *Living in the End Times*. London: Verso.

Žižek, S. (2011). *The Parallax*. Available at http://www.youtube.com/watch?v=vdwF3j1F2pg. Accessed 20 September 2016.

Žižek, S. (2012a). *Less Than Nothing: Hegel and the Shadow of Dialectical Materialism*. London: Verso.

Žižek, S. (2012b). *The Year of Dreaming Dangerously*. New York and London: Verso.

Žižek, S. (2012c). *The Heart of the People of Europe Beats in Greece*. Available at http://www.youtube.com/watch?v=SWtn7iECkyY. Accessed 20 September 2016.

Žižek, S. (2013a). 'Neighbours and Other Monsters: A Plea For Ethical Violence', in Žižek, S., Santner, E., and Reinhardt, K. (eds.) *The Neighbour: Three Inquiries in Political Theology*. Chicago: The University of Chicago Press, pp. 134–190.

Žižek, S. (2013b). 'The Necessity of a Dead Bird' in Blanton, W. and de Vries, H. (eds.) *Paul and the Philosophers*. New York: Fordham University Press, pp. 175–185.

Žižek, S. (2014). *Absolute Recoil: Towards a New Foundation of Dialectical Materialism*. London: Verso.

Žižek, S. (2016). *Against the Double Blackmail: Refugees, Terror and Other Troubles with the Neighbours*. London: Allen Lane.

Žižek, S. (2018). 'Marx Reads Object-Oriented Ontology', in Žižek, S., Ruda, F., and Hamza, A. *Reading Marx*. Cambridge: Polity Press, pp. 17–61.

Žižek, S. and Daly, G. (2004). *Conversations with Žižek*. Cambridge: Polity Press.

Žižek, S. and Dupuy, J-P. (2014). *Žižek and Dupuy: Religion, Secularism, and Political Belonging*. Available at https://www.youtube.com/watch?v=NEEBYNNpX9o. Accessed 20 September 2016.

Žižek, S. and Gunjević, B. (2012). *God in Pain: Inversions of Apocalypse*. New York: Seven Stories Press.

Žižek, S. and Milbank, J. (2009). *The Monstrosity of Christ: Paradox or Dialectic?* London: The MIT Press.

CHAPTER 3

Bonhoeffer's Social Theology

FROM DOGMATICS TO SOCIOLOGY…

Before turning to a Žižekian critical reading of Bonhoeffer's *Sanctorum Communio*, it is appropriate to take a look at the grounds of the theological exploration, appropriation and engagement with social philosophy in his thesis—the theological influences during his studies at the Friedrich Wilhelm University in Berlin (later Humboldt University). I will argue that it was the liberal theological faculty that introduced and, in a way, projected Bonhoeffer into a reflection upon the social philosophical thinkers, such as Hegel.

At the time of Bonhoeffer's arrival for his studies in Berlin in 1924, the University there was a stronghold of nineteenth-century liberal theology. Its theological faculty boasted prominent thinkers who were trained in the theology of Albrecht Ritschl and represented various reactions to or modifications of his thought—Ernst Troeltsch, Karl Holl, Reinhold Seeberg and Adolf von Harnack.[1] They moved away from Ritschl's disinterest in culture and the philosophy of religion and his isolation of theology from other intel-

---

[1] To that list we could add Karl Holl, who attempted to relate Luther to the whole modern development of the West. While Troeltsch had rejected Luther as a medieval man, Holl was convinced of his relevance and through him developed an understanding of religion as conscience. The latter represented the 'higher plane', a place in man where God might encounter him and show him his possibilities (Holl 1959, p. 48). It is because of this inward focus of Holl's thought that he is not included in the consideration here. It suffices to say that even though Bonhoeffer developed a passion for Luther's thought in Holl's seminars

© The Author(s) 2019
B. Koltaj, *Žižek Reading Bonhoeffer*,
Radical Theologies and Philosophies,
https://doi.org/10.1007/978-3-030-26094-1_3

lectual disciplines (Mackintosh 1937, pp. 181–183). For his understanding of the decline of religion, Troeltsch drew upon Max Weber's conception of sociology and Neo-Kantian thought. By his concentration upon the church, the theme of the redemptive community and seeking a synthesis with Hegelian metaphysics, Seeberg placed a conservative view of church history at the service of the Liberal Spirit.[2] Von Harnack, on the other hand, substituted Ritschl's centrality of ecclesiology for a broad sweep of cultural interests and an individual spirit which drew its strength from the heroic transcendence of history and nature. Their thinking influenced Bonhoeffer's own intellectual development, its social philosophical concern or orientation, content and manner, be it positively or negatively.

Ernst Troeltsch

It could be said that the systematic theologian of the History of Religions School[3] Ernst Troeltsch provided the most radical liberal reaction against Ritschl. Unlike von Harnack and Seeberg, he did not look for an irreducible essence or absolute principles of Christianity, but instead desired to complete the process initiated by Schleiermacher and construct a modern Christianity under the auspices of philosophy of religion, the psychological analysis of religious consciousness and the religious idea as it manifested itself in history (Troeltsch 1911, p. 6). Deeply influenced by Hegel, he argued that even though Christianity is the highest religious form with its perfect expression of the unity of God with man, it must recognise that it is limited and conditioned, and that its idea can now maintain itself by means of its own intrinsic resources. Therefore, that idea must be guarded against any ecclesiastical or religious encroachments:

> If the absolute authority has fallen which, in its absoluteness, made the antithesis of the divine and human equally absolute, if in man an autonomous principle is recognized as the source of truth and moral conduct, then all conceptions of the world which were specially designed to maintain that gulf

(Bethge 1961, p. 4), he reacted against the notion of conscience as a contact point between man and God. See DBWE 1: p. 51; DBWE 8: p. 362.

[2] This is observed in the lectures Seeberg gave to students on 'the principle truths of the Christian religion' in 1901–1902. See Cremer (1903).

[3] The term Religionsgeschichtliche Schule denoted a group of German Protestant theologians associated with the University of Göttingen in late nineteenth century.

between the human and divine, fall along with it. With it falls the doctrine of the absolute corruption of mankind through original sin, and the transference of the ends of life to the heavenly world in which there will be deliverance from this corruption. In consequence, all the factors of this present life acquire an enhanced value and a higher impressiveness, and the ends of life fall more and more within the realms of the present world with its ideal of transformation. (Troeltsch 1912, pp. 22–23)

The departure of this 'absolute authority' results in its place being taken by a 'truth and morality producing autonomous principle' in Man that is not in the possession of any religious or otherwise community. Troeltsch certainly had no illusions about the future course of world history, the outcome of the growth of what he called 'militaristic, nationalistic bourgeois states', but his emancipation rather recalls Žižek's own negativity of the Cross. Given its Hegelian dialectical motor, it is of no surprise that Troeltsch's argument here reminds one of Žižek's own Hegelian model of religion, where Christianity represents the final stage in the autonomy of Man, resulting in the community of abandoned solidarity, without recourse to the big Other or indeed an afterlife. This emphasis on the present life of Man was at the forefront of Troeltsch's sociological approach to the doctrine of the church presented in his *Die Soziallehren der christlichen Kirchen und Gruppen* [Social Teachings] (1923).

Even though Troeltsch died before Bonhoeffer could attend his lectures, his thought very much pervaded the subjects on offer and influenced the topic and approach of Bonhoeffer's own dissertation—to produce an understanding of the church outside the terms of general religious principles, setting forth its structure in terms of a sociological analysis carried into the service of dogmatics. While Troeltsch focused on the historico-sociological shapes and conditions of the church, 'the intrinsic sociological idea of Christianity, and its structure and organization' (Troeltsch 1923, pp. 33–34), Bonhoeffer wished to present a genuinely theological concept of the church, all the while insisting that Troeltsch was correct in seeing the church as an empirical structure because 'revelation means nothing beyond, but an entity in this historically and sociologically shaped world' (Bethge 1963, p. 34). Taking over his sociological tools, Bonhoeffer examined the spatial question of faith in community, rather than engaging in discussion over the temporal problems of faith and history. Later, in *Ethics* and the *Letters*, he attempted to come to terms with the basic questions Troeltsch had raised. Thus in the letter on June 8th which outlines the implication of the world-come-of-age for Christianity, Bonhoeffer stated to Bethge that liberal theology began to apprehend it, specifically mentioning Troeltsch's name in parenthesis (8 June 1944 in DBWE 8: p. 428). Thus Troeltsch's influence on the development of Bonhoeffer's thought is not to be over-looked and there are traces of it in all of his writings, but foremost in his sociological and modern *qua* contemporary orientation.

Reinhold Seeberg

This sociological concern with the modern man was certainly also char-acteristic of Bonhoeffer's dissertation supervisor and historian of dogma Reinhold Seeberg, who taught at the University from 1898 to 1927, and his *Lehrbuch der Dogmengeschichte* [Text-Book of the History of Doctrines] (1953). The work represented an argument against Ritschl's dismissal of dogmatics, instead of attempting to preserve the Christian faith by express-ing it in a form intelligible to modern man, a sort of rewriting of dogma for a modern age.[4] Yet what proved crucial for Bonhoeffer's thought was Seeberg's focus on the moral and social dimensions of theological reflec-tion, grounded in his conviction that theology ought to be life-related and experience-focused rather than purely theoretical. He convinced Bonho-effer about the social reality of existence, in history and community. The disciple attended all of his systematic theology seminars, where he observed his rigour and pursuit of knowledge, which led him to approach Seeberg about supervising his dissertation. This theme of sociality became Bonho-effer's lens through which he considered theology.[5]

Seeberg and Bonhoeffer's shared sociological conviction centred upon a particular field of theology—ecclesiology. Seeberg's ecclesiology was part of his dialectical historical understanding of the Trinity, wherein the church was understood as the visible, tangible and incarnate Holy Spirit, and inter-

---

[4] See Seeberg's preface to the English translation of his *Die Grundwahrheiten der christlichen Religion* (1908, pp. v–viii). Seeberg's task was rooted in an understanding of the mind as the contact point between man and God, a religious a priori possessing the intrinsic capacity for becoming aware of his being and activity, which Bonhoeffer challenged in *Act and Being* (1996). See also Seeberg (1927a, p. 104) and Bethge (1994, pp. 87–89).

[5] However, Green (1999, p. 24) is quick to rightly point out that the complex set of concepts Bonhoeffer uses to explicate sociality are not simply taken over from Seeberg, but in discussion with others.

preted the social reality of existence (Seeberg 1927b, p. 357f.).[6] It was in this context that Bonhoeffer proposed in his thesis a 'Christian philosophy of spirit [...] that will provide a direction for Christian philosophy' (DBWE 1: pp. 43–44 [30]). This proposal is masterfully laid out in the prologue and deserving of a full quote:

> The goal of the following ecclesiological study is a dogmatic-theological reflection on the church in light of insights from social philosophy and sociology. Creating a real conceptual connection between theology and both social philosophy and sociology is the basic task and also the difficulty in this essay, whose concrete subject matter is the idea of the church as sanctorum communio. The dogmatic character of the work prevails; both disciplines of social science are to be made fruitful for theology.

> Thus the basic problem can be defined as the problem of a specifically Christian social philosophy and sociology. My intention is to discuss neither a general sociology of religion, nor genetic-sociological questions; rather, I intend to show that an inherently Christian social philosophy and sociology, arising essentially out of fundamental concepts of Christian theology, is most fully articulated in the concept of the church.

> The more I have focused on this problem, the more clearly I have recognized the social intention of all fundamental Christian concepts. 'Person', 'primal state', 'sin', and 'revelation' appeared fully understandable only in relation to sociality [...].

> I hope this study will be seen as a modest contribution to a 'philosophy of the church' as was recently called for by Reinhold Seeberg in his Christliche Dogmatik [cf. Seeberg, Dogmatik, 2, 385], namely one which not only clarifies the nature of the church and of religious community, but which 'would result in new understanding of the cohesion of the spirit of humanity [...]. My [...] wish in presenting this study is to contribute something to the understanding that our church, profoundly impoverished and helpless though it appears today, is nevertheless the sanctorum communio, the holy body of Christ, even Christ's very presence in the world. (DBWE 1: pp. 22–23 [5])[7]

---

[6] This thoroughly Hegelian understanding of the church, in contrast to Žižek, results in Seeberg's attempt to relate the significance of the church to history in general.

[7] This final sentence also lays the backdrop for Bonhoeffer's criticism of Barth; He was disapproving of dialectical theology's neglect of the critical questions posed by liberal theology, specifically the sociological dimensions of church, interaction with the world and other disciplines and interpretation of dogma—the very concerns of this thesis. Neglect of these resulted in an inability to ground an ontology in Christ, provide a dogmatic base for the empirical

The first paragraph makes clear Bonhoeffer's determination to make both disciplines of social science 'fruitful for theology', despite the challenge presented by such a reflection on theological thought about the church in light of their insight. His conviction regarding 'the social intention of all fundamental Christian concepts',[8] as well as his desire to develop 'a real conceptual connection between theology and both social philosophy and sociology', speaks strongly of Seeberg's influence upon the form of his thought and also his later explorations of questions about what it means to be human in the concrete contingencies of life.

Following the completion of *Sanctorum Communio*, Seeberg suggested that Bonhoeffer proceeds with a historical investigation of ethics, such as the ethics of Scholasticism, or to move onto discussing the method of interpretation of Scripture (Bethge 1967, p. 132). Instead, Bonhoeffer's *Act and Being* (1996) discussed God's revelation epistemologically in light of the clash between the transcendental philosophy of liberal theology and Barth's scepticism about its capacity for critical reflection (to be discussed later).[9] Thus Bonhoeffer's second dissertation was not supervised by Seeberg, but by his successor Wilhelm Lütgert. Bethge (1967, pp. 69–72) remarks that after 1933, when the national socialists made expansion of the German Reich their official policy and some of Seeberg's thoughts

church and develop a concrete ethic. While Bonhoeffer did point out the shortcoming of his liberal Berlin professors as the reduction of God to man, he also criticized Barth for fixating his attention on the transcendent at the expense of revelation as concrete and apprehensible in its community—the church. Rather than a disciple of one or the other, Bonhoeffer was developing his own critical approach in reflection on both, one that appreciated the strengths of liberal theology or Barth, while also pointing out their errors. It will become abundantly clear in the reading of *Sanctorum Communio* that in the development of his thought, recourse to both proved a crucial role. For a general discussion of Barth's impact on Bonhoeffer see Pangritz's *Karl Barth in the Theology of Dietrich Bonhoeffer* (2000). For examples of interpretations of the relationship between Barth and Bonhoeffer, see Prenter's 'Dietrich Bonhoeffer and Karl Barth's Positivism of Revelation' (1967, pp. 93–130), and Ott's *Reality and Faith* (1972, pp. 58–61, 120–142). Green's *Bonhoeffer: A Theology of Sociality* (1999) attempts to present Bonhoeffer's sociality in contrast to Barth, while DeJonge (2012) and Mawson (2018, pp. 13–38) show Bonhoeffer developing a distinctive 'person-theology' in contrast to both Barth and the liberal theology in Berlin.

[8]According to Richard Roberts (2005, pp. 375–377), it also qualifies *Sanctorum Communio* as a classic illuminating the relation between theology and the social sciences.

[9]A thorough presentation of Bonhoeffer's second dissertation can be found in 'Bonhoeffer's *Act and Being*: The Priority of the Other as Critique of Idealism', in Floyd (1988).

on community appealed to values that nurtured nationalism, Bonhoeffer's break with the latter became complete. Nonetheless, Seeberg's influence upon the form and socio-philosophical orientation of Bonhoeffer's thought should not be overlooked.[10]

Von Harnack

Finally, and of no less importance, was the influence of the church historian Adolf von Harnack.[11] Of Bonhoeffer's Berlin professors, von Harnack alone had a personal relationship to his family—he was a friend of Bonhoeffer's father and both families lived in Grunewald, which was a neighbourhood of academics.[12] After retiring from teaching at Berlin (from 1888 until 1921), he personally chose Bonhoeffer as one of a handful of students who worked with him in his seminars on church history after retirement. The latter described the experience in a letter as 'too closely associated with my whole personality for me to be able ever to forget it' (Bethge 1967, p. 34). It is understandable, then, that von Harnack strongly influenced Bonhoeffer's intellectual development.

Von Harnack's thought was characteristically liberal insofar as his thought in pursuit of knowledge was without limits and marked by a confidence in the human spirit and ability to pursue objectivity under the scrutiny of reason.[13] In contrast to Troeltsch's understanding of dogmatic theology as a possibility for neo-Protestantism, or Seebergs redrafting of dogma in modern metaphysical language, he adopted yet a different approach. His *Lehrbuch der Dogmengeschichte* [*History of Dogma*] (1890) narrated the history of dogma as an obscuration of the Gospel through

---

[10]Volume 17 of *BDWE: Register und Ergänzungen*, lists a total of 168 references to Seeberg, 134 of these before *Act and Being.* This goes to show the influence the latter has had on Bonhoeffer's formation as a thinker, not only as a teacher, but also in Bonhoeffer's challenge of or response to his thought.

[11]Volume 17 of the German edition of *BDWE: Register und Ergänzungen* lists 134 references to Harnack. Unlike those to Seeberg, these appear throughout Bonhoeffer's writings, after the publication of his second dissertation. Certainly, he remains in Bonhoeffer's view an influence of a much more positive disposition.

[12]A description of the personal relationship between them is beyond the scope of this thesis. For an insight into that, see Bethge (1967, p. 72).

[13]A good account of von Harnack's liberal theology can be found in Rumscheidt's *Adolf von Harnack: Liberal Theology at Its Height* (1988).

Hellenization, concluding that the task of contemporary theology is to continue destroying dogma:

> Moving forward, Christianity must learn that even in religion the simplest is the hardest, and that everything that burdens religion only blunts its gravity. Therefore, the goal of all Christian work, even of all theological work, can only be this – to discern ever more distinctly the simplicity and the gravity of the Gospel, in order to become ever purer and livelier in spirit, and ever more loving and brotherly in action. (von Harnack 1890, p. 764)[14]

With that conviction he founded in 1891 the Commission on the Church Fathers, intending to publish a critical edition of the Greco-Christian literature up to the year 325,[15] one which would instead focus on the way belief shapes one's life. Bonhoeffer admired the epistemological rigour with which the church historian sought to engage or present theology to the modern man. Of particular influence was von Harnack's positive perception of 'the world', compared to the isolationist attitude of his teachers—something he clearly expressed in the text of his address at von Harnack's funeral (DBWE 10: pp. 379–381).

While the influence of von Harnack on Bonhoeffer's intellectual formation was immense and multifocal,[16] it is within the remit of this brief section (as outlined above) to focus on the following areas of Bonhoeffer's thought, which have been shaped by his teacher: his ethical concern oriented towards action, the maturity of the world come-of-age, the notion of arcane discipline and the emphasis on Jesus' humanity.

---

[14]This is my own translation of the original German [*Fortschreitend muss die Christenheit lernen, dass auch in der Religion das Einfachste das Schwerste ist, und dass Alles, was die Religion belastet, ihren Ernst abstumpft. Darum kann das Ziel aller christlichen Arbeit, auch aller theologischen, nur das sein, immer sicherer die Schlichtheit und den Ernst des Evangeliums zu erkennen, um in der Gesinnung immer reiner und lebendiger, in der That immer liebevoller und brüderlicher zu warden.*] For von Harnack, the archetypal hero was Luther, who discarded dogma and substituted it for an evangelical view (ibid., pp. 691–764).

[15]By 1924 forty-five volumes had appeared, most of them edited by von Harnack himself.

[16]Rumscheidt delivers a glimpse into von Harnack's influence in the formation of Bonhoeffer's theology in the *Cambridge Companion to Dietrich Bonhoeffer* (Rumscheidt 1999, pp. 50–70 at p. 54). A very helpful introduction to Harnackian characteristics of Bonhoeffer's thought can be found in Kalternborn's (1973) illuminating study of von Harnack as Bonhoeffer's teacher. See in particular pp. 125–128 and the more detailed analysis that follows. Alternatively, Kaltenborn's brief contribution to Klassen in English relies on that work. See 'Adolf von Harnack and Bonhoeffer' in Klassen (1981, pp. 48–57).

The ethical orientation of Bonhoeffer's thought was already visible in *Sanctorum Communio*, where Christ existing as community poses the question of how the community should act.[17] Later, at the end of his stay at Union Seminary, Bonhoeffer set out an understanding of the import of Christianity for the world as the deciding contribution of American Christianity: 'Taking seriously the kingdom of God as a kingdom on earth is biblically sound and is justified compared to an understanding of the kingdom as one beyond' (DBWE 12: p. 241). Indeed, in all Bonhoeffer's works the ethical, and specific questions of ethical implications of Christianity, assume utmost importance. Bonhoeffer contemplates the gravity of the ethical in contrast to knowledge of good and bad in *Ethik*:

> The knowledge of good and evil appears to be the goal of all ethical reflection. The first task of Christian ethics is to supersede that knowledge. This attack on the presuppositions of all other ethics is so unique that it is questionable whether it even makes sense to speak of Christian ethics at all. If it is nevertheless done, then this can only mean that Christian ethics claims to articulate the origin of the whole ethical enterprise, and thus to be considered an ethic only as the critique of all ethics. (DBWE 6: pp. 299–300)

This understanding of Christianity's subversion of the ethical preoccupation with the knowledge of good and evil lends itself to Žižek's own reading of the atonement as an act suspending the Law, or in Bonhoeffer's words, 'a critique of all ethics' (ibid.). Indeed, it can be read as a critique of modernity's preoccupation with knowledge (as an act).

The described ethical orientation is situated within a world which, for both von Harnack and Bonhoeffer, is characterised by maturity or has come-of-age. In both of their thought, this concept of *Mündigkeit*, that is maturity or come-of-ageness, performs a crucial function in understanding Christianity today. Thus, in his *Bericht über die Ausgabe der griechischen Kirchenväter der drei ersten Jahrhunderte*, von Harnack argues that of all religions Christianity best expresses the *Mündigkeit* of the Greeks and Romans (1906b, p. 166). He also remarks that it is unworthy of a people come-of-age 'to be patronized and bound to the inner spheres of religion'

---

[17] For Bonhoeffer the emphasis lies on community, rather than von Harnack's individual. That does not mean that Bonhoeffer ignores the individual, but rather that the two are inseparable.

(ibid., pp. 89–90).[18] For Bonhoeffer also the maturity of the world engages or co-determines the purpose of ecclesiology, its role and identity today. The church, he contends in *Ethik*, can no longer be the purpose in and of itself, but exists for the world that has come-of-age.[19] If it fails to do so, it also profanes the gospel, which itself has brought the world to maturity. Here is how he then expresses this again in *The Letters*:

> Thus our coming of age leads us to a truer recognition of our situation before God. God would have us know that we must live as men who manage their lives without him. The same God who is with us is the God who forsakes us (Mark 15:34!). The same God who makes us to live in the world without the working hypothesis of God is the God before whom we stand continually. Before God, and with God, we live without God. God consents to be pushed out of the world and onto the Cross; God is weak and powerless in the world and in precisely this way, and only so, is at our side and helps us. Matt. 8:17 makes it quite clear that Christ helps us not by virtue of his omnipotence but rather by virtue of his weakness and suffering! (16 July 1944 in DBWE 8: pp. 478–479)

This following of Jesus into the world became the central theme of Bonhoeffer's *Letters and Papers*. In it one finds descriptions of a 'world-come-of-age', in which humans operate autonomously, without sensing a need to refer to either the divine grace or truth. In the world-come-of-age, people no longer require God as a working hypothesis, whether in science, in human affairs in general, or increasingly even in religion (8 June 1944 in DBWE 8: p. 267ff.). The older view of God as God-of-the-Gaps was false and as man became more and more independent God was pushed out of increasingly larger dimensions of life, with theology retreating to the inner world of man. Bonhoeffer sought to provide a response to the world-come-of-age and called for Christians to understand it better than it understands itself (8 June 1944 in DBWE 8: p. 269ff.). Bonhoeffer discussed Christological concerns in light of their ontological and ethical import in a modern world, which seemed to operate without God's involvement, observed in the scientific approach, but also in the terrors of both World Wars. This is succinctly revealed in the line: 'What keeps gnawing at me is the question,

---

[18] My own translation of the original German ['auf dem innerlichsten gebiete, dem der Religion, bevormundet und gebunden zu werden'].

[19] See 'Church and World I' in DBWE 6: pp. 339–351, and 'On the Possibility of the Church's Message to the World' in DBWE 6: pp. 352–362.

what is Christianity, or who is Christ actually for us today?' (30 April 1944 in DBWE 8: p. 362). His Christology was the driving force of his ecclesiology, where the church as community was the locus of Christ's presence today, and the life of the community revolved around imitating Christ as a vicarious representative.[20]

Conviction about the *Mündigkeit* of the world plays a part in another sphere of von Harnack's influence—Bonhoeffer's concept of 'arcane discipline' protecting the riches of Christianity from profanation. Thus Bonhoeffer's contention on 5 May 1944 that 'there are degrees of cognition and degrees of significance. That means, an "arcane discipline" must be re-established, through which the mysteries of the Christian faith are sheltered against profanation' (5 May 1944 in DBWE 8: p. 373)[21] can be read alongside von Harnack's contention that 'what matters is not the form but the reverence with which one lays hold of the mystery of the person of Christ and then submits one's life to the spirit of Christ' (1906a, p. 296).[22] The parallelism in the wording is not coincidental, even though 'profanation' is perceived differently—by Harnack in relation to those segments of the church that held to some form of untouchable orthodoxy (von Zahn-Harnack 1951, p. 131), while Bonhoeffer argued for a protection from the assertions of German Christians that what was being carried out in Germany was the will of God. In light of this Bonhoeffer calls for an intellectual discussion that will challenge the world:

> It is not for us to predict the day – but the day will come – when people will once more be called to speak the word of God in such a way that the world is changed and renewed. It will be a new language, perhaps quite non-religious, but liberating and redeeming like Jesus' language, so that people will be alarmed and yet overcome by its power – the language of a new righteousness and truth, a language proclaiming that God makes peace with humankind and that God's kingdom is drawing near. (18 May 1944 in DBWE 8: p. 390)

[20] See DBWE 1: pp. 120, 157, 189; DBWE 2: p. 120; DBWE 12: p. 323. See also Phillips (1967, p. 48).

[21] See also Staats (1981, p. 105).

[22] My own translation of the original German: [Nicht auf die Fassung kommt es an, sondern auf die Ehrfurcht, mit der man das Geheimnis der Person Christi umfasst und das eigene Leben unter den Geist Christi beugt].

Finally, Bonhoeffer's thought reflects von Harnack's emphasis on the humanity of Jesus. Admittedly, von Harnack prioritises Christ's human nature when he says:

> [T]he thesis: 'the life of Jesus was not purely human', can only mean: the life of Jesus offers brush-strokes, for which our history does not possess any analogies. Any other formulation is not permitted or possible for a scientific man [...]. (von Zahn-Harnack 1951, p. 187)[23]

or indeed 'If you are assuming that the life of Jesus was not purely human, you also deprive it of its peculiarity' (von Harnack 1906b, p. 223).[24] In contrast, Bonhoeffer maintains that the humanity of Jesus cannot be separated from his divinity.[25] Nonetheless, there remains an emphasis on the humanity of Jesus, fully expressed in *the Letters*, where he writes to Bethge:

> In the last few years I have come to know and understand more and more of the profound this-worldliness of Christianity. The Christian is not a homo religiosus, but simply a human being, in the same way that Jesus was a human being – in contrast, perhaps, to John the Baptist. (21 July 1944 in DBWE 8: p. 541)

By positioning the humanity of Jesus in contrast to the Baptist and designating the *homo religiosus* as negative, Bonhoeffer seeks to protect the humanity of Jesus against any 'religionalising' imposition of religion. In other words, Christ's humanity ought to be presented together with his divinity, while refusing to be overtaken by it, for it alone prevents any invocation of the 'deus ex machina':

> Human religiosity directs people in need to the power of God in the world: God as deus ex machina. The Bible directs people toward the powerlessness

---

[23] My own translation of the original German: [... die These: 'das Leben Jesu war kein rein menschliches' darf nur lauten: Das Leben Jesu bietet Züge, für die wir in der Geschichte Analogien nicht besitzen. Eine andere Formulierung kann und darf ein wissenchaftlicher Mann nicht brauchen...].

[24] My own translation of the original German: [Behauptest Du, das Leben Jesu sei kein rein menschliches, so entziehst Du auch dem Glauben sein Eigentümliches...].

[25] See, for example, 'The Image of Christ' in DBWE 4: pp. 281–289.

and suffering of God; only the suffering God can help. (16 July 1944 in DBWE 8: p. 479)[26]

What remains is the paradox of pointing at the man Jesus and proclaiming that this is God (DBWE 4: p. 225), the man existing for others, rather than man in himself. In *Outline of a Book* (3 August 1944 in DBWE 8: pp. 499–504), Bonhoeffer writes under Chapter Three:

> The church [...] must tell people in every calling what a life with Christ is, what it means 'to be there for others' [...] It will have to see that it does not underestimate the significance of the human 'example' (which has its origin in the humanity of Jesus and is so important in Paul's writings!). (ibid., pp. 503–504)

Another letter deserving of mention can be directly compared with the *Das Wesen des Christentums*, in which von Harnack wishes 'to remind humanity over and again that a man named Jesus Christ was in their midst' (von Harnack 1902, p. 1). On 21 August 1944 Bonhoeffer writes, 'If this earth was deemed worthy to bear the human being Jesus Christ, if a human being like Jesus lived, then and only then does our life as human beings have meaning' (21 August 1944 in DBWE 8: p. 515). Despite their differences in relation to the divine nature of Jesus, Bonhoeffer very much shared the emphasis on his humanity with von Harnack, both in implication and application.

Perhaps their difference in relation to the divine is illuminated even further by Bonhoeffer's criticism of von Harnack's overt confidence in the human ability to comprehend. Rumscheidt describes this confidence as follows: '[In] liberal theology [...] the distance between the knower and the known [...] is reduced to the extent that what is known cannot be a limit on the knower' (Rumscheidt 1999, p. 54). Bonhoeffer, however, in his notion of sociality in *Sanctorum Communio* (DBWE 1: p. 51) and

---

[26] 'The Incarnation, Jesus' words and deeds, and his death on the Cross are integral elements of this image. It is an image different from the image of Adam in the original glory of paradise. It is the image of one who places himself in the very midst of the world of sin and death, who takes on the needs of human flesh, who humbly submits to God's wrath and judgment over sinners, who remains obedient to God's will in suffering and death; the one born in poverty, who befriended and sat at the table to eat with tax collectors and sinners, and who, on the Cross, was rejected and abandoned by God and human beings – this is God in human form, this is the human being who is the new image of God!' (DBWE 4: p. 284).

then again in *Act and Being* (DBWE 2: p. 88), argues for limits that are imposed by the other and are as such insurmountable methodologically and ethically. He concludes that when those limits are transgressed, as in the case of von Harnack's confident liberal theology, it is revealed that the subject does not know the other—man or *God*—epistemologically at all, but knows only oneself.

Bonhoeffer's references to von Harnack began to recede with Karl Barth's prominence in his thought from the late 1920s.[27] However, as Bethge reports, in *The Letters* the references pick up again, due to Bonhoeffer's desire 'to become better acquainted with particular aspects of nineteenth-century literature and rehabilitate the tradition of the forefathers, from Keller to Harnack, from Pestalozzi to Dilthey, over against more modern existentialist tendencies' (Bethge 1967, pp. 844–846). Among works of others, Bonhoeffer asked for Harnack's *Geschichte der Königlich Preussischen Akademie* [The History of the Prussian Academy of Sciences] (1900)[28] and expressing a sadness that so few people appreciate the intellectual achievements of the eighteenth and nineteenth centuries (29–30 January, 2 March 1944, in DBW 8: p. 279, p. 316). This comment reveals the continued influence and context of von Harnack within which Bonhoeffer developed the orientation, concern and emphasis of his own thought.

It has hopefully become clear that Bonhoeffer's Berlin faculty has left an immense intellectual imprint on the development, content and overall concern of his work. Bethge sums up the formative influences as follows: 'Troeltsch's interest in the sociological realities of Christianity, [...] Harnack's intellectual incorruptibility, and Seeberg's philosophical openness' (Bethge 1963, p. 28). They laid the foundation to Bonhoeffer's sustained engagement of theology with social philosophy and his understanding of the church and sociological realities of Christianity in a mature modern world, including the corresponding interpretation of dogma. An understanding of this background is necessary in order to fully appreciate the

---

[27]This was not solely down to Barth, but also due to the political circumstances, argues Bethge (1967, p. 126). Having said that, while von Harnack's influence receded, it certainly wasn't absent. Thus in his 'lectures on the History of twentieth-century systematic theology' he devotes an entire chapter to 'Wesen des Christentums'.

[28]Von Harnack was asked to write the work in connection with the celebration of its 200th anniversary in 1900, because of his contribution to the natural and medical sciences for the Prussian Academy of Sciences. He was a member of the Prussian Academy of Sciences in Berlin, director of the Prussian State Library and president of the Kaiser Wilhelm Society (now the Max Planck Society for the Advancement of Science) after 1911.

philosophical dimension of his thought, observed in statements such as 'The church is church only when it is there for others' (3 August 1944 in DBWE 8: p. 503). Indeed, his intellectual formation at Berlin serves as the ground for his 'Christ existing as church-community' (DBWE 1: p. 121), the key principle around which his thought revolves. Thus, importantly, what started as a term in Hegelian dialectics under Seeberg, became an essential concept for Bonhoeffer's growing understanding of sociality, first embodied in his dissertation *Sanctorum Communio*. This will be examined next, when his engagement with Hegel will also enable a critical reading of the work alongside Žižek's thought. For now, however, a supplementary note on Hegel's influence is in order, since he is not among the most common thinkers consulted in consideration of Bonhoeffer's intellectual formation.

On the Influence of Hegel

Hegel's notion of rationality as God (or the Absolute) realising itself through a dialectical process in history shaped the intellectual modern theological environment[29] and his idealist philosophy had an important part to play in the development and content of Bonhoeffer's thought at Berlin.[30] Unfortunately, Hegel has not been given the appropriate attention in examinations of Bonhoeffer's intellectual formation,[31] something Jacob Holm links to an uncritical acceptance of the simplified opposition between Bonhoeffer and Hegel that persisted until the 1980s (Holm 2002, pp. 64–65). Thus, for example, in his early account of Bonhoeffer's intellectual biography, Bethge claims that Bonhoeffer's second dissertation is

---

[29]Twentieth century modern theologians have engaged with Hegel in diverse ways: Karl Barth in *Prolegomena to Church Dogmatics* (1975), Karl Rahner in *The Trinity* (1970), Wolfhart Pannenberg in *Revelation as History* (1968), while Jürgen Moltmann in *The Trinity and the Kingdom* (1981) considered his integration of history in the Trinity. Moltmann's *The Crucified God* (1974) and Eberhard Jüngel's *God as the Mystery of the World* (1983) and *Unterwegs zur Sache* (1972) engaged with Hegel's death of God, Rahner's (1976) affirmation of reality as rational, Hans Urs von Balthasar's (1961, 1973–1982, 1985–1987) genres of epic, lyric and drama, Pannenberg's (1963) concepts of rationality and universal history or Hans Küng's (1987) approach to incarnation.

[30]For an introduction to Hegel and Bonhoeffer, see Floyd (2008, pp. 83–119).

[31]Unfortunately, it is not only Hegel but the overall philosophical influences of Bonhoeffer's intellectual formation have not been given the required attention. See Frick's essay 'Bonhoeffer and Philosophy' (2017, pp. 166–182).

'basically addressing philosophers, whom he schematically finds guilty of the original sin of idealism, namely imprisonment in the self' (Bethge 1967, p. 97).[32] Perhaps Bonhoeffer's own early treatment of Hegel contributed to that insofar as *Sanctorum Communio* lacks most references to specific texts but also fails to substantiate his generalisations about Hegel and the diverse movement of German idealism (see Marsh 1994, p. 89). Furthermore, an examination of his footnotes reveals that he mostly relies upon others' presentation of Hegel.[33] Possibly a combination of all these contributed to a lack of consideration of Hegel's influence upon the development of Bonhoeffer's thought.

Change came about after the publication of Oswald Bayer's article 'Christus als Mitte: Ethik im Banne der Religionsphilosophie Hegels' in 1985 (later published as a chapter in his *Leibliches Wort*, 1992, pp. 245–260), evidenced by the publication of student notes from Bonhoeffer's 1933 lectures on Hegel's *Philosophy of Religion* in 1988 as *Dietrich Bonhoeffers Hegel-Seminar* (Tödt 1988).[34] Those very lectures reveal an appreciation for Hegel, whose thought is to be 'judged as a whole'.[35] After that, in the nineties, Charles Marsh examined the way Bonhoeffer read his own idea of Christian community in *Akt und Sein* against Hegel's.[36] Holm concluded his 2002 observation with the statement that Hegel's positive impact upon Bonhoeffer is still not fully recognised or even acknowledged (Holm 2002, p. 65). While Frick (2017, pp. 172–174) provided a brief

---

[32]Admittedly, Bethge goes on to say that the philosophers did not recognise themselves in this characterisation, and later sided with critics of Bonhoeffer's conceptual oversimplifications (pp. 97–99).

[33]For example, a heavy reliance upon Emmanuel Hirsch is observable in Bonhoeffer's criticism of the idealist misconception of the subject, including a brief outline of the resulting distorted community in which individuals surrender absolutely and dissolve into it. DBWE 1: pp. 193–198, cf. Hirsch (1926, p. 66f.).

[34]These student notes reveal Bonhoeffer's interest in the theological dimensions of *Phenomenology of Spirit* and *Lectures in the Philosophy of Religion*.

[35]On an occasion when a student in Bonhoeffer's class pointed out a passage in Hegel that he deemed as non-christian [nichtchristlich], and thus dismissing his Philosophy of Religion, Bonhoeffer responded: 'Man soll einen Autor nicht von einem negative Satz aus angreifen oder interpretieren; man soll fragen, was er mit dem Ganzen meint oder will' [One ought not to attack or interpret an author solely on the basis of a negative sentence; but rather inquire about its meaning or purpose] (ibid., p. 137).

[36]'Christ as the Mediation of the Other' in Marsh (1994, pp. 81–110).

insight, it is only the most recent additions of Robinson (2018)[37] and Mawson (2018)[38] that provide an indispensable insight into the effect of Hegel on Bonhoeffer's social ecclesiology.

I will thus highlight that rather than a matter of simple disagreement, Bonhoeffer's treatment of Hegel in *Sanctorum Communio* is also an attempt to develop his thought.[39] Marsh aptly observes that his approach is 'less concerned with overcoming Hegel than in thinking along with the philosopher on the meaning of God's presence in the complex drama of divine worldliness' (Marsh 1994, p. 91). Consequently, as will be observed, Bonhoeffer's own thoughts are distinctly Hegelian and retain that form and dialectically tense content, even while being developed. Indeed, Bonhoeffer's engagement with Hegel and the sociological structure of the church functions as a necessary social philosophical background of and formal model for his later thought, including *The Letters*.[40] In a way, then, it is entirely appropriate to at least discuss Bonhoeffer as a Hegelian,[41] even though his development or appropriation of Hegel is creative and critical. Hopefully, my critical reading will contribute—albeit in a very limited way as this is not its primary aim—to the demonstration of the foundational role Hegel has played in the development of Bonhoeffer's thought, for the latter's engagement with Hegel's communitarianism, be it in reaction to his understanding of the subject-object relationship or the utilisation of the concept of objective spirit, is indispensable and highly formative.

[37] Robinson's work argues that there is more to Bonhoeffer's use of Hegel than his polemic against idealism.

[38] Mawson ('The Concrete Community', 2018, pp. 150–175) devotes an entire chapter to show how Bonhoeffer's engagement with Hegel's concept of objective spirit allows him to consider the existing church with its concrete forms and functions.

[39] I am far from arguing that Bonhoeffer wasn't critical of Hegel, but rather pointing out how Hegel still shapes his thought positively rather than merely negatively. For an example of a straightforward critique of Hegel, see *The Letters* 16 July 1944 in DBWE 8: p. 477, wherein Bonhoeffer accuses Hegel of pantheism ('Kant is basically a deist; Fichte and Hegel are pantheists').

[40] Cf. Marsh (1994, p. 175, n. 11). Recently, there has been an indispensable contribution to consideration of Hegel's importance for Bonhoeffer by Robinson (2018) who offers an account of the development of Bonhoeffer's thought with respect to Hegel. In light of his findings, Robinson arges that interpretation of Bonhoeffer's works requires fuller reckoning with Hegel's thought (2018, pp. 25–27).

[41] Marsh has observed 'whether Bonhoeffer turns out to be a Hegelian by default is a question that must not be ignored' (ibid., p. 80).

The Foundation Has Been Laid

This brief exploration of the emergence of Bonhoeffer's social theology during his studies at the Theological Faculty in Berlin clearly positions him as a critical theologian in pursuit of a theology reflective of its modern cultural context and its challenges. Next, I will critically explore the direct result of such a reflection—his 1927 doctoral dissertation entitled *Sanctorum Communio: eine dogmatische Untersuchung zur Soziologie der Kirche* [*Sanctorum Communio: A Theological Study of the Sociology of the Church*] (DBW 1, 2005; DBWE 1, 2009).[42]

This theologico-sociological reflection brought together a Barthian theology of revelation and Hegel, Weber and Troeltsch, resulting in a 'theology of sociality' built upon a relational view of personhood. The social form of revelation, described as 'Christ existing as community', elevated interrelatedness between 'I' and 'Other' to the highest importance, at the heart of the way one understands God, self and other.[43] Yet, Bonhoeffer's dissertation was far from a simple harmonisation of theology with modern thought. More radically it explored the social intention of basic Christian concepts. It argued that insofar as the concept of God ought to be conceived as formed in relation to persons and community, the relationship between 'I' and 'Other' is to be understood as providing an ethical boundary for one another (DBWE 1: pp. 554–557). A boundary where the other is encountered as a limit introduces a notion of sin as a breaking of that limit, whether the Other is God or a fellow being (see 'Sin and Broken Community' in DBWE 1: pp. 107–121). Sin thus denies the freedom of the other, turning them into an image of oneself. This is where Bonhoeffer introduced the concept of *stellvertretung* [vicarious representative action] as the willingness not merely to allow the other to exist, but to allow the other to place upon me the burden of their freedom to be who they are (DBWE 1: pp. 155ff., 293ff., 303f.). For Bonhoeffer, this was the essence of Christ's messianic vocation and ethical challenge for humanity.

I will reflect upon *Sanctorum Communio* in dialogue with or context of Žižek's theology of abandonment and allow it to challenge Bonhoeffer's claims. Like Bonhoeffer about his endeavour, I too am aware of the com-

---

[42] Karl Barth described *Sanctorum Communio* as a 'theological miracle', finding it hard to believe it was written at the age of twenty-one (Barth 2003, p. 4; 2010, p. 533).

[43] As will be shown next, Bonhoeffer's personalism and attention to interrelatedness is derived from the phenomenology of Max Scheler's value personalism.

plexities of reflecting on his thesis from the perspective of Žižek's theology of abandonment but am not deterred from making them fruitful for theology. For it is only this kind of reflection upon theological thought in its intellectual context that exposes its strengths and weaknesses, if engaged openly and without presuppositions. Thus my reading will not begin with a fencing of certain Bonhoeffer's tenets as not for discussion or even pre-determining certain Žižek's arguments as flawed or wrong and not to be engaged. It will not start by assuming a position of 'who is right' and therefore needs to prove the interlocutor as wrong. Instead, this will be a fully open and critical reflection that does not pre-determine its outcome but calls into question the very framework of conventional theological analysis and theory production.

In Pursuit of a Genuine Form of Community

Sanctorum Communio, Bonhoeffer's first thesis, received the highest approbation from Seeberg and the Theological faculty in Berlin, but received little attention until after Bonhoeffer's death, as part of a renewed interest in the body of his work.[44] What set the work apart was its ambition to deal with sociological issues theologically or from a theological perspective. Bonhoeffer carried out his undertaking of a dialogue between theology and sociology with conviction and confidence aided by his liberal theological intellectual formation at Berlin and its own persuasion about the need for theology to engage other intellectual disciplines.[45] In the first chapter, after providing his definitions of social philosophy and sociology, Bonhoeffer reflects on the import of social philosophy and states that 'the concern of sociology is to trace the many complex interactions back to

[44] The work was first published only three years after his doctoral exam in 1927 but it was truncated and received only three reviews. In the 1960s, versions that included more of the original dissertation were published but it was not until 1986 when the full text was included as the first volume of the *Dietrich Bonhoeffer Werke* (DBW). The English translation part of the *Dietrich Bonhoeffer Works* (DBWE) is based on that edition. See the editor's introduction to DBWE 1: pp. 9–13.

[45] For a description of the original character of *Sanctorum Communio* in that respect, see Dramm (2001, pp. 67–70). The work has only recently received a fitting examination from Michael Mawson in his *Christ Existing as Community* (2018). Mawson surveys the reasons for its oversights and challenges the criticisms of Bonhoeffer's selective consideration of sociology ('Theology and Social Theory', 2018, pp. 39–55), offering a thorough exposition and a strong case for consideration of the work on its own.

certain constitutive acts of spirit that comprise the distinctive characteristic of the structure [of community]' (DBWE 1: p. 30). His pursuit in *Sanctorum Communio* is, then, just that—a sociological attempt to locate the constitutive acts of a true community, which he considers is exclusively the structurally distinctive community of saints. Thus both Bonhoeffer and Žižek search for the structure of a genuine community and find its religious form enlightening, one from an ethical perspective that is distinctly religious and personalist, the other from one which is forthrightly materialist and ontological.

Collective Person

In order to employ social philosophy and social theory in pursuit of a theology of sociality,[46] *Sanctorum Communio* begins by engaging in a dialectical discussion of personhood as the foundation of sociality, but also as existing only in sociality. To denote this relational view of personhood, or interrelatedness, Bonhoeffer employs the term 'collective person' [*Gesamtperson*], a term originally used by the philosopher Max Scheler (1874–1928) in *Der Formalismus in der Ethik und die materiale Wertethik* (2005a). There the term describes the distinctive unity of the execution of social acts,[47] which are inherently directed at other persons and are only fully executed in relation to others, in contrast to the intimate or singularising acts.[48] Together these acts show that the person is both an individual and a member of a community or collectivist, and that the individual person is formed and realised only in the context of sharing the responsibility for community. Bonhoeffer agrees with this relational view of personhood—indeed, his use of the term 'person' is completely relational in statements such as 'for the individual to "exist", others must necessarily be there', and therefore personhood is possible and real only in sociality, i.e. responsibility towards the other (DBWE 1: p. 51). This is what Green has in mind when he says that Bonhoeffer 'insists equally on the irreducible, independent integrity of the individual person, and on the fact that this person exists essentially in relation to others' (ibid., p. 30). Bonhoeffer's personalism is marked by

---

[46] As laid out in the work's foreword; see DBWE 1: pp. 21–23.

[47] These include promising, commanding and obeying.

[48] These are acts of self-consciousness, self-love and self-respect, directed at the self and fulfilled with reference only to the self (ibid., p. 511).

the dialectic tension between individuality and communality, where one is not overtaken by the other.

Bonhoeffer uses his personalist perspective of the collective person where '[t]he You sets the limit for the subject' (ibid., p. 51) to challenge Hegel's Idealist subject-object relation. Hegel sought to overcome the conscious gap between the individual and the world, or the subject and the object, in Part A of *Phenomenology of Spirit* (1977): 'Consciousness'[49] and argued that perception of something as external is nothing but self-consciousness, our appropriation of the world around us. Thus the object cannot be considered as detached, apart from the subject, together with whom it forms a whole. Indeed, consciousness of self and the external world are part of a comprehensive, evolving, rational unity—the Absolute. Bonhoeffer considers that the Other is in Hegel's talk of consciousness reduced to a mere object of the subject's perception and is in that sense subsumed by it.[50]

---

[49] Part A (1977, pp. 58–103) comprises three chapters: Chapter 1: Sense-Certainty: or the 'This' and 'Meaning', pp. 58–66; Chapter 2: Perception: or the Thing and Deception, pp. 67–78; Chapter 3: Force and the Understanding: Appearance and the Supersensible World, pp. 79–103.

[50] DBWE 1: p. 41 [20], p. 45. However, Bonhoeffer's objection doesn't seem to consider how Hegel's thought develops from 'consciousness' to 'self-consciousness', which is the title of Part B. Thus in Chapter 4: The Truth of Self-Certainty (Hegel 1977, pp. 104–138), Hegel examines the intersubjective conditions of consciousness. Not only does the subject's consciousness of the object as something distinct from oneself require awareness of self as a subject for whom something is distinct, but that itself depends on one's recognition [*Anerkennung*] of other self-conscious subjects as such (as self-conscious subjects for whom any object of consciousness will be thought as also existing). This means that the subject's self-consciousness of the other depends on the other recognising themselves as a self-conscious subject. As we shall see later, this complex pattern of mutual recognition constitutes Hegel's objective spirit. There is thus a notable change in *Phenomenology*, from consideration of individual (self)consciousness in earlier chapters, to an exploration of what grounds them—the patterns of intersubjectivity. To quote Žižek: 'This seems to be the lesson of Hegel's intersubjectivity—I am a free subject only through encountering another free subject—and the usual counterargument is here that, for Hegel, this dependence on the Other is just a mediating step/detour on the way toward full recognition of the subject in its Other, the full appropriation of the Other. But are things so simple? What if the Hegelian "recognition" means that I have to recognize in the impenetrable Other which appears as the obstacle to my freedom its positive-enabling ground and condition? What if it is *only* in this sense is that the Other is "sublated"?' See Žižek (2013, p. 142).

Bonhoeffer seems to have missed this topic in his consideration of the *Phenomenology*. Rather than boldly claiming that this is a sign of his secondary familiarity with Hegel, it should be noted that attention to Hegel's intersubjective conditions of consciousness gathered momentum only with Kojève and onwards. However, it is this missed movement in Hegel's thought that makes for an interesting comparison when Bonhoeffer claims that 'there

In support of his argument, Bonhoeffer outlines four conceptual models of social basic-relation which demonstrate that every concept of community is essentially related to a concept of person but which fail to maintain the dialectical tension between them (DBWE 1: pp. 34–57): Aristotle's metaphysical ontological model, in which the essential being 'lies beyond individual-personal being'; the Stoic school model, in which the human being becomes a person 'by subordination to a higher imperative' (ibid., p. 37) and which Bonhoeffer compares with the Christian concept of a person,[51] although he still locates the essential being outside the individual; the Epicurean model, which he understands as mere individualism; and the Cartesian epistemological model, which remains in the subject–object relationship, where 'the knowing I becomes the starting point of all philosophy' (ibid., p. 40). Bonhoeffer observes that all four of these models are based upon sameness, not unity, where 'it is the destiny of the human species to be absorbed into the realm of reason, perform a realm of completely similar and harmonious persons, defined by universal reason or by one spirit and separated only by the different activities' (ibid., p. 43). Along parallel lines the idealist subject-object schema, he argues, ends up denying the community by overtaking or eradicating distinctiveness and resulting in sameness, leading Bonhoeffer to conclude that they do not result in true community (ibid., pp. 41–43, 80), since they are merely epistemological rather than sociological concepts.

Far from advocating a vulgar form of individualism, Bonhoeffer in turn insists upon intersubjectivity and is clear that personhood emerges and exists only in meeting with the Other:

> [T]he person ever and again arises and passes away in time. The person does not exist timelessly; a person is not static, but dynamic. The person exists always and only in ethical responsibility; the person is re-created again and again in the perpetual flux of life. (ibid., p. 48)

The theoretical framework and drive here is social rather than epistemological, hence the preference for the word 'person'. This is the context of

would be no self-consciousness without community—or better, that self-consciousness arises concurrently with the consciousness of existing in community' (DBWE 1: p. 70). See also Marsh (1994, pp. 88–91).

[51] In this conception the individual and universal are closely interconnected. The importance of this will become clearer later on.

statements asserting that there is a 'fundamental synthesis between social and individual being' (ibid., p. 75), that the individual belongs with the other 'even though, or precisely because, the one is completely separate from the other' (ibid., p. 56)[52] and that 'social relations must be understood, then, as purely interpersonal and building on the uniqueness and separateness of persons' (ibid., p. 55).

How can Bonhoeffer's understanding of intersubjectivity be compared to Žižek's ontological assertion that any attempt to account for oneself is always conducted within a certain intersubjective context and reveals our constitutive exposure to the Other (Žižek 2008, p. 45)? The difference is made clear in the following paragraph from *The Neighbour*:

> My very status as a subject depends on its link to the substantial Other: not only the regulative-symbolic Other of the tradition in which I am embedded, but also the bodily-desiring substance of the Other, the fact that, in the core of my being, I am irreducibly vulnerable, exposed to Other(s). And far from limiting my ethical status (autonomy), this primordial vulnerability due to my constitutive exposure to the Other grounds it: what makes an individual human and thus something for which we are responsible, toward whom we have a duty to help, is his/her very finitude and vulnerability. Far from undermining ethics […], this primordial exposure/dependency opens up the properly ethical relation of individuals who accept and respect each other's vulnerability and limitation. Crucial here is the link between the impenetrability of the Other and my own impenetrability to myself: they are linked because my own being is grounded in the primordial exposure to the Other. Confronted with the Other, I never can fully account for myself. (Žižek 2013, p. 138)

Bonhoeffer's and Žižek's intersubjectivity differs in its grounding—ethics as pre-existing and grounding ontology for the first and ontology grounding ethics for the latter.

For Bonhoeffer synthesis between social and individual being is based upon the 'concrete ethical barrier' (DBWE 1: p. 50) that exists between persons. He asserts in a dialectical manner that while personhood emerges in sociality, this sociality is established upon the barrier between individuals. Therefore '*only when my intellect is confronted by some fundamental barrier*' do I enter the social sphere (ibid., p. 45). What is this barrier? Following

---

[52]Bonhoeffer here, in footnote 12, refers back approvingly to Fichte's recognition that persons cannot exist at all without others to spark their personhood-encounter.

Scheler, who asserts that the core of the person, irreducible to any physical or psychic characteristics, is not given in perception by the Other (Scheler 2005b, p. 238), Bonhoeffer insists on the impossibility of knowing the Other as an independent subject in a cognitive way (DBWE 1: p. 45). If that is attempted, then the Other is no longer an independent subject but purely an object of the knowing mind, leaving the social sphere for the epistemological. Therefore, from page 45 onwards, Bonhoeffer argues that in order to avoid the Other becoming purely an object they must remain an 'alien I' (ibid., pp. 45, 52).

The use of the word 'alien' lends itself nicely to a contrast with Žižek's perspective which, concerned with the real of the subject or its core before and after symbolisation, considers the Other as monstrous (Žižek 2013, p. 162). In comparison to Bonhoeffer's Schelerian personalist theoretical apparatus, Žižek's subjectivity is thoroughly Lacanian for the subject is located on the borders of the Real and the Symbolic Order, with everything one can know about them being located in the Symbolic (Žižek 1996, p. 43). However, besides the constant surplus of the subject of the other, Žižek insists upon the surplus of the subject itself. Furthermore, that which cannot be known directly is what the subject is in itself, therefore locating the subject in the lack. He speaks about the inhuman which makes the human human (Žižek 2013, pp. 159–160; 2018, pp. 46–57) and the hole in the order of being: I fully am not as an isolated Self, but in the thriving reality part of which I am.[53] 'I will never be able to account for myself in front of the Other, because I am already nontransparent to myself, and I will never get from the Other a full answer to "who are you?" because the Other is a mystery also for him/herself' (Žižek 2013, p. 138). Not only is there more to the other subject than what I can know, but, what is more radical, the subject of the first or second person is that which cannot be known—the lack or gap itself. Bonhoeffer speaks of inability and impermissibility to recognise the other in an absolute manner, but for Žižek the absolute other and self are recognised, but is not known (ibid., p. 143). Žižek's impenetrability of the subject (whether I or the Other) is thus radically contrasted with Bonhoeffer's mere impenetrability of the

---

[53] Cf. Bonhoeffer in DBWE 1: p. 80: 'in relations with others, I do not merely satisfy one side of my structurally closed being as spirit; rather, only here do I discover my reality, i.e., my I-ness […] community and individual exist in the same moment and rest in one another. The collective unit and the individual unit have the same structure'.

Other. The being's ontological impenetrability of the former is completely distinct from the Other's ethical impenetrability of the latter.

Rather than merely a Bonhoefferian impenetrability of the Other, Žižek demonstrates that the Real of the subject is recognised only through the psychoanalytical introduction of the unconscious. On the other side, Bonhoeffer's use of 'real' in order to distinguish the ethical sphere from the epistemological when he says that 'only the experience of the barrier as real is a specifically ethical experience' is far from an ontological or psychoanalytic category (DBWE 1: p. 47). Therefore, while a cursory reading of the *Sanctorum Communio* would suggest that Bonhoeffer's struggle of the epistemological with the ethical perception of the Other can be compared to Žižek's struggle of the Symbolic and the Real of the subject, a closer reading shows a fundamental difference in the understanding of the subject. From Žižek's perspective Bonhoeffer's personalist consideration of the subject is limited or partial in its restricted ethical ruminations about the Other without a proper ontological foundation. It will be argued later that Bonhoeffer's consideration ultimately results in a sociality of separation.

Ethical Ontology

For Bonhoeffer the subject emerges in the ethical encounter with the Other or the experience of the 'concrete ethical barrier': 'The You sets the limit for the subject and by its own accord activates a will that impinges upon the Other in such a way that this other will becomes a You for the I' (ibid., p. 51).[54] Yet this ethical ontology is in stark contrast to Žižek's own ontological foundation for the relation of persons. Immediately the use of the word 'you' alerts the reader to a contrast of the subject knowing itself authentically but not the Other—it is an ontology based on separation. Here the Other addresses me with an unconditional transcendent (ibid., p. 52) call and constitutes me as an ethical subject:

> The I comes into being only in relation to the You; only in response to a demand does responsibility arise. 'You' says nothing about its own being, only about its demand. This demand is absolute. What does this mean? The whole person, who is totally claimless, is claimed by this absolute demand.

---

[54] Cf. DBWE 1: p. 50: 'One cannot even speak of the individual without at the same time necessarily thinking of the 'other' who moves the individual into the ethical sphere.'

But this seems to make one human being the creator of the ethical person of the other, which is an intolerable thought. (ibid., p. 54)

Bonhoeffer's insistence that the Other is a 'person in concrete, living individuality' (ibid., p. 48) is a sign that this is a completely heteronomous injunction, captivated within the symbolic rather than a recognition of the surplus which disrupts it. It is the ethical which calls the subject into being in a 'concrete, living individuality', rather than the subject in its intersubjective inhumanity grounding the (ethical) action. Far from an ontology, it is ethics: to the question about what constitutes being, Bonhoeffer answers ethics. But this ethic is completely external, an inescapable command coming from an entirely alien sphere, not from a solidarity of the vulnerable, but rather from the Other, who has now become the transcendent and 'overcomes' me, demanding obedience if I am to be constituted as a subject.[55]

Bonhoeffer theoretically analyses the time when faced with this ethical call as 'moment'—a time dimension where the claim of ethics is effectual in concrete time and 'only when I am responsible am I fully conscious of being bound to time' (ibid., p. 48). Bonhoeffer is not merely arguing against a sort of universally valid decision as coming from being in full possession of a rational mind, but rather reiterating his understanding of subjectivisation or the emergence of the subject: 'I enter the reality of time by relating my concrete person in time and all its particularities to this imperative—by making myself ethically responsible' (ibid.). Bonhoeffer thus reconceives the relation between subjectivity and transcendence by advocating the existence of the subject as grounded in its openness to a transcendent Otherness. His understanding of 'concrete' and 'moment' denotes a particularity at the expense of any notion of universality, for any other concept of person fragments the fullness of life of the concrete person. Insofar as all that exists is an ethical call deciding the continual emergence or fading away of the subject, this moment knows nothing but the particular.

How, then, does Bonhoeffer's moment compare to Žižek's 'truth-event'? As explored in Chapter 2, in 'The Politics of Truth, or, Alain Badiou as a Reader of St. Paul' in *The Ticklish Subject* (1999, pp. 127–170), Žižek proposes that revolutionary change only comes from an 'event' or location

---

[55] In that sense a Žižekian challenge to Bonhoeffer runs parallel to his challenge of the Levinasian account of the emergence of the Ethical. See Žižek (2013, pp. 142–151).

of the political act and subject, specifically the marginalised or excluded. This focus on the location and the marginalised is in contrast to Bonhoeffer's focus on time and the concrete. Whereas Žižek focuses on the excluded, those unseen and barely discernible as a tic in the current order, Bonhoeffer focuses on the injunction of those temporally present. Bonhoeffer would no doubt dismiss Žižek's reference to the universal as idealist aberration, yet Žižek's conception of universalism as being embodied in the excluded is in stark contrast to Bonhoeffer's recognition of those presenting their particular interests (Žižek 2003, p. 112). What about those who cannot be seen because they are excluded, unseen or *inhuman*? Žižek adopts Agamben's figure of the *Muselmann*[56]—the living dead of the concentration camp—as someone 'who fully witnessed the horror of the concentration camp and, for that very reason, is not able to bear witness to it' (Žižek 2013, p. 160).[57] Such a subject, reduced to the inhuman, is not present in Bonhoeffer's grounding of the subject temporally upon a response to the ethical demand of the present particular; neither can 'I' respond. It highlights Bonhoeffer's temporal concreteness of particularity at the expense of universality. Žižek in turn grounds the subject spatially upon the recognition of the universal lack, of that very inhuman:

> What if it is precisely in the guise of […] a Muselmann that we encounter the Other's call at its purest and most radical? What if, facing a Muselmann, one hits upon one's responsibility toward the Other at its most traumatic? (ibid., p. 162)

In Žižek's understanding universalism is the result of a great process of struggle of the excluded that opens with an event. For him this is the 'intrusion of the traumatic Real that shatters the predominant symbolic texture' (Žižek 1999, p. 142). It is thus necessary to detach oneself from Bonhoeffer's 'concrete' situation, for it is only in this way that universality follows (Žižek 2003, p. 17f.). Anything else does not represent a meeting with the subject *qua* the Real of the Subject. Does Bonhoeffer not advocate avoiding the troubling excess, rather than exposing the self to

---

[56]This slang term was used by prisoners and guards in Auschwitz to refer to a concentration camp prisoner who has been reduced to no more than a shadow by starvation, exhaustion and resignation.

[57]Žižek here refers to Agamben (2002).

the real of the other (cf. Žižek 2013, p. 9)? This is the only way to meet the Real of the given order rather than merely its semblance, and as such a constitutive act of a 'true community' that Bonhoeffer and Žižek are searching for. This surplus, the Real, the inhuman, the alien or the monstrous, is what Žižek understands as the theological, and its recognition, concomitant with a detachment from that which is present, represented, included—or to use Bonhoeffer's words, concrete and particular—represents an Event and breaking in or emergence of the true community. Much like in his understanding of the new community, recognition and detachment are the distinctive characteristics of the structure of genuine community. This tension between Bonhoeffer and Žižek will next be observed in Bonhoeffer's grapple with Hegel's concept of objective spirit.

Objective Spirit

In the final section of Chapter Three (DBWE 1: pp. 97–106), 'The Primal State and the Problem of Community', Bonhoeffer takes up a discussion of Hegel's objective spirit.[58] Hegel proposed the concept as an embodiment of the Absolute in objective patterns of social interaction and the cultural institutions, the relational ties between individual wills conscious of their diversity and particularity, but beyond their individual control. As such it concerns philosophical questions of law, moral philosophy, political philosophy and history, in contrast to his philosophy of subjective spirit, which is a sort of philosophy of mind in the contemporary sense and deals with, among other things, anthropology and psychology. Bonhoeffer's own understanding of the concept is guided by Seeberg's *Christliche Dogmatik* (1927a, p. 505ff.) and Freyer's *Theorie des objektiven Geistes* (Freyer 1923, p. 53ff.).[59] He finds much value in the concept and its 'monumental perception' of the spirit of sociality extending beyond the individual (DBWE 1: p. 74),[60] and adopts it in order to develop a dialectical understanding of the emergence of the communal subject:

---

[58]A developed version of Hegel's philosophy of objective spirit as philosophy of right is found in *Elements of the Philosophy of Right* (1991), originally published in 1821 as a textbook to accompany Hegel's lectures at the University of Berlin.

[59]For a valuable secondary insight into Bonhoeffer's understanding and appropriation of the concept, see Kotsko (2005) and Nowers (2013).

[60]See also p. 102.

[W]here wills unite, a 'structure' is created – that is, a third entity, previously unknown, independent of being willed or not willed by the persons who are uniting. This general recognition of the nature of objective spirit was a discovery of the qualitative thinking that became dominant in romanticism and idealism [...]. Two wills encountering one another form a structure. A third person joining them sees not just one person connected to the other; rather, the will of the structure, as a third factor, resists the newcomer with a resistance not identical with the wills of the two individuals. Sometimes this is even more forceful than that of either individual [...]. Precisely this structure is objective spirit [...] the persons themselves experience their community as something real outside themselves. (DBWE 1: pp. 98–99)

The objective spirit here is understood as the ineradicable core of the community—it enables and directs it and 'to withdraw from it is to withdraw from the community. It wills historical continuity as well as the social realisation of its will' (ibid., p. 100). This 'bond' or entity of the objective spirit is already in place and is encountered by a person wishing to enter an already existing community, where members also interact with each other only by its means.[61] The objective spirit is the heart of community.

To distinguish his understanding of the spirit from that of Hegel, Bonhoeffer insists that it does not absorb the individual (DBWE 1: p. 103). His insistence is parallel to that which is observed in his critique in Chapter Two of the four models of social-basic relation as enforcing sameness and the rejection of the Hegelian subject–object model as considering the other as an object of the subject's perception—it is based upon a conviction that each time the ethical boundary or limit of the relationship between 'I' and 'Other' has been transgressed. This is what he understands as sin ('Sin and Broken Community' in DBWE 1: pp. 107–121), as will be discussed later. For now, it is appropriate to summarise by noting that for Bonhoeffer, objective spirit is the tension or meeting place between the individual and the community and it is within this tension that a person exists:

Thus we are not dealing here with the conception of some spirit entity, called spirit of the people, that arises of its own natural strength from metaphysical depths. Rather, in the dialectical movement through which alone persons originate, individual collective persons come into being as well. Only with this insight does the richness of the monadic image of social life become clear. Collective persons are self-conscious and spontaneous. (ibid., p. 103)

---

[61] Language is one such means; see DBWE 1: p. 69.

Bonhoeffer is here pursuing a dialectical conception of the objective spirit and introduces the concept of 'individual collective person' as 'one that transcends all individuals but would be incomprehensible without the correlate of personal, individual being' (ibid., p. 77). It is thus a personalist description of interaction or the relationship between the individual and community, where the individual is 'self-contained' but discovering its being in the engagement and shaping of community (ibid., p. 79). This unity, Bonhoeffer contends,

> does not abolish the specific reciprocal movement of community. Individual persons remain completely separate from one another. The collective person is metaphysically autonomous in relation to the individuals, though at the same time genetically dependent. (ibid., p. 105)

This contention is established upon the earlier presentation of basic relations given within the personhood of every human being—a net of sociality (ibid., pp. 65–80), which is characterised by openness on the one hand (the capacity and necessity of a person to participate in sociality with others), but also closedness on the other (the unity, integrity and irreducibility of the person) (ibid., p. 67). 'The unity and closedness of the whole person is posited along with its sociality' (ibid., p. 75), refuting the priority of either personal or social being.[62]

Bonhoeffer's personalist rejection of Hegel's universalism, or at least Bonhoeffer's reading of it as already noted above, is that the latter is itself based on exclusion by destroying the particularity of the individual. In other words, its inclusion is achieved upon its exclusion. It resonates strongly with more current multi-cultural suspicion of suppression or exclusion of those that do not fit the notion of the universal. It is thus but a false solution. The history of the twentieth century has shown that underneath the concept of universality often lie instincts of domination, racism and sexism of a particular group at the expense of the other, who is effaced and suppressed (at any cost).

The question then becomes whether the same criticism can be directed at Žižek and his argument for and conception of universality. Is it ultimately

---

[62] See also DBWE 1: p. 80: 'God does not desire a history of individual human beings, but the history of the human *community*. However, God does not want a community that absorbs the individual into itself, but a community of *human beings*. In God's eyes, community and individual exist in the same moment and rest in one another.'

hiding the same exclusivism and an attempt at articulating the interests of a particular post-Marxist Eurocentric perspective when he calls for an undermining of globalisation from the standpoint of universal Truth (Žižek 1999, p. 211)? Is this what is really at the heart of his materialist utilisation and interpretation of Christian theology in which the murder of Christ the particular enables the emergence of the universality of Galatians 3:22?[63]

As I have demonstrated in the chapter on Žižek's community of the Holy Spirit, his challenge is rather that universality is the very principle of negativity which drives these particularities in antagonism to prevent the notion of totality.[64] According to his Lacanian understanding of Hegel, universality is this negativity or tension that prevents a certain particularity from ever achieving self-closure. Rather than abolishing differences it articulates them (Žižek 2003, p. 112). He reminds us that this is why Hegel calls it 'concrete universality' (Žižek 2006, p. 30)—it is an awareness of the present state of affairs, revealing internally unsolvable conflicts and emerging at the point of exception or marginalisation: '[T]he whole point of the Pauline notion of struggling universality is that true universality and partiality do not exclude each other, but universal Truth is accessible only from a partial engaged subjective position' (ibid., p. 35).

Bonhoeffer also speaks of the community as struggling. He recognises that the unification of will is constituted upon the 'inner conflict of individual wills' (DBWE 1: p. 86) and observes 'that strife [Kampf] is recognised as a fundamental sociological law and basically is sanctified [...]. Genuine life arises only in the conflict of wills; strength unfolds only in strife' (ibid., pp. 84–85).[65] However, in the next sentence he qualifies this with a statement that there has been no concrete and productive conflict in the genuine sense since the Fall, thus raising the problem of sin and pointing to the need for the community of 'separate persons' (ibid., p. 83) to be maintained by someone else—God. The contrast becomes even more accentuated when

[63]Žižek (1999, p. 157; 2003, p. 17f.).

[64]A good and concise introduction to Žižek's understanding of Hegelian universality can be found on pp. 28–36 in *The Parallax View* (2006).

[65]Bonhoeffer refers here to Hobbes as in all likelihood the first to articulate the purely social meaning of strife when talking about *bellum omnium contra omnes*. The reference is missing but the Latin phrase occurs in *De Cive or The Citizen* (New York: Appleton-Century-Crofts 1949, pp. 13, 29, 104), while in *Leviathan* (Project Gutenberg 2002) Hobbes speaks of 'warre of every one against every one [or man]' in Chapter XIII of the Naturall Condition of Mankind, pp. 94, 96 and XIV of the First and Second Naturall Lawes, pp. 98, 102.

Žižek distinguishes concrete universality from abstract universality, which is maintained by the big Other, be it the big Other of really existing Christianity (as in 'real-socialism') or capitalism. This abstract universality is mediated and regulated (Žižek 2013, p. 143) and remains trapped within particularity insofar as it disavows 'the antagonism that inheres to the notion' of 'Christianity' and 'frees the universal notion of antagonisms [no more Greek, nor Jew, etc.] of the way it is embedded in the system, by relegating this aspect to just one of its historical subspecies' (i.e. they are now all Christian) (Žižek 2006, p. 34).[66] As we shall see later, this is indeed how Bonhoeffer reads Galatians 3:22. Here is how Žižek understands it:

> [T]he universal dimension he [Saint Paul] opened up is not the 'neither Greek nor Jew but all Christians,' which implicitly excludes non-Christians; it is, rather, the difference Christians/non-Christians itself which, as a difference, is universal, that is to say, cuts across the entire social body, splitting, dividing from within every substantial ethnic. (ibid., p. 35)

Žižek's materialist Christianity suspends the particular in its name along the line of Lenin's repetition of the paradigmatic Christ-event in his advocation of actual freedom (Žižek 2001a, p. 114). This is the 'Christian experience' to which Žižek refers as necessary for concrete universalism, the recognition or realisation that Christ stands for a break with all totalities and cosmic schemes and enables an unplugging from one's symbolic community. Instead of the indiscriminate, postmodern talk about differences, Christ divides between good and bad in accordance with the Gospel, saying, 'Do you suppose that I came to grant peace on earth? I tell you, no, but rather division' (Luke 12:51). Only in this way, Žižek argues, is the relationship between the universal and particular properly dialectical and the resulting universality concrete. As previously noted, according to him Christian love resists the gentrification of the neighbour and instead accepts its radical impenetrability. This kind of universality or a new collective no longer relies on an identity, but is instead struggling (Žižek 2013, p. 154). It is not against the background of universal hatred, but of universal indifference, where one is indifferent towards all and in this way loves the indi-

---

[66] This is slightly paraphrased and applied to real-existing Christianity, while in the work it serves to elucidate the abstract universality of 'alternate' modernities.

vidual. 'There is neither Jew nor Greek, there is neither slave nor free, there is no male and female, for you are all one in Christ Jesus' (Galatians 3:28).

No wonder Žižek interprets the resurrection in a Hegelian manner as the new community and identical with the Holy Spirit, for in doing so he avoids resurrection of the big Other and rests upon his absence. So, when Bonhoeffer writes that the essence of community is not commonality but rather reciprocal will, Žižek would respond that in this case the will is not their own but rather that of the big Other, who abstracts the community and prevents any 'conflict of individual wills'. It seems that, from this perspective, Bonhoeffer's drive to avoid a vulgar absorption of the individual by the community and to maintain separateness of persons solely by God results in the opposite—an abstraction of unity into particularisation. Instead, Žižek proposes that only Christ-like unplugging or division is the constitutive act of the spirit of this new community.

The difference between Bonhoeffer's[67] and Žižek's understanding of Hegel is clear. While Žižek would consider Bonhoeffer's understanding overly simplistic and restrained by Seeberg and Freyer, his own understanding of Hegel is particular and strongly Lacanian.[68] Nonetheless, Bonhoeffer's personalism, which he wishes to differentiate from the idealist universalism of exclusion, seems to result in an abstraction itself. This will be explored further in the next section, with reference to that section of his thesis in which he engages the thus far explored concepts of social philosophy with theology.

Indispensability of Theology

In the major section of his thesis, that is, Chapter 5, entitled 'Sanctorum Communio', Bonhoeffer presents a case for this distinctly theological community of saints grounded in, established and governed by God. He does so by engaging the thus far developed personalist perception of community with theology, developed and aided by the Hegelian conception of objective spirit described above which is equipped with the Holy Spirit,

---

[67] In footnote 42 on p. 75 Bonhoeffer concludes: 'Thus our turning against idealist theory is clear; equally clear, of course, is what we have to learn from it.'

[68] A similar difference can be observed by Žižek and by his fellow critical theorist Ernesto Laclau (2001), who, in contrast to Hegelian concrete universality which 'sublates' all antagonisms into a higher unity, prefers the logic of irreducible antagonisms.

and thereby demonstrates the structure of a genuine community in the community of saints. The reason for the engagement, Bonhoeffer argues, is because the personalist perception of community falls short—as does Hegel's conception of objective spirit—for it rests upon an inadequate conception of person which ignores the fundamental ontological concept of sin (guilt) and God (DBWE 1: p. 48). Without treatment of these, any discussion of being oversteps the ethical barrier and plays God—again, as exemplified in the Idealist case where the subject subsumes the Other as an object.[69] Bonhoeffer thus goes about engaging the idealist and personalist conceptions with these theological concepts in order to demonstrate how community is necessarily grounded in them.[70]

The Necessity of God…

For Bonhoeffer any form of community without the community with God is not authentic (DBWE 1: p. 157).[71] The importance of including the conception of God lies in the origin of the incomprehensibility of the Other—it lies in God the 'impenetrable You' (ibid., p. 34). In other words the subject is grounded in the openness to the unfathomable and transcendent Otherness of God.[72] Furthermore the concept must be in appropriate form, rather than what is observed in idealism's consideration of the subject and community with its inappropriate 'immanentist concept of God or the identification of human and divine spirit' (DBWE 1: p. 197), as Hegel's understanding of the Absolute materialised in the historical community (Hegel 2006, pp. 470–489). Following Seeberg (1927a, p. 73ff.), Bonho-

---

[69] In *Lectures on the Philosophy of Religion* (2006, pp. 442–445), Hegel understands the Fall primarily as self-consciousness. While the form of the Genesis narrative is but an image, the content communicates humanity achieving knowledge of good and evil—cognition (ibid., pp. 446–451). Being self-conscious, humanity is also self-estranged, aware of its good and evil. Evil is tendency to follow desires and remain within natural being as selfish, while good is reaching beyond natural towards infinitude of thought as social—spirit. Hegel's interpretation of the Fall is thus much like Žižek's positive, or at least that which enables self-cognition as the beginning of the sublation to the pure realm of the spirit—the subject must become social.

[70] Parallel to my reading of Bonhoeffer's argument as a dialectic of God, sin, and church-community, see Mawson's dialectic of creation, sin, and reconciliation (2018, Chapters 4, 5, and 6, pp. 77–149).

[71] Again, this is Bonhoeffer's contention with Scheler. See also Mawson (2018, pp. 92–100).

[72] Cf. Žižek (2013, p. 138).

effer calls for a 'voluntarist' concept of God, where the latter is the original will and in the encounter with which the human will is subjected in the process to being grasped, first intuitively and then intellectually (DWE 1: p. 49 [53]). In contrast to this, the immanentist drive of Hegel's identification of the Holy Spirit with the corporate spirit of the community, where God's will and human will are effectively collapsed into each other, ends up in a deprivation of a divine transcendence and an overbearing concept of unity (ibid., p. 198).[73] Such a community is then broken insofar as it originates in its failure to recognise the human person in its 'creatureliness', which rests only in relation to the Divine (DBWE 1: p. 49). Its conflict or tension or 'meeting of wills' is not a necessary part in maintaining the conditions of freedom of the individual, but rather a way of transgressing it, stemming from the original transgression of creatureliness—the Fall (ibid., pp. 84–85).[74] For it is only in God that a true meeting of wills takes place and individuals are able to understand each other.[75] Outside of God any conception of person and corresponding community is based on the 'shared sinfulness' of transgression (ibid., pp. 108–109).

Bonhoeffer thus maintains that the 'conception' of community rests not only upon an appropriate understanding of person but that they both depend on the conception of God—they are 'inseparably and essentially interrelated' (ibid., p. 34). Only within this model is the concrete character of the community and the individual present as 'absolute and intended by God' (ibid., p. 45). In other words, 'only through God's active working does the other become You to me from whom I arises' and in this way 'every human You is an image of the divine You' (ibid., p. 54). God is here conceived not merely as the transcendence that enables and maintains the

---

[73]While Bonhoeffer does recognise that Hegel retains an emphasis on the concrete individual life, he mentions that the latter also 'considers it to be merely a form of universal spirit' (DBWE 1: p. 197).

[74]This is why Bonhoeffer earlier asserted that since the Fall, conflict of wills is not productive.

[75]In offering this contention, Bonhoeffer shows some qualified appreciation of Fichte's treatment of the problem of the synthesis of the World Spirits, wherein the latter enquires about the common origin of persons so as to enable their mutual understanding. See DBWE 1: pp. 43–44 [8].

relationship between the subjects, but as the integral part of the relationship itself.[76]

According to this understanding the ethical barrier between persons comes from God, as well as the claim of the Other upon the subject and the latter's ensuing ethical responsibility (ibid., pp. 36–37, 49). Bonhoeffer describes this moment in a Kierkegaardian manner as a 'threat of absolute demand' causing 'infinite anxiety [Angst]' (ibid., p. 49) and argues that it is missing in the idealist model insofar as the claim comes from below or within, rather than the divine which transcends the human person. Interestingly, in 'Building Blocks for a Materialist Theology' in *Parallax View*, Žižek instead appropriates Kierkegaard to argue for the already discussed suspension of the ethical (Žižek 2006, pp. 68–123). He reads the account of Abraham's sacrifice as the subject's overcoming of the ethical coordinates or the Symbolic Order by faith and standing in an absolute relation to the Absolute, by betraying the very ethical substance of their being (Žižek 2001b, p. 14). Žižek and Bonhoeffer both focus on the threatening or terrible moment of the call to responsibility, but while Bonhoeffer insists that it needs to come from the transcendent, Žižek convincingly argues that with the suspension of the big Other the 'ethical' act is no longer transposed or sustained by it, but the responsibility is fully assumed by the subject (Žižek 2010, p. 134). Only here can a full understanding of humanity arise.

The question is ultimately about which of the two proposed an authentic form of responsibility, not only with regards to its source but also its absolute value $|r|$—its real magnitude without regard to its sign [again chiming Kierkegaard]. What is its distance from 0, if 0 is the signless pure act of will and distance the assumed responsibility, irrespective of its sign $|r| = r \operatorname{sgn}(r)$? For the sign returns the sign only, irrespective of the absolute value of responsibility: $\operatorname{sgn}(r) = \frac{|r|}{r}$ (insofar as $r \neq 0$). The problem with Bonhoeffer's assertion is that the sign—from the transcendent perspective—has no value and does not affect the absolute value of responsibility. The absolute value of responsibility $|r|$ is determined only in the distance between absolute values of both $r_{\check{z}}$ and r_B or their distance from 0. To include the divine in the determination of the absolute value of the difference of both responsibilities is—to use Žižek's word—a perversion, for

[76]DBWE 1: p. 55: 'One might then speak here of the human being as the image of God with respect to the effect one person has on another.' Bonhoeffer's later description of how one person becomes Christ for the another builds on this.

proper or true or thorough responsibility [*qua*] is ever only absolute, one that exclaims: we are alone.

No doubt, Bonhoeffer would reply that the truth about things as such, particularly in relation to judgements about the value of responsibility, is perceived only in the eyes of God, therefore any talk of absolute value falls short or is incorrect. That is also the reasoning behind his claim that the community of saints can never be grasped with sociological insights and is only understandable from within—*cum ira et studio*[77]—with the eyes of (Christian) faith (DBWE 1: p. 33). In contrast to Žižek, the theology of Bonhoeffer in *Sanctorum Communio* is distinctively dogmatic and still Barthian, upholding the positivism of revelation by arguing that 'faith is not a possible method by which to gain academic knowledge; rather, by acknowledging the claim of revelation, faith is the given prerequisite for positive theological knowledge' (ibid., p. 127). For Bonhoeffer there is no absolute value or knowledge apart from or outside God.[78]

However, does this restriction to God not functionally abstract its object, be it the ethical act or community? Does Bonhoeffer's first and foremost ethical intersubjectivity, which is grounded and sustained by God, not characterise an abstract community insofar as it originates, is maintained and ends in the external? Is it true that a concept of person is misunderstood apart from God? Is it not rather that Bonhoeffer's ethics is based on a God as a third agent who gentrifies the surplus or monstrous of the Other, the big Other anchoring, pacifying the monstrous and regulating any engagement with the Other (Žižek 2013, p. 144)? God functions as the ultimate authentic foundation for community which manages the terrifying real Other. However, the encounter of the Other through God is not experience of the real Other, but rather gentrified, for what is met in the encounter is God. Certainly, it might no longer be conducted as an ethnic encounter; it does raise a new identity of 'Christian', but it is far from a collective of the alien, what Žižek calls a struggling universality, where the Other is encountered as it is, 'the ambiguity of the Real embodied, the extreme/impossible point at which opposites coincide, at which the innocence of the Other's vulnerable nakedness overlaps with pure evil' (ibid., p. 162). From a functional

---

[77] [with passionate zeal]. This is in contrast to Tacitus, *Annals*, 1,1: *sine ira et studio* [without passion and bias].

[78] Along these lines Løland (2018, p. 161) accuses Žižek of 'decisionism (p. 162) where everything is left up to the human beings.

perspective Bonhoeffer's community rests upon God's obscuration of the neighbour by proclaiming it as the site from which the divine call to ethical responsibility emanates. His theological insistence upon the subject's being ultimately residing in a voluntarist conception of God is conducted at the expense of the Other. Žižek proposes a conception of community that seemingly does not abstract, a 'pure voluntarism' (Žižek 2016, p. 107), within which humanity is freed through Christ's suspension of the ethical on the Cross and realisation that the big Other does not exist, enabling the grasp of the human will and responsibility. The resulting terrible freedom is a refutation of Bonhoeffer's claim that the idealist model has 'no understanding of the moment in which the person feels the threat of absolute demand' (DBWE 1: p. 49). *Absolute* demand is only such if its magnitude is perceived without regard to its sign.

Beyond deus-ex-machina?
Perhaps Bonhoeffer's later tantalisingly brief but suggestive remarks in *The Letters* (DBWE 8), wherein he reflects on the conception of a 'religionless Christianity' offer more prospect? Does his incarnated transcendence enable an escape from abstraction?

In the letters, written to his friend and theological confidant Eberhard Bethge between April and August 1944, Bonhoeffer invokes the concept in imagining the form of faith that would take in the ruins of the post-war Christian West—a conception of Christianity distinct from its perception as a religion.[79] For Bonhoeffer the concept of religion is 'only a historically conditioned and transient form of human self-expression' (ibid.), which is marked by an inwardness and consideration of God as omnipotent coming to aid of human weakness (DBWE 8: p. 479). However, he contends, this religious understanding belongs to an epoch that has come to an end through the historical, scientific and socio-political development (DBWE 8: pp. 425–426) that has led to the 'autonomy' and 'coming-of-age' of the world itself (DBWE 8: p. 362).[80] Bonhoeffer thus attempts to consider the form Christianity ought to take in such a radically religionless world.

---

[79] The unfinished manuscript that explored it has been lost; what remains are the letters and an 'Outline for a Book'.

[80] Bonhoeffer's consideration of historical development toward autonomy is in no small part due to his reading of Wilhelm Dilthey, as demonstrated by Ralph Wüstenberg's *Theology of Life* (1998, pp. 136–145).

A specific concern comes to the fore in Bonhoeffer's conception of Christianity as religionless—how to 'talk about God without religion?' (DBWE 8: p. 364). In other words, how is Christianity to speak of God, if his understanding as a stopgap or working hypothesis is 'increasingly pushed out' (DBWE 8: p. 450), 'ever on retreat' (DBWE 8: p. 406) or 'losing ground' (DBWE 8: p. 426)? His solution is to demonstrate that the very absence of the religious concept of God demonstrates the presence of the Christian God. Drawing attention to the incarnation of God in Jesus Christ and his ultimate act of love by his death on the Cross, Bonhoeffer demonstrates that the Christian God establishes his presence precisely by abandoning us, consenting 'to be pushed out of the world and onto the cross' (DBWE 8: p. 479). This leads Bonhoeffer to reformulate the transcendence of God, which is no longer considered as 'infinite, unattainable tasks, but the neighbour within reach in any given situation. God in human form!' (DBWE 8: p. 490). 'Participation in the being of Jesus' (DBWE 8: p. 501) thus replaces participation in a religiously conceived omnipotent God as solving the problems of this world. In a world without God as the stopgap, God's transcendence is experienced in the incarnation of Jesus. Bonhoeffer wishes to assert that God is still very much present in a world that has come to function and cope without Him.

It is thus important to acknowledge then that Bonhoeffer's letter on 16 July 1944, stating that 'Before God, and with God, we live without God' (DBWE 8: pp. 478–479), is actually Bonhoeffer's affirmation of God's presence in this world. In other words, for Bonhoeffer, God does not die and empty himself completely in Jesus the man but rather, in Jesus, opens a way to participate in transcendence. To paraphrase, while no longer functioning as a stopgap, God still orders the world.

… and Recognition of Sin

The other concept that Bonhoeffer deems as indispensable to any theory of the subject and community and which has specific implication is that of sin (ibid., p. 58). Here too idealism is accused of failing to give it due consideration and neglecting the impact of the Fall on the 'primal state' and consequent sociological structures of community (ibid., pp. 59–60). Sin or the Fall, then, has a real qualitative historical character and Bonhoeffer argues that 'history in the true sense only begins with sin' (ibid., p. 63). It isolates the individual from God and consequently the Other, but at the same time, since Adam's Fall marks the Fall of the whole humanity, places them into the deepest, most immediate bond with humanity—a bond of culpability. This is where the communality of humanity resides for Bonhoeffer:

> Now since in the individual guilty act it is precisely the humanity of human beings that has been affirmed, humanity has to be considered a community. As such it is also a collective person that has the same nature as each of its members. (ibid., p. 145)

This nature of culpability places subjects in isolation from and in bondage to each other and into a constant overstepping of the borders between them, thus rupturing the community with God and the Other. The 'sinful humanity' which resides in each and every individual and deserves condemnation is foundational to and indispensable in consideration of any community (ibid., p. 124).

In Chapter 4, 'Sin and Broken Community' (ibid., pp. 107–122), Bonhoeffer engages in an exposition of the social basic-relations between I and You after the Fall, which replaced love with selfishness, obfuscated morality to the point that it is visible only in the structures of legal order and brought about consciousness (of good and evil). Thus when individuals hear the Law and recognise their guilt they emerge as ethical persons, albeit in isolation. Their sense of culpability only intensifies upon grasping that this is the status of whole humanity—sin is a 'supra-individual deed' (ibid., p. 108). Not that man sins because the first man sinned and they are of the same biological species; rather, they share ethical personhood, where the individual is part of the ethical intersubjective. Therefore, as an individual sin, they do so as a member of the human race, which means that 'all humanity falls with each sin' (ibid., p. 115). 'Sin is the sign of belonging to the old humanity, to the first Adam; consciousness of guilt reveals to individuals their connection with all sinners' (ibid., p. 121). Bonhoeffer asserts in a dialectical manner that 'the experience of ethical solidarity is based upon the utmost singularity of the person' (ibid., p. 117), concluding that humanity is therefore a [dialectically] comprehensive [ethical] community:

> The collective person of humanity has one heart. Participation in its ethical nature is demonstrated by individuals through every act of repentance and recognition of culpability. Wherever individuals recognize themselves both as individuals and as the human race, and submit to the demand of God, there beats the heart of the collective person. (ibid., p. 121)

The concepts of sin, guilt and the Fall which form the distinctive foundation of the subject and community, Bonhoeffer claims, are overlooked by idealist philosophy:

> For idealism, origin and telos remain in unbroken connection and are brought to synthesis in the concept of 'essence'. Nothing in between – sin, on the one hand, and Christ, on the other – can essentially break this eternal, necessary connection [...]. Such a view of history as an unbroken straight line basically eliminates everything specifically Christian. In this view, neither sin nor redemption alters the essence of history. (ibid., pp. 59–60)[81]

Is that also the case for Žižek? The latter considers the Fall as absolutely necessary, for it creates the conditions of 'salvation'. However, there is a fundamental difference insofar as for him there is no state from which humanity falls or (original community), rather 'the Fall creates that from which it is a Fall—or, in theological terms, God is not the Beginning' (Žižek 2010, p. 93). It is then an Event which enables Adam and Eve to undergo a paradigm shift through which they realise what they already are or were—naked and mortal:

> So when God announces the punishment, he just spells out what Adam and Eve have already realized in noticing that they were naked, namely, their misery as two weak mortal beings [...]. It is not that the Fall is followed by redemption; rather, the Fall is identical to Redemption, it is 'in itself' already Redemption. (Žižek 2014, p. 127)

This logic was already observed in Žižek's reading of Romans 7 (Žižek 1999, pp. 147–149), where, according to him, the Law is given to point out its inherent transgression and thereby leads to its suspension and assumption of the subject's full responsibility in acting. It therefore contrasts Bonhoeffer's move to incorporate the ethical into God by making him the origin of our morality.[82] Bonhoeffer upholds the Law as holy and good due to revealing the deficiency or brokenness of the community, and understands Christ's redemptive role as fulfilling the Law by love (DBWE 1: pp. 148–151). On the other hand, Žižek asserts that Christ rather suspends the Law by love and abolishes its logic of sin and punishment by bringing

---

[81] See also p. 62.
[82] Cf. Žižek (2014, p. 130).

it to the point of self-relating. For him also the Fall is foundational and indispensable in the formation of community but without regard for the *ex post facto* sign which abstracts community (cf. Hamza 2016, p. 173).

The factor of difference between Bonhoeffer and Žižek is sin. For Žižek, the Law itself is 'bad' (causes sin), whereas Bonhoeffer points to the agency of sin and protects the holiness of the law. The problem is thus not the law but sin—in other words, the problem is we (see Løland 2018, pp. 137–147). While with Žižek there is an eventual realisation of the problem or contradictory character/inherent transgression of the law, for Bonhoeffer it enables us to realise our guilt—the law is holy and good but we are sinful; the problem is sin, not the law says Bonhoeffer. He would not doubt point to the wider Paul's text that preserves the sanctity of the law—Žižek's omission of Romans 7:12. As Løland (2018, p. 145) concludes: 'While for Paul "the law is spiritual' (Romans 7:14), Žižek's use of Romans 7 is directed against any sort of spiritualisation of the law, whether the law is regarded as Jewish or non-Jewish.'

Bonhoeffer insists upon a broken community where sin and guilt are fundamental elements of its ontology—no matter how much emphasis is laid on grace and the presence of God. That is why the first step towards a transcendental redeeming of such a dysfunctional community is a recognition of guilt and the resulting shame before God's gaze. What happens to this guilt and shame if we accept Žižek's suspension of the big Other? Does the guilt disappear? Žižek's poignant observation is that this guilt or shame does not arise from 'the Benthamic-Orwellian notion of the panopticon society in which we are (potentially) observed all the time and have no place to hide from the omnipresent gaze', but rather from 'the prospect of *not* being exposed to the Other's gaze all the time, so that the subject needs the camera's gaze as a kind of ontological guarantee of his or her being' (Žižek 2013, p. 180). The terror for Bonhoeffer seems to be that there is only us, inconsistent, ambiguous and lacking, and therefore he grounds the subject and community in the redeeming big Other by the notion of sin and guilt.

Is Bonhoeffer's argument here not an example of Feuerbach's false essence of Christianity that alienates man as himself and man from community and its own 'perfections'? His famous dictum that in order 'to enrich God, man must become poor; that God may be all, man must be nothing'

(Feuerbach 1989, p. 26)[83] certainly seems to hold true with Bonhoeffer's *pecatorum communio* [community of sinners], where not only is that which is attributed to God withheld from the community of man itself but the deprived state of humanity also forms the basis of sociality.[84]

In the next section it will be described how, according to Bonhoeffer, God enters the broken community by revealing himself in and as Christ and redeems it by creating the church *qua* a new community no longer grounded upon culpability—Christ existing as community.

Only in the Church-Community

After considering the derivation of the social form derived from the idealist metaphysical as flawed due to its inappropriate conception of God and sin and therefore to be rejected (DBWE 1: p. 28), Bonhoeffer attempts to demonstrate the preferred and apposite social from the theological in the community of saints [*sanctorum communio*], where the conceptions of 'person, community and God have an essential and indissoluble relation to one another' (ibid., p. 22). This community of God—as in church of God—is presented as representing the source for any and all social considerations in theology (ibid., pp. 86, 122–123).

When Bonhoeffer writes about the 'community of saints', he has in mind the concrete or empirical[85] church, not a 'religious community, but the empirical church as the *sanctorum communio* present in its actual embodiment' (ibid., p. 180). The term *sanctorum communio*, derived from the Apostles' Creed and Augustine's community of Christ, was brought to Bonhoeffer's attention by his supervisor's use of it to portray the church as a distinctly visible social body in its worship and cooperation (ibid., p. 141). Bonhoeffer, however, wishes to highlight that the church is not isolated or secluded and focuses on its participation in the basic forms of society, such as the subject or sociality (ibid., p. 152). The full dialectical character of this participation is demonstrated in the observation that while these basic forms take on a new form they remain the same and are sublated

---

[83] Might one not understand the passage from the gospel of John Chapter 3, where John the Baptist meets Jesus at the baptism, in this way? In verse 20 John utters the following: 'He must increase, but I must decrease!', thus projecting the predicates of perfection onto Jesus and then pushing himself into obscurity.

[84] DBWE 1: pp. 148–149, cf. Feuerbach (1989, p. 27).

[85] Empirical as in grounded in reality and thus suitable for deduction. See DBWE 1: p. 97.

upon encountering God. It is only through this interaction that the new basic relation of the church is constituted (ibid., p. 261). For Bonhoeffer *sanctorum communio* or the empirical church thus represents a 'form of community *sui generis*' (ibid., p. 266), a dialectically unique structure where the divine and human come together (ibid., p. 126).

To elaborate and lay bare the existing sociality of the community of saints which is sublated through its encounter with God, Bonhoeffer adapts and appropriates Hegel's sociological category of the objective spirit discussed earlier, by 'equipping' it with the Holy Spirit. Insofar as the human objective spirit is the ineradicable core and bond of the community that gets its character from the historical context, this very historicity 'implies that it is fallible and imperfect as far as its understanding and will are concerned' (ibid., p. 215). It is therefore only through its meeting with the divine in the Holy Spirit that it is *aufgehoben* to a building and bearing of the church (ibid., p. 152). Yet the objective spirit and Holy Spirit remain distinct as observed in their function (ibid., pp. 203–204, 214) and are not to be confused: while the function of the first is to enable a degree of continuity, the latter actualises the church here and now (ibid., p. 208).[86] Thus both concepts bring about the two natures, or constituent elements of the church: while its actions are not simply those of the Holy Spirit (ibid., p. 214), the latter changes and influences the objective spirit, thus performing its redemptive role by impacting and maintaining it, lifting this fallible community into God's community (ibid., pp. 126, 143, 280–281). Indeed, Bonhoeffer understands the objective spirit, as corrupt as it may be, as the Holy Spirit's vehicle (ibid., p. 215) and explores the institutions of the church's objective spirit along the lines of Hegel's account of the spirit in the modern state (1991, pp. 275ff.). To that end an individual congregation is contrasted with the universal church (DBWE 1: pp. 223–226), whereas Hegel contrasts the family and the state. To summarise, Bonhoeffer's understanding of the church-community form as distinctive from the basic forms of society and yet in dialectical relationship with them is in its foundation Hegelian, for it is founded upon the concept of objective spirit as objective patterns of social interaction.[87]

---

[86] From this page onwards Bonhoeffer engages in an exegesis of the role of the Holy Spirit in the establishment and continuation of the church community, thus also distinguishing his understanding of objective spirit from the idealist. Cf. DBWE 1: p. 145.

[87] Even though the concept of the objective spirit is not mentioned specifically in most of the works that follow *Sanctorum Communio* and *Act and Being*, this Hegelian foundation of

To the challenge that the basic sociological forms are merely overcome by God, Bonhoeffer responds that while this community is marked by ambiguity and the emphasis is on God as its sole source and maintainer (DBWE 1: p. 216), the community participates in those acts through its active being.[88] This dialectic is best illustrated in Bonhoeffer's concept of *Stellvertretung*, or vicarious representative action, denoting representation in place of another or intercession on behalf of another and originating in Christ who bore the sins of humanity and accepted the punishment on Calvary.[89] This fundamental theological concept throughout Bonhoeffer's writings, which appears already in *Sanctorum Communio* rather than being a later development of *Ethics*,[90] is achieved by transforming Hegel's conception of the Spirit existing as community[91] into 'Christ existing as church-community'.[92] The line between human and divine agency is obscure here, fully expressed in the statement that 'in our intercession we can become a Christ to our neighbour' (DBWE 1: p. 187).[93] Insofar as Christ's being-for-other is the experience of transcendence, the church participates in this being when it is there for others.[94] Not only is Christ 'at all times a real presence for the church' (DBWE 1: p. 139),[95] but the church is the real presence of Christ, where 'Christ truly is' (ibid., pp. 140, 158).[96] Bonhoeffer again highlights the dialectical participation between

the dynamic of church-community persists. Kotsko's helpful article (2005) draws attention to its prominence in Bonhoeffer's 1933 lectures on Christology, *Discipleship* and *The Letters*, the first with regards to the presence of Christ in the human community, the second with regards to the church's doctrine and, the latter, with regards to the changing form of the church, specifically religiosity.

[88] Also, the church is not a triumphalist community where sin is absent, but instead the bringing in of a divine reality. See Luca D'Isanto (1992, p. 143).

[89] DBWE 1: pp. 79, 120, 146, 148, 155ff., 178, 184, 191.

[90] Cf. DBWE 6: pp. 231, 235, 257–258, 288, 404.

[91] 'The realization of the Spirituality of the Community' in Hegel, *Lectures on the Philosophy of Religion* (2006) 3:339ff.

[92] DBWE 1: p. 121: 'It is "Adam", a collective person, who can only be superseded [abgelöst] by the collective person "Christ existing as church-community"'.

[93] See also pp. 178–180.

[94] Cf. DBWE 8: p. 501.

[95] Bonhoeffer is here referring to 1 Corinthians 12:2ff. and Romans 12:4ff.

[96] Likewise, Bonhoeffer asserts, the Holy Spirit also is 'only in the church-community, and the church-community is only in the spirit: "Ubi enim ecclesia ibi et spiritus; et ubi spiritus

the divine and human agency of this community centred in the figure of Christ.

Bonhoeffer's upholding of the church as the presence of Christ can be compared to Žižek's own upholding of Christ's continued presence as the emancipatory collective of the Holy Spirit community (Žižek 2012a, pp. 85–86). The latter explains this Christological aspect through the use of the folk song 'Joe Hill' about the murder of a trade union organiser. The song takes on the form of Joe's post-mortem apparition to someone in a dream. To their insistence that Joe is dead, he responds, 'What they forgot to kill went on to organize' (quoted in Žižek 2012a, p. 68). What survives, Žižek argues, is that which is more than the body—the excess or immortal part, the Real of the subject—and therefore not as the body or ghost but in the context of its intersubjective exposure, the 'collective'. With regards to Christ, the body dies as the site of overcoming the law and any attempt to 'resurrect' it by looking for him outside the community is seen as a mistake 'which Christ corrects with the famous words: "Where two or three are gathered in my name, I will be there"' (ibid., p. 86). Could this not be read in parallel with Bonhoeffer's assertion that 'there is no relation to Christ in which the relation to the church is not necessarily established as well' (DBWE 1: p. 127)? Of course, for Bonhoeffer the presence of Christ is only possible because resurrection actually occurred,[97] whereas for Žižek it is the very absence of the resurrection that makes the presence of that which is more than the body of Christ possible in the Holy Spirit community. However, it would be a mistake to consider Žižek's understanding as some kind of a mystical power through memory. Instead, it is engagement with the Real of Christ. Perhaps again Bonhoeffer's own understanding is also stretched further in the later stages of his thought (*The Letters*), when he wonders about the church, the ethical challenge to be a *stellvertretender* [vicarious representative] with reference to God's place in the world:

> Before God, and with God, we live without God. God consents to be pushed out of the world and onto the Cross; God is weak and powerless in the world and in precisely this way, and only so, is at our side and helps us. Matt. 8:17

---

dei, illic ecclesia et omnis gratia" [for where the church is there is the Spirit; and where the spirit of God is, there is the church and every kind of grace]' (DBWE 1: p. 144).

[97] DBW 12: p. 312: 'Only where the risen Christ is understood as the ground and the prerequisite for Christology is it possible to grasp his presence as person.' Cf. pp. 330–331, 359.

makes it quite clear that Christ helps us not by virtue of his omnipotence but rather by virtue of his weakness and suffering! (16 July 1944 in DBWE 8: pp. 478–479)

The import of Christ and his social embodiment is common and foundational to both Bonhoeffer[98] and Žižek.[99]

Bonhoeffer's emphasis on Christ-existing-as-community, compared to Hegel's God-existing-as-community, becomes of central importance in the preservation of divine transcendence and its relationship to man as the source of subjectivity and intersubjectivity:

> The cord between human beings and God that was cut by the first Adam is tied anew by God, by revealing God's own love in Christ, by no longer approaching us in demand and summons, purely as You, but instead by giving God's own self as an I, opening God's own heart. The church is founded on the revelation of God's heart. But since destroying the primal community with God also destroyed human community, so likewise when God restores community between human beings and God's own self, community among us also is restored once again. (DBWE 1: p. 145)[100]

The preservation of transcendence is what sets apart the church community as a model for any other community in the first place (ibid., pp. 103, 146). While the latter is a fallen community composed of individuals in sin and enmity with each other and God, the church is built upon Jesus as the essential difference who brought fallen humanity into community with God and thereby also re-established the community with one another. Bonhoeffer reiterates that 'true' community requires recognition of the fallen humanity in Adam: 'the transformation into a new community-of-God is possible only if the deficiency of the old is recognised' (ibid., pp. 148–149). This is not a simple recognition that mankind was wrong in 'excluding' God

---

[98] Bonhoeffer's focus on the import of Christ for community is only further accentuated in *Life Together* (DBWE 5: p. 34.): 'Our community consists solely in what Christ has done to both of us.' Note the word 'to' rather than 'for', denoting that Christ has done something to our sociality, rather than a mere punitive character.

[99] Žižek agrees on the crucial role of Christ for the community as he calls for continual repetition of the act of Christ as a community (e.g. Žižek 2001a, p. 105). Indeed, despite adopting Hegel's focus on the Spirit and describing the new community as the Holy Spirit, he advocates the central role of Christ and the incarnation (Žižek 2010, pp. 371–375).

[100] See also pp. 138–139.

and ought now to 'include' him, but rather one of that is only bound by sin and the necessity of Christ's soteriological death on the Cross (ibid., p. 124).[101] Bonhoeffer then develops the implication of this for the action of this community: 'what characterises the Christian notion of vicarious representative action is that it is vicariously representative strictly with respect to sin and punishment' (ibid., p. 155). The authentic community and its life is for Bonhoeffer only possible within the framework of sin and punishment (Žižek 2013, p. 177). The church community's difference from any other form of community, not only because of its relationship with God but fundamentally because of its recognition of lostness without God, qualifies it as a model to be followed.[102]

The above observed problematic of guilt re-emerges in Bonhoeffer's consideration of the church as a community-form paradigm and is again illuminated with reference to the law (ibid., pp. 148–151). Bonhoeffer describes or explains Christ and his vicarious representative action as fulfilling the Law. He upholds it as holy and good and concludes that Christ's 'love had to become complete by fulfilling the Law – that is, the claim of God and of human beings – even to death' (ibid., p. 149). Žižek, as observed in the chapter on his theology, instead interprets Christ's death as traumatising the Law and suspending the logic of sin and punishment by committing a senseless act outside social convention—an act that overcomes the Law. Thus while Bonhoeffer considers the community itself as broken because of sin, Žižek considers the community as broken because of the utmost Symbolic Law and calls for its suspension. Rather than a person dying to sin (ibid., p. 123), Žižek speaks of the person dying to the Law of the Symbolic and coming to existence outside of the legal-ethical. The terror for Bonhoeffer again seems to be that there is only humanity, opaque and monstrous, and therefore he grounds the community in the constant and all-knowing gaze of the redeeming big Other.

---

[101] That is why Bonhoeffer (DBWE 1: p. 155) also chastises Ritschl for his denial of the 'punitive character of the suffering of Jesus', when the latter argues that the notion of punishment originated in the context of a legal relationship and therefore ought to be rejected in the Christian religion. See Ritschl (1882, pp. 364f., 472ff.).

[102] Despite a marked difference with regards to sinfulness, Bonhoeffer's assertion of the church as a paradigm for other communities reveals as Hegelian not only its form, founded upon the concept of objective spirit as objective patterns of social interaction, but also its function.

The church also becomes a model for any other community because of its preservation of the dialectical balance between the individual and community, which is only enabled by, in and through God, specifically through Christ who becomes the 'pioneer of a new humanity' (ibid., p. 136). Christ's action as a *stellvertreter* then functions as a model for the vicarious representative action of the church in place of another, rather than merely on their behalf, where their fate is accepted as own.[103] It is through this action that the true collectivity of the church emerges—'Christ existing as church-community' (ibid., p. 190),[104] where the individual and community are one (ibid., p. 165).[105] Bonhoeffer makes it very clear that this unity is not established upon uniformity of will or shared purpose, but is brought about by God as the transcendent. In fact, it finds its embodiment

precisely where the seemingly sharpest outward antitheses prevail, where each person really leads an individual life [...] where wills clash [...] it might very well lead them to remember the One who is over them both, and in whom both of them are one. (ibid., p. 192f.)

It is only in communion with God that this clashing of wills manifests a single collective person [*Gesamtperson*] (ibid., p. 193), a unity rather than unanimity.[106] Specifically, the vicarious representative action, which is founded, grounded and takes place in Christ, characterises a collectivity from the perspective of Christ—not anthropocentric egalitarianism, but rather equal status in the eyes of God as described in Galatians 3:28 (ibid., pp. 204, 207).[107] Bonhoeffer presents the New Testament view of the church arguing for its clear expression as a community transcending 'all national and political boundaries' (ibid., pp. 135–139 at p. 135).[108] In

---

[103] Cf. DBWE 1: pp. 118–121, 188.

[104] Cf. pp. 121, 130, 136, 139, 141, 189f., 207, 211, 214, 216, 231, 260, 275, 280, 288. Also see DBW 11: pp. 269, 271f.

[105] Bonhoeffer infers that this holds also for each individual community as the concrete form of the whole: 'the church-community as a whole is real only in the individual congregation' (DBWE 1: p. 135).

[106] 'The Christian idea of equality does not allow for an egalitarianism' (DBWE 1: p. 207).

[107] Insofar as the collectivity of the church is from the perspective of God, it therefore also depends and is acted upon in faith. See DBWE 1: p. 202.

[108] Bonhoeffer views the adoption of the established Greek term ἐκκλησία denoting political assembly to describe this community as opportune, yet the rest of the quote reveals its

being from the perspective of God, this act is directed towards the independent neighbour as 'alien' rather than the perception of the subject (ibid., p. 169). Insofar as it does not emerge from the subject it avoids the latter's absolutisation, maintaining the freedom of the other. At the same time the ability to assert oneself against the knowing subject is limited by the objective spirit, the collective person of the community of individuals, thus avoiding absolutisation of the Other and maintaining the freedom of the subject and community. Together the independence of all three is preserved—the subject (and community), the Other and the ethical claim which remains regardless of whether the action is taken or not.[109] Together with the neighbour, this claim and the act itself is grounded in God as the ultimate Other and seeks to establish God's rule over humanity (ibid., p. 170). It is a love that is marked by surrender to the Other, neighbour and God, where 'I love the You by placing myself, my entire will, in the service of the You' (ibid., p. 169) because God unreservedly surrenders to me (ibid., pp. 173, 177).[110] Bonhoeffer claims that taking part in *Stellvertretung* marks the form of community which does not create community at the expense of the individual (ibid., pp. 203–204)[111] but rather preserves the collective person and a true ethical encounter:

> Paul speaks of the church of God. As such it is God's reality of revelation, and the individual is really only a part of it – a part, however, as a whole person, as someone elected by God within the church-community […]. With the notion of the organism, therefore, Paul wants to express, on the one hand, that all belong to the body of Christ, who is the unity of all members; Paul wants to express belonging to God's church community, in which alone the individual can live. But, on the other hand, from this membership there falls

problem: '[…] it is universal and yet "one people". It is, besides Gentiles and Jews, the "third people".' The term "third people" exposes that while Bonhoeffer's community of the saints overcomes some boundaries it creates a new one. This will be discussed next.

[109] This claim is what Bonhoeffer has in mind when he writes that 'each one bears the other's burden' (DBWE 1: p. 188)

[110] In describing this type of 'being-for-each-other' [*Das Füreinander*], Bonhoeffer draws on the scriptural accounts of how Moses and Paul were willing to set themselves outside of communion with God for the sake of their people. This is considered as 'the abyss into which intercession can lead the individual' (p. 185).

[111] This again is first and foremost in reference to Hegel, or rather Bonhoeffer's understanding of Hegel as the immanentist metaphysician of the Spirit with an epistemological consciousness of religion (DBW 1: pp. 131–132).

the demand, or rather the obvious consequence of operating with the whole (ibid., p. 138 [29]).[112]

Yet Bonhoeffer's claim that the grounding of the Other, ethical claim and act in God enables a true collectivity, where the individual is not overcome by community, is problematic from a Žižekian perspective.[113] Insofar as the perspective is from God it does not represent an engagement with the monstrous Other but rather an abstraction or Symbolic image—as a sinner in need of redemption, brother/sister in faith or Christ—and therefore a distortion. It is not as if the subject catches a glimpse of the mysterious real Other through God—the Other exists only in its relation to the big Other rather than its constitutive exposure to the subject (Žižek 2013, pp. 146–147). This claim is thus heteronomous and from above, not only as a command from the neighbour, but further as a command from God. Consequently, the ethical is not genuine for it originates in God rather than in the subject's constitutive exposure to the Other. It is rather vulnerability or finitude and dependency as described earlier that makes one responsible towards the other (ibid., p. 138). Therefore Bonhoeffer's collective person is but an abstraction and does not describe a properly ethical intersubjectivity. While it might overcome an ethnic collectivity (Galatians 3:22) based on race, political status, even gender, it does not overcome God and remains abstract. While the big Other overcomes one set of symbolic differences it replaces them with a new set, where the Other is known only through and according to the big Other.[114]

Perhaps here again Bonhoeffer's understanding regarding the ethical is stretched further during his stay in New York, when he describes something that is prima facie akin to Žižek's suspension of the ethical:

---

[112] This is in reference to Paul's notion of the church as the body of Christ in 1 Corinthians 12.

[113] Bonhoeffer's argument is here along the lines of Milbank who, in *The Monstrosity of Christ*, argues for a paradoxical constitution of the subject, where God is not only the maintainer of community but its sole source, or embodment. Žižek, in contrast, talks about the subject and the new revolutionary community being constituted in the parallax dialectical view as revelation meaning absolute kenosis. See Milbank, 'The Double Glory, or Paradox versus Dialectics: On Not Quite Agreeing with Slavoj Žižek' in Žižek and Milbank (2009, p. 110ff.).

[114] It is interesting to observe an argument of similar logic in Løland's (2018, pp. 5.3–5.4) counterproposal (to Žižek's universalism) of Nancy Fraser's consideration through the prism of justice of recognition.

Christians stand in freedom, without any backing, before both God and the world; they alone bear the entire responsibility for how they will deal with this gift of freedom. Through precisely this freedom, however, Christians become creative in their ethical actions. Acting according to principles is unproductive and merely reflects or copies the law. Acting in freedom is creative. Christians draw the forms of their ethical activity out of eternity itself, as it were, put these forms with sovereignty in the world, as deed, as their own creations born of the freedom of God's children. Christians create their own standards for good and evil; only Christians themselves provide the justification for their acts, just as they alone bear responsibility for them. Christians create new tablets, new decalogues, as Nietzsche said of the Overman. Indeed, Nietzsche's overman is not, as he imagined, the opposite of the Christian; without realizing it, Nietzsche imbued the Overman with many of the features of the free Christian as described and conceived by both Paul and Luther. (DBWE 10: pp. 366–367)

While the suspension of the ethical is comparable, Bonhoeffer still insists that suspension itself is from God and claims its exclusivity to the Christian identity.[115] This is in clear contrast to Žižek, who understands the Christian core as subverting any identity, including and foremost the divine, and asserts that it is only from this standpoint that the ethical is suspended. The ethical is not truly suspended with Bonhoeffer, for his position remains identitarian.[116] In that sense the difference between his own Christian identity and Nietzsche's non-or-over-identitarian Übermensch is clear: while both can create new decalogues, only one does so by rising above the identitarian, while the other remains firmly within it (cf. Frick 2017—Understanding Bonhoeffer—pp. 97–101).

This revealed the sociologically dangerous potential in Bonhoeffer's transcendent community of saints—that of identity politics. His illuminating critique of the traditional and Bonhoeffer's understanding of Galatians 3:28 as suspending identities only through the creation of a new one,

---

[115]Cf. 1, p. 156, where Bonhoeffer speaks of *Stellvertretung* as 'not an ethical possibility or standard, but solely the reality of the divine love for the church-community: it is not an ethical, but a theological concept'.

[116]This is also the challenge of Dahill (2013, p. 78) when she argues that Bonhoeffer's 'articulation that *all* social forms, including marriage, are open to the transforming revelation of Jesus Christ' reverts to patriarchal views of mandates and order. Dahill (2013, p. 83) spots the potential in some (not all) parts of *Letters and Papers*, where Bonhoeffer imagines God from below, rather than God being located above, so that divine authorisation does not become 'confused with the positions of those in power'.

hangs like a sword of Damocles, particularly in light of Bonhoeffer's immediate context.[117] The short-sightedness of his fellow German Christians to recognise the full problem of the Aryan paragraph and lack of concern for their neighbours, whether or not they are Christian, highlights this entrapment within the particular at the expense of the universality it excludes. Upon this consideration, it seems that Žižek's drawing of attention to the theological character as the excess or monstrous, transcendental, never submitting to an identity but rather blurring the hypostasised boundaries between them irrevocably, ought to be considered carefully.

Bonhoeffer's problematic divine personalism is opposed by Žižek's challenge to pursue a community without symbolic differences, including those imposed by God as the big Other, one that does not have to be contrasted with egalitarianism and within which unreserved surrender to each other takes place without an injunction, grounded upon respect and acceptance of each other's vulnerability and limitation. In *The Monstrosity of Christ* (Žižek and Milbank 2009, pp. 301–303), Žižek describes such an ethical stance with the help of Agota Kristof's *The Notebook*, which is the first volume of her trilogy entitled *The Notebook: The Proof—The Third Lie* (1997). The story revolves around young twins who live with their grandmother and stand for authentic ethical naivety at its purest, in that they are spontaneously and without empathy doing what needs to be done in order to meet their neighbours' needs. 'With more people like this, the world would be a pleasant place in which sentimentality would be replaced by a cold and cruel passion', Žižek concludes (ibid., p. 303).

Such a community looks beyond Symbolic difference and is not identitarian; characterised by love or, as Žižek calls it, the ethics of indifference, it is a community:

> where I am indifferent toward all, the totality of the universe, and as such, I actually love you, the unique individual who stands/sticks out of this indifferent background. Love and hatred are thus not symmetrical: love emerges out of universal indifference, while hatred emerges out of universal love. (Žižek 2013, p. 183)

---

[117] Pugh notes: 'In the context of Bonhoeffer's life, we see the manifestation of one of Western Christianity's greatest failures. Its inability to dissociate itself from the military and political apparatus of Nazi Germany [...]; all these things serve to illustrate that Christianity in that situation had become nothing more than an enfeebled and useless religion' (Pugh 2008, p. 17).

This kind of love is different from Bonhoeffer's 'universal' love which is, as already observed, focused only on those present in the gaze of the big Other. Even if it is argued that all are present in this guise, it is still a love based on abstraction and furthermore allows for no existence of the subject outside of it. Love of universal indifference, on the other hand, is based on the constitutive exposure of the subject and its monstrous excess, a universality that does not exclude but is itself the excluded from the Symbolic—the sempiternally present inhuman human. This love is, according to Žižek, also exemplified in Christ's injunction in Luke 14:26: 'If anyone comes to me and does not hate his father and his mother, his wife and his children, his brothers and sisters – yes, even his own life – he cannot be my disciple'. Rather than being a love of Symbolic features it is obligatory indifference to those in preference to the existing excess and in that way a love of all.

Žižek: No Abstraction, Please!

While Bonhoeffer and Žižek agree on the sociality of theological concepts, as well as the theological essence of social concepts and therefore theology's relevance in pursuit of community, they disagree on their form. For Bonhoeffer true community is possible only through, with and from God, whereas for Žižek the big Other abstracts it. This difference emerges from their respective understanding of theology. While Bonhoeffer considers it to be foremost the study of the divine grounding—study of God—Žižek deems it as the study of the alien or monstrous, the Real. Whereas Bonhoeffer seeks to apply the theological concepts of God, sin and the church to demonstrate the shortfall of the social-philosophical concepts of person and community, Žižek also employs theological concepts of Christ, the Fall and the Holy Spirit community for sociological implication, but not to reveal the divine truth and instruction; rather, he does so to reveal the cracks and fissures of the current or given order, intimating the existence or presence of excess.

From Žižek's perspective Bonhoeffer's Schelerian personalism betrays a very limited and second-hand understanding of Hegel's subject–object relationship, where universality is reduced to totalitarianism of the subject. His alternative of the collective person rests upon an ethical barrier between persons, asserting the inability and impermissibility to recognise the Other but also placing them in a relationship of ethical responsibility. According to Žižek, this ethical constitution of the subject and impenetrability of the Other is partial for it lacks an ontological foundation of the subject itself as unknowable. Insofar as intersubjectivity is located in the unknowable excess of the subject (and the Other), he considers Bonhoeffer's impenetrability restricted to the Other as resulting in a sociality of separation, where the Other is always alien in their particularity and thus a source of heteronomous ethical demands.

This tension is also observed in Bonhoeffer's grapple with Hegel's concept of objective spirit, which he uses to illustrate the dialectically tense spirit of sociality, within which community emerges. He wishes to preserve the individual in contrast to his understanding of Hegel's transgression of the ethical boundary, where the particular individual is overcome by the universal. Žižek corrects Bonhoeffer's understanding of universalism by pointing out that it should instead be conceived as struggling, a principle of negativity constantly driving particularities in antagonism to prevent the notion of totality. According to Žižek, Bonhoeffer's sociality of separation seeks to preserve the individual but ends up sacrificing sociality.

Of course, for Bonhoeffer this is only the foundation, for in the final chapter of the thesis he grounds the community in the divine by engaging the sociological concepts of community with theological concepts of God, sin and church. Thus God, the transcendent Other, becomes the Other that grounds the subject, its relationship to the Other and the ethical claim of the community. However, by doing this Bonhoeffer abstracts them, for the subject, its relationship to the Other and the community no longer have absolute value apart from God, who assigns identity and orders engagement. Furthermore, their first assigned value is that of sin, for the individual and the community needs to recognise itself as sinful and guilty, in need of redemption from God.

Bonhoeffer then describes how God enters the broken community by revealing himself in and as Christ and redeems it by creating the church *qua* a new community no longer grounded upon culpability but in God—Christ existing as community. This community, where the subject, the Other and the ethical claim of the community are all maintained by God, is for him the true community and the source for any and all social considerations in theology.

From Žižek's perspective, however, Bonhoeffer's attempt to escape the sinful totalitarianism of universality results in a total domination of the transcendent big Other, who abstracts all the concepts by assigning a new identity to the subject, the Other and the community. It does not represent an engagement with the Real but rather the construction of a new yet still Symbolic reality. The terror for Bonhoeffer seems to be that there is only us, inconsistent, ambiguous and lacking; therefore, he grounds the subject and community in the redeeming big Other by the notion of sin and guilt. Rather than grounding social forms and resolving their dialectical tensions in God, Žižek challenges Bonhoeffer to venture beyond the regulating of the big Other, where the latter's role is suspended and the Real subject emerges, to embrace the inconsistent and lacking struggling universality, not only to contest the *deus ex machina* as Bonhoeffer attempts in *The Letters*,[118] but, from an ethical concern, to contest and surmount the *deus superanus*—the sovereign ordering the 'reality', including 'sociological forms and relations'—identity.

The Žižekian reading of Bonhoeffer's social theology of *Sanctorum Communio* thus highlights its problems. The final section of this chapter will further practically explore it by applying Bonhoeffer's social typology to contemporary struggles for change.

Applying Bonhoeffer's Reasoning to the Struggle for Social Change

> A people is 'community' in the specific sense, not something that has grown but only as something willed, namely willed-community – recognised as an end in itself, is a value, for all community is community of will. (DBWE 1: p. 89)

The Sociological Problem

In Section C of *Sanctorum Communio*'s third chapter, entitled 'The Sociological Problem' (DBWE 1: pp. 80–106), Bonhoeffer presents and discusses a typology of social forms through the lens of the objective spirit (ibid., pp. 86–97). In pursuit of an authentic form, he distinguishes between three types within which 'wills unite': society, the mass and community.[119] He then proceeds to contrast the meeting of wills in each type

---

[118] 16 July 1944 in DBWE 8: p. 479.

[119] This criterion of 'a meeting of wills' also explains the difference with Scheler's typology, upon which Bonhoeffer relies. In contrast to Bonhoeffer, Scheler identifies four different types

and argues that, while in society and the mass wills will beside each other, resting upon common interests or reaction respectively, it is only in community that wills will together, resting on purposeful acts of will (ibid., p. 83). Thus while the mass and society are temporary [*innerzeitlich*] and limited by time [*zeitbegrenzt*], insofar as they rest upon coincidence of wills and their rationale, the community exists at the limits of time [*grenzzeitlich*] (ibid., p. 96).

The contrast Bonhoeffer draws between the forms of sociality reveals a dialectical tension between these forms and can be employed in a post-Marxist analysis of contemporary struggles for social change—their form and relation to the hoped-for goal—a new beginning. Therefore, first, the perversion of contemporary capitalist society will be discussed through the lens of Bonhoeffer's understanding of the problems of the social form of society. Then the contemporary movements for social change Occupy and Black Lives Matter (BLM) will be explored through the lens of the social form of the mass, its response to society and its limits. Finally, its limits will enable us to draw attention to its dialectically tense relation with a new beginning through the lens of the social form of community.

Society (as Unethical)

Bonhoeffer's consideration of the form of society as 'shallow, suspicious and egotistic' (ibid., p. 91) lends itself nicely to Žižek's own view of the contemporary global neo-liberal society as perverse and serving only the interests of capital.

Having no substance beyond its coming together in pursuit of a common goal, society needs to be tied together with written documents and agreements, which ensure society's adherence to that goal. In that sense, Bonhoeffer argues, the society itself is used extensively in this pursuit and 'the only reason this is not called unethical is that it is based on consent and applies equally to all' (ibid., p. 90). What Bonhoeffer's acute observation conveys is the functional perversion of contemporary society's legal framework in the service of particular interests. Even though the legal framework

---

of communities: the herd/mass, life-community [*Lebensgemeinschaft*], society [*Gesellschaft*], and collective person [*Gesamtperson*]. Out of them all, Scheler contends, only the latter (collective person) is the most profound level of community, characterised by a sense of solidarity rather than psychic contagion, over-identification with community or common interest. He also contends that the church is by far the most expansive collective person, including all finite persons—past, present and future. See 'Unser Personbegriff im Werhältnis zu anderen Formen Personalistischer Ethik' in Scheler (2005a, pp. 522–595).

was originally set up as a tool to ensure society's adherence to its stated purpose, it becomes the telos of society which itself serves the order—from serving the will of the people to people serving its will or the will of particular interests, to be precise. This is why Žižek describes the current global society as postpolitical, trapped in service to the legal philosophy of capitalism, ensuring that particular economic interests are set up as the legal order (Žižek 2010, pp. 118–119). Politics itself is in the service of the legal philosophy of the greater economic system. A double instrumentalisation is observed: of society in service to the legal system and of the legal system in the service of economic interests. In this role, law obscures or abstracts the deeper social and institutional problems. Bonhoeffer's remark about the form of society as shallow, suspicious and egotistical thus also holds for the contemporary global society.

Bonhoeffer also asserts that any society is transitory (DBWE 1: p. 94), and this temporality has recently been shown in numerous calls for a change of the global order, such as the Occupy movement or BLM. In the discussion of such movements Žižek calls for a construction of new political subjects who break out of the legal entanglement and ground a new collective space. These struggles will be explored next through the lens of Bonhoeffer's form of the mass.

Mass (as Reflex)
In contrast to society as a rational willing of wills, Bonhoeffer uses the term 'mass' to describe social bonding where wills come together as a mechanical response to certain stimuli (ibid., pp. 93–96). Given its purely mechanical nature, Bonhoeffer does not consider this form of sociality as genuine and only discusses it as human 'because it is composed of conscious beings' (ibid., p. 93). Furthermore, he infers that because of its mechanical nature any bonding is accidental and vanishes as soon as the stimuli disappear—it is temporary [*innerzeitlich*]. However, does Bonhoeffer abandon consideration of the function and form of mass too hastily? I will show that while movements for social change such as Occupy and BLM can be regarded as a response to the current socio-political conditions, they are far from purely mechanical and are full of potential for the emergence of an alternative—a new beginning.

Occupy and Black Lives Matter

Occupy, the diverse and multifocal international movement against social inequality and economic injustice, could be considered as corresponding to Bonhoeffer's social type of mass, for it emerged as a response to the external provocation of neoliberal conditions and infringement of social rights and well-being. The social movement derived from the protests against budget cuts imposed by the University of California in response to the post-2007 financial crisis, as students occupied campus buildings under the slogan 'Occupy Everything, Demand Nothing'.[120] It first received widespread attention at the 'Occupy Wall Street' protest in Zuccotti Park in September 2011 against the global financial system and within a month had spread around the globe. Soon there were localised protests in cities in eighty-odd countries against the way in which national and international politics have been thwarted in their service to the interests of large corporations. Insofar as Occupy emerges in and embodies the response to a set of wider socio-political stimuli it can, according to Bonhoeffer, be considered as mass.

BLM, the international activist movement against violence and systemic racism towards black people, could also be considered as corresponding to Bonhoeffer's social type of mass, for it also emerged as a response to the external provocation of police violence again black people. The social movement derived from the protest in Ferguson, Missouri where the murder of Mike Brown by Darren Wilson, a white police officer took place and spread across the United States and has at least twenty-six chapters. More than a mere protest against police violence, the movement highlighted racism as engrained in the economic system of capitalism—systemic racism in the United States and beyond. Insofar as BLM also emerges in and embodies the response to a set of wider socio-political stimuli it can, according to Bonhoeffer, be considered as mass.

It is interesting to note the connection between BLM and Occupy. In her critical *From Black Lives Matter to Black Liberation* (2016, pp. 145–148) Keeanga-Yamahtta Taylor briefly presents how the protests called after the execution of Troy Davis in Georgia marched to the Occupy Wall Street encampment begun only a week before Davis' execution. The convergence enabled a perception of the 'entanglement of racial and economic inequality' (p. 146). She notes that while Occupy is often portrayed

---

[120]Bady and Konczal (2012).

as 'white', there were significant discussions or actions against racism at its Oakland, Wall Street and Chicago encampments, and draws particular attention to the efforts of 'Black Occupy' (p. 146). Most of all, Taylor contends that Occupy 'relegitimized street protests, occupations and direct actions', while the violent crackdown on Occupy encampments in Winter of 2011 turned many protesters to BLM. It therefore makes sense to discuss these two movements for social change side by side.

In agreement with Bonhoeffer, the structure of Occupy and BLM corresponds to the nature of its emergence,[121] set-up and unfolding in response to the existing politics as democratically compromised. The individual Occupy protests function as a platform for participatory democracy, where anyone can contribute to leader-less discussions, analysing the local situation and issuing statements with alternatives in due time. There is no privileging and rushing of decisions. Thus, for example, the movement in London released a statement on corporations and called for an end to tax evasion by wealthy firms in late November 2011, after initial occupation outside St. Paul's on October 15th (Occupy London 2011). Likewise, BLM describes itself as a decentralised and leaderless network, allowing its followers to 'act on what they want to do without the restraint of others weighing in' (Taylor 2016, p. 176).[122] The anti-hierarchical structure of both movements, with direct access for all in its consensus-based decision-making process, is a response to the really existing hierarchical politics.

Where the difference begins to emerge is with Bonhoeffer's consideration that in the mass 'the boundary of personhood is lost' (DBWE 1: p. 93) and the individual is no longer a person but an anonymous particle of the mass—'drawn into it and directed by it' (ibid., p. 94). However, is it true that the Occupy's bonding 'is not supported by the separateness of the person and thus cannot last' (ibid.)? Is this observed in their slogan, 'We are the 99%'—individuals morphed into a faceless mass? Quite the opposite, for the protests embody the individualisation of those considered faceless in the financial global order. Thus the slogan was originally launched as a Tumblr blog page in August 2011, making visible individuals and their stories of social inequality and economic injustice. Furthermore,

---

[121]Cf. DBWE 1: p. 93.

[122]This is acknowledged by the civil rights activist DeRay McKesson: 'But what is different about Ferguson… what makes that really important, unlike previous struggle, is that – who is the spokesperson? The people. The people, in a very democratic way, become the voice of the struggle' (quoted by Taylor 2016, p. 175).

its participatory democracy is anything but totalitarian. In the same way, the democratic structure of BLM gives everyone a voice and embodies the individualisation of those considered as faceless of racist police violence, such as Mike Brown or Troy Davis. Thus, even though Occupy and BLM are a movement of response, the emerging sociality is far from overcoming by the mass.

Interestingly, Bonhoeffer observes that the social form of mass 'creates the most powerful experiences of unity' (ibid., p. 94), but quickly notes that this perception is a confusion of mass-unity and community. While the former rests 'on the parallel direction of the wills of a number of persons' (ibid., p. 93), the latter rests upon a true meeting of wills. As such, Bonhoeffer argues, it is unable to create a social form [*Sozialgebilde*] (ibid., p. 88). As previously noted, Occupy's and BLM's unity is not a totalitarianism of mass (rather it is particularised); the question now is whether it is able to create a social form. However, it is important to stress that no social movement is the alternative or the hoped-for goal in itself. Taylor quotes the historian Barbara Ransby (2016, p. 175); 'a movement that itself is not the goal but instead aims to construct a community'. Therefore, the mass-unity of an emerging movement is such in the current condition/global order and the alternative will emerge only after the latter is subverted. While both movements perform the role of a catalyst for social change, they are not the community yet. However, without it and its mass-unity change is impossible, for the overcoming of Capitalism as the big Other tying the people together must begin from the position of this recognition. Otherwise, any 'alternative' will remain part of this system or 'society'. While the mass is not yet the alternative, it is its necessary and, as we shall see, potential catalyst.

It is with regards to its potential for an alternative that Occupy has been criticised for its lack of clearly defined goals. Thus the political theorist of non-violence Gene Sharp warned that 'the protesters don't have a clear objective, something they can actually achieve. If they think they will change the economic system by simply staying in a particular location, then they are likely to be very disappointed. Protest alone accomplishes very little'.[123] Žižek, who himself addressed the protesters in Zuccotti Park in October 2011,[124] in 'Occupy Wall Street, Or, the Violent Silence of a New Beginning' (2012b, pp. 77–89) warned against the protests ending in mere

---

[123]Sharp (2011).
[124]Žižek (2011).

rejection of the current order and called for a start to the laborious task of imagining an alternative. However, Žižek at the same time defended the movement by affirming the essentiality of its initial pure negativity:

> [O]ne always has to begin this way, with a formal gesture of rejection that is initially more important than any positive content—only such a gesture opens up the space for a new content. In the psychoanalytic sense, the protesters are indeed hysterical actors, provoking the master, undermining his authority; and the question with which they were constantly bombarded, 'But what do you want?' aims precisely at precluding the true answer—its point is: 'Say it in my terms or shut up!' In this way, the process of translating an inchoate protest into a concrete project is blocked. (ibid., p. 84)

He thus dismissed the calls for a list of clear objectives and negotiations as compromise of the movement's radical nature and potential and called for a thorough consideration in making 'feasible and legitimate' but 'de facto impossible' demands (ibid.), such as universal healthcare, which disturb the very core of the hegemonic ideology. The movement's lack of clearly defined goals is thus not only due to its mechanical nature, but represents the only way to avoid being subsumed within the current order and to subvert it.

In her critical *From Black Lives Matter to Black Liberation* (2016) Keeanga-Yamahtta Taylor also recognises that the reforms which BLM put forward, like those of the mentioned statement from Occupy's London chapter, are 'only building blocks that can lead to larger and more transformative struggles' (p. 183). It is important to understand that Taylor does not speak of being reasonable in one's demands; The demand is still impossible, but rather is a specific impossible that is part of a larger impossible—the issue of police violence as part of the state violence against Black people but also 'the wider phenomenon of economic exploitation and inequality that pervades all of American society...' (Taylor 2016, p. 194).[125] This recognition of the true condition of the wider society is what distinguishes a movement from a simple reaction to a particularity. It is what unites people as a movement of resistance and a collective force with the power to transform social conditions'. The impossible demands

---

[125]Taylor (2016, pp. 197–205) gives examples of people who recognized the interconnectedness of the Black struggle and the wider socialist struggle—Malcolm X, Martin Luther King, John Watson.

of Occupy and BLM are a sign of their perceptiveness as a movement, rather than a mere protest of reaction.

Instead, I propose that various arguments about the inability of Occupy or BLM to produce 'reasonable' demands and a 'viable' alternative end up being preoccupied with the particularity of the movements, rather than the conditions that compelled them. When they attempt to define them as mere reaction and without potential, such arguments are an attempt to inscribe meaning—meaning that obscures, abstracts and seeks to take away the movement's transforming power. Far from emerging movements such as Occupy or BLM representing merely a mechanical reaction to the neoliberal conditions, a sort of reflex which is unable to bring about anything concrete, they are rather where the emerging alternative is to be located. In other words, mass carries the potential to become a 'critical mass', reaching the point at which it converges into something more than a mechanical reaction—a community. It is to a discussion of the characteristics or parameters of this alternative in the social form of community that we turn next.

Community (as Transcendent)

As noted in the introduction to this chapter, Bonhoeffer regards community alone as an authentic social form, as its essence is not commonality but reciprocal will. Accordingly, its telos as the essence of community cannot be elaborated:

> A community may have a rational telos, but its very essence is not absorbed by that telos, nor identical with it. Instead, community as such is characterised by value, as is history, and, as value-bearing, transcends inner historical limitations. (DBWE 1: p. 95 [114])

Rather than having a purpose/goal-oriented or applied essence, the community's essence is completely objectless—that is its value. The community is an end in itself and thus pure will (ibid., p. 89). It is due to this grounding that it exists at the limits of time [*grenzzeitlich*] or outside time, manifesting in the present, the past and the future, and is therefore transcendental.[126] That is why, Žižek observes, it 'can' (as in "has the potential to") manifest in various guises, Christianity, Ancient Greek

---

[126]In elaborating this point the idealist Bonhoeffer is most visible: 'The concept of community thus also contains the idea of infinite time, whose only limit is the boundary of time.

democracy, Lenin's Bolshevik revolution, Eastern Europe's undermining of Communism in the 1980s or indeed the Occupy or BLM. Interestingly, this objectless essence is also highlighted in Taylor's quote of Donna Murch:

> I have no words to express what is happening in Ferguson […] drawing in people from all over the U.S., […] It looks explicitly not only to St. Louis city and county police and other municipal law enforcement, but also to the Imperial Wars of Middle East as sites of murder and trauma. The call repeated over and over is Stokely Carmichael's: 'Organize, Organize, Organize.' And this growing youth movement has all the ancestral sweetness of kinship. In the words of a local hip-hop artist/activist, 'Our grandparents would be proud of us'. (Murch quoted by Taylor 2016, p. 158)

It is this transcendence that attracts Žižek to the theological considerations of the revolutionary moment of the community and informs his understanding of its pure externality 'from above' as 'grace'.[127] For both Bonhoeffer and Žižek, this formative 'moment' is manifested in history but is not restricted to it or by it. Rather, in contrast to the form of society which exists only within history coming 'to an end with the satisfaction of the individual's wishes' (DBWE 1: pp. 95, 101), the transcendent value itself breaks in and shapes history. This also means that community is not historically verifiable and is from that perspective invisible, even though it is always present and part of the historical community (ibid., pp. 216, 223–226):

> The empirical church lives in history. Just as the individual spirit, as a member of the church, has particular tasks at particular times, so the objective spirit of the church has an individual character; that is, it is different at any given time. It gets its character from the historical context. But the fact that the objective spirit is part of history necessarily implies that it is fallible and imperfect as far as its understanding and will are concerned. (ibid., pp. 214–215)

It is thus exactly in and through its particularity of understanding and will that community is transcendent.

The "duration" of community is identical with the duration of history. Of course, we speak of community as an idea, not as an empirical entity' (DBWE 1: p. 95 [114]).

[127] See 'Introduction: From Christ to Lenin… and Back' in Žižek (2001a, pp. 1–5).

The transcendental of this form of community, which for Bonhoeffer and Žižek is a theological category, also means that it is only understood within its actuality, not outside it. Bonhoeffer's assertion that the church can be 'understood fully only from within, on the basis of its own claim; only on this basis can we develop appropriately critical criteria for judging it' (ibid., p. 127), can be compared with Žižek's statement that it is cognitively accessible only from within (Žižek 2001a, p. 105). Indeed, to an outsider, the community does not make sense and remains pure idealist utopia. That is why the radical demands of Occupy and BLM are perceived as impossible and why if an alternative is to emerge, it will have to be judged according to its own criteria, its radical core.

Moreover, in keeping with its transcendent dialectical nature, this knowledge precedes it; community is established upon already existing knowledge and acknowledgement. Bonhoeffer thus highlights the necessity of faith, which, together with revelation, is 'not a possible method by which to gain academic knowledge; rather, by acknowledging the claim of revelation, faith is given the prerequisite for positive theological language' (DBWE 1: pp. 127, 133[23]). For Žižek, faith is the miracle (Žižek 2001a, p. 148) that enables the traversing of fantasy by acknowledging revelation as the impossible becoming possible and thus enables a political act, which might seem impossible from the current coordinates, yet once it arrives, it always already was and becomes 'routine' (Žižek 2010, pp. 13–14).[128] Žižek and Bonhoeffer contend that the community logically establishes its own foundation in itself. Thus when the 'irrational' demand of Occupy or BLM is met and the coordinates of the current situation are overcome, it will be of the future perfect.

It is this impossibility of the authentic community that marks it as distinct to any other form. It is possible, Bonhoeffer argues, 'to deduce certain impulses towards community that become visible in the empirical formation of community; but this still does not lead to the concept of the church' (DBWE 1: p. 133). Accordingly, while it is possible to deduce certain impulses towards Žižek's struggling community from various movements, including Occupy and BLM, it is important not to confuse the movement with community as such. They are but the necessary 'place' where the distinct community can emerge when revelation is believed or taken seri-

---

[128] Cf. DBWE 1: p. 144. Also see again section 2.7.1.

ously.[129] Thus any analysis of the movement for social change as the end result ends in failure.

The empirical form of the community has a will and life of its own. Bonhoeffer describes it as guided by the Spirit (ibid., p. 209),[130] while Žižek presents this in Christ's act which, while irrational, from within the existing coordinates, actually suspends them (Žižek 2000, pp. 133, 135, 143). This is what the breaking in of community does with the existing forms of sociality: it suspends them. Yes, within the realm of other forms of society the acts of the community are perceived as madness. Is this not also the case with the discussed movements, whose refusal to produce a clear list of goals is frowned upon from the perspective of the global political order? That is why the movement's demands ought not to be 'feasible' and 'legitimate', but 'de facto impossible' in order to change the very coordinates of the situation. Failure to do so would be to remain within the particular capitalist world order.

This statement brings us to the final characteristic of the new community—its contingency. Despite its absolute necessity it is only a historical potentiality and even then incredibly fragile. Since, as already observed, for Žižek (2001a, p. 105) its emergence through various 'new beginnings' is only a possibility, the Occupy and BLM movements carry the potential to bear an alternative, but this is not ensured. Furthermore, the community is incredibly fragile. Bonhoeffer writes about it, saying that the church 'continues to fall again and again, it comes into being anew, passes away, and comes into being once more' (DBWE 1: p. 213).[131] Just as Lenin's revolution led to the perverse ideology of Stalinism, the communality of the Arab Spring was taken over by religious fundamentalists, so too the Occupy and BLM movement, without the proper stance in relation to what happened in Zuccotti Park or Ferguson, that is by accepting the rules of the game or the coordinates dictated by the system, can transform its radicality into perversion.

---

[129]Cf. DBWE 1: p. 144.

[130]From page 208 onward Bonhoeffer engages in a description of the empirical form of the church.

[131]Of course, for Bonhoeffer this is because of sin, in that the community of saints is still a community of sinners [*peccatorum communio*].

Žižek: No Hope for Social Change?

This section has examined Bonhoeffer's understanding of the sociological function of the forms of society, mass and community in analysis of the contemporary capitalist society as selfish and perverse, the responsive nature of challenges posed to it by emerging movements, such as Occupy and BLM, as well as the transcendence of the alternative social form. With the help of Žižek, contrasting the two revealed the dialectical tension between their sociological function—the necessary responsive-to-the-current-conditions-of-society character of movements for social change, their essentiality and potential, but also their difference from the transcendent form of their hope for a new beginning—a new form of sociality. Far from them merely excluding each other, they instead embody a tense relationship where one emerges at the cracks of the other. To paraphrase Bonhoeffer, every society is limited by time, mass emerging on its borders temporarily, only in order for the possibility of transcendental community, which is, however, inherently fragile. It is the negative dialectical relationship between them that enables an understanding of and hope for social change. This, their ontological, grounding is something that Bonhoeffer fails to consider. His insistence upon sinfulness prevents society from seeing the failure of its own form and unable to imagine or bring about an alternative. Within the paradigm of *Sanctorum Communio*, the only solution is God's creation of a new community. However, this identity is one of abstraction, as was already observed in the last chapter with regards to Holsclaw and again here, and alienates the subject and the society from each other and themselves. Furthermore, the emphasis that change is not possible lest it come from God leaves humanity incapacitated in the existing coordinates.

REFERENCES

Agamben, G. (2002). *What Remains of Auschwitz: The Witness and the Archive*. Translated by D. Heller-Roazen. Stanford: Stanford University Press.

Bady, A. and Konczal, M. (2012). 'From Master Plan to No Plan: The Slow Death of Public Higher Education', *Dissent Magazine* (Fall) [Online]. Available at http://www.dissentmagazine.org/article/from-master-plan-to-no-plan-the-slow-death-of-public-higher-education. Accessed 20 September 2016.

Barth, K. (1975). *Church Dogmatics I.1: Doctrine of the Word of God: Prolegomena to Church Dogmatics*. Edinburgh: T&T Clark.

Barth, K. (2003). *Church Dogmatics III.4: The Doctrine of Creation—The Command of God and the Creator.* Study edition. Translated by G.W. Bromiley. London and New York: T&T Clark.

Barth, K. (2010). *Church Dogmatics IV.2: The Doctrine of Reconciliation.* Study edition. Translated by G.W. Bromiley. London and New York: T&T Clark.

Bayer, O. (1992). *Leibliches Wort: Reformation und Neuzeit im Konflikt.* Tübingen: J.C.B. Mohr.

Bethge, E. (1961). 'The Challenge of Dietrich Bonhoeffer's Life and Theology', *The Chicago Seminary Register,* 51(2), pp. 1–38.

Bethge, E. (1963). 'The Challenge of Dietrich Bonhoeffer's Life and Theology', in Smith, R.G. (ed.) *World Come of Age.* Philadelphia: Fortress Press, pp. 22–88.

Bethge, E. (1967). *Dietrich Bonhoeffer: Theologe – Christ – Zeitgenosse.* München: C. Kaiser Verlag.

Bethge, E. (1994). *Dietrich Bonhoeffer: Eine Biographie.* Gütersloh: C. Kaiser.

Bonhoeffer, D. (1996). *Dietrich Bonhoeffer Works. Volume 2: Act and Being—Transcendental Philosophy and Ontology in Systematic Theology.* Translated by M. Rumscheidt. Minneapolis: Fortress Press.

Cremer, A.H. (1903). *Die Grundwahrheiten der christlichen Religion nach Dr. R. Seeberg.* Gütersloh: Bertelsmann.

Dahill, L.E. (2013). '"There's Some Contradiction Here": Gender and the Relation of *Above* and *Below* in Bonhoeffer', in Frick, P. (ed.) *Bonhoeffer and Interpretive Theory: Essays on Method and Understanding.* Frankfurt am Main: Peter Lang, pp. 53–84.

DeJonge, M.P. (2012). *Bonhoeffer's Theological Formation: Berlin, Barth, and Protestant Theology.* Oxford: Oxford University Press.

D'Isanto, L. (1992). 'Bonhoeffer's Hermeneutical Model of Community', *Union Theological Seminary Quarterly Review,* 46, pp. 135–148.

Dramm, S. (2001). *Dietrich Bonhoeffer: Eine Einführung in sein Denken.* Gütersloh: C. Kaiser and Gütersloher Verlag. English: (2007) *Dietrich Bonhoeffer: An Introduction to His Thought.* Translated by T. Rice. Peabody: Hendrickson Publishers.

Feuerbach, L. (1989). *The Essence of Christianity.* Translated by G. Elliot. New York: Prometheus Books.

Floyd, W.W. (1988). *Theology and Dialectics of Otherness: Bonhoeffer and Adorno.* Lanham: University Press of America.

Floyd, W.W. (2008). 'Kant, Hegel and Bonhoeffer', in Frick, P. (ed.) *Bonhoeffer's Intellectual Formation.* Tübingen: Mohr Siebeck, pp. 83–119.

Freyer, H. (1923). *Theorie des objektiven Geistes.* Leipzig and Berlin: B.G. Teubner.

Frick, P. (2017). *Understanding Bonhoeffer.* Tübingen: Mohr Siebeck.

Green, C.J. (1999). *Bonhoeffer: A Theology of Sociality.* Cambridge: Eerdmans.

Hamza, A. (2016). 'Going to One's Ground: Žižek's Dialectical Materialism', in Hamza, A. and Ruda, F. (eds.) *Slavoj Žižek and Dialectical Materialism*. New York: Palgrave Macmillan, pp. 163–175.

Hegel, G.W.F. (1977). *Phenomenology of Spirit*. Translated by A.V. Miller. Oxford: Oxford University Press.

Hegel, G.W.F. (1991). *Elements of the Philosophy of Right*. Translated by H.B. Nisbet. Cambridge: Cambridge University Press.

Hegel, G.W.F. (2006). *Lectures on the Philosophy of Religion*. Translated by R.F. Brown, P.C. Hodgson, and J.M. Stewart. Oxford: Clarendon Press.

Hirsch, E. (1926). *Die idealistische Philosophie und das Christentum: Gesammelte Aufsätze*. Gütersloh: C. Bertelsmann.

Hobbes, T. (1949). *De Cive or The Citizen*. New York: Appleton-Century-Crofts.

Hobbes, T. (2002). *Leviathan. Project Gutenberg* [Online]. Available at https://www.gutenberg.org/ebooks/3207. Accessed 7 October 2016.

Holl, K. (1959). *The Cultural Significance of the Reformation*. New York: Meridian.

Holm, J. (2002). 'G.W.F. Hegel's Impact on Dietrich Bonhoeffer's Early Theology', *Studia Theologica*, 56(1), pp. 64–75.

Jüngel, E. (1972). *Unterwegs zur Sache: Theologische Bemerkungen*. München: Chr. Kaiser Verlag.

Jüngel, E. (1983). *God as the Mystery of the World*. Grand Rapids: Eerdmans.

Kaltenborn, C.J. (1973). *Adolf von Harnack als Lehrer Dietrich Bonhoeffers*. Berlin: Evangelische Verl. Anst.

Kaltenborn, C.J. (1981). 'Adolf von Harnack and Bonhoeffer', in Klassen, A.J. (ed.) *A Bonhoeffer Legacy: Essays in Understanding*. Grand Rapids: Eerdmans, pp. 48–57.

Kotsko, A. (2005). 'Objective Spirit and Continuity in the Theology of Dietrich Bonhoeffer', *Philosophy & Theology*, 17(1 & 2), pp. 17–31.

Kristof, A. (1997). *The Notebook: The Proof—The Third Lie*. Translated by A Sheridan, D. Watson, and M. Romano. New York: Grove Press.

Laclau, E. (2001). 'Hegemony: The Genealogy of a Concept', in Laclau, E. and Mouffe, C. (eds.), *Hegemony and Socialist Strategy*. London and New York: Verso, pp. 7–46.

Løland, O.J. (2018). *The Reception of Paul the Apostle in the Works of Slavoj Žižek*. New York: Palgrave Macmillan.

Mackintosh, H.R. (1937). *Types of Modern Theology: Schleiermacher to Barth*. London: Nisbet & Co Ltd.

Marsh, C. (1994). *Reclaiming Dietrich Bonhoeffer: The Promise of His Theology*. New York and Oxford: Oxford University Press.

Mawson, M. (2018). *Christ Existing as Community: Bonhoeffer's Ecclesiology*. Oxford: Oxford University Press.

Moltmann, J. (1974). *The Crucified God*. Translated by R.A. Wilson and J. Bowden. New York: Harper & Row.

Moltmann, J. (1981). *The Trinity and the Kingdom: The Doctrine of God*. New York: Harper & Row.

Nowers, J. (2013). 'Hegel, Bonhoeffer and Objective Geist: An Architectonic Exegesis', in Clar, A.C. and Mawson, M. (eds.) *Ontology and Ethics: Bonhoeffer and Contemporary Scholarship*. Eugene: Pickwick Publications.

Occupy London. (2011). 'Help Us Draft the Global Statement for the Occupy Movement', *The Guardian*, 15 November. Available at http://www.guardian.co.uk/commentisfree/2011/nov/15/draft-statement-occupy-london. Accessed 20 September 2016.

Ott, H. (1972). *Reality and Faith: The Theological legacy of Dietrich Bonhoeffer*. Translated by A.A. Morrison. Philadelphia: Fortress Press.

Pangritz, A. (2000). *Karl Barth in the Theology of Dietrich Bonhoeffer*. Grand Rapids: Eerdmans.

Pannenberg, W. (ed.). (1963). *Offenbarung als Geschichte*. Göttingen: Vandenhoeck und Ruprecht. English: (1968) *Revelation as History*. Translated by E. Quinn. New York: Macmillan.

Phillips, J.A. (1967). *Christ for Us in the Theology of Dietrich Bonhoeffer*. New York: Harper & Row.

Prenter, R. (1967). 'Dietrich Bonhoeffer and Karl Barth's Positivism of Revelation', in Smith, R.G. (ed.) *World Come of Age*. London: Collins, pp. 93–130.

Pugh, J.C. (2008). *Religionless Christianity: Dietrich Bonhoeffer in Troubled Times*. London: T&T Clark.

Rahner, K. (1970). *The Trinity*. Translated by J. Donceel. New York: Herder and Herder.

Rahner, K. (1976). *Grundkurs des Glaubens: Einführung in den Begriff des Christentums*. Freiburg: Herder.

Ritschl, A. (1882). *Die Christliche Lehre von der Rechtfertigung und Versöhnung: Vol. 1*. Bonn: A. Marcus.

Robinson, D.S. (2018). *Christ and Revelatory Community in Bonhoeffer's Reception of Hegel*. Tübingen: Mohr Siebeck.

Roberts, R.H. (2005). 'Theology and Social Sciences', in Ford, D.F. and Muers, R. (eds.) *The Modern Theologians*. Oxford: Blackwell, pp. 375–377.

Rumscheidt, M. (ed.). (1988). *Adolf von Harnack: Liberal Theology at Its Height*. London: Collins.

Rumscheidt, M. (1999). 'The Formation of Bonhoeffer's Theology', in de Gruchy. J.W. (ed.) *The Cambridge Companion to Dietrich Bonhoeffer*. Cambridge: Cambridge University Press, pp. 50–70.

Scheler, M. (author), Frings, M.S. (ed.). (2005a). *Gesammelte Werke II: Der Formalismus in der Ethik und die materiale Wertethik: Neuer Versuch der Grundlegung eines ethischen Personalismus*. Bern: Francke Verlag.

Scheler, M. (author), Frings, M.S. (ed.). (2005b). *Gesammelte Werke VII: Wesen und Formen der Sympathie – Die deutsche Philosophie der Gegenwart.* Bern: Francke Verlag.

Seeberg, R. (1908). *The Fundamental Truths of the Christian Religion.* Translated by G.E. Thompson and C. Wallentin. London: Williams & Norgate.

Seeberg, R. (1927a). *Die Christliche Dogmatik: Band 1.* Erlangen: Deichert.

Seeberg, R. (1927b). *Die Christliche Dogmatik: Band 2.* Erlangen: Deichert.

Seeberg, R. (1953). *Lehrbuch der Dogmengeschichte.* Darmstadt: Wissenschaftliche Buchgesellschaft.

Sharp, G. (2011). 'Q&A: Gene Sharp', *Al Jazeera,* 6 December. Available at http://www.aljazeera.com/indepth/opinion/2011/12/20111213179492201.html. Accessed 20 September 2016.

Staats, R. (1981). 'Adolf von Harnack im Leben Dietrich Bonhoeffers', *Theologische Zeitschrift,* 37, pp. 94–122.

Taylor, K.-Y. (2016). *From #BlackLivesMatter to Black Liberation.* Chicago: Haymarket Books.

Tödt, I. (ed.). (1988). *Dietrich Bonhoeffers Hegel-Seminar 1933: Nach den Aufzeichnungen von Ferenc Lehel.* München: Chr. Kaiser.

Troeltsch, E. (1911). *Die Bedeutung der Geschichtlichkeit Jesus für den Glauben.* Tübingen: J.C.B. Mohr.

Troeltsch, E. (1912). *Protestantism and Progress: A Historical Study of the Relation of Protestantism to the Modern World.* Translated by W. Montgomery. London: Williams & Norgate.

Troeltsch, E. (1923). *Die Soziallehren der christlichen Kirchen und Gruppen.* Tübingen: J.C.B. Mohr.

von Harnack, A. (1890). *Lehrbuch der Dogmengeschichte.* Freiburg: J.C.B. Mohr.

von Harnack, A. (1900). *Geschichte der Königlich Preussischen Akademie der Wissenschaften zu Berlin.* Berlin: Reichsdruckerei.

von Harnack, A. (1902). *What Is Christianity.* Translated by T.B. Saunders. London: Williams & Norgate.

von Harnack, A. (1906a). *Reden und Aufsätze: Band 1.* Giessen: Alfred Töpelmann.

von Harnack, A. (1906b). *Reden und Aufsätze: Band 3.* Giessen: Alfred Töpelmann.

von Zahn-Harnack, A. (1951). *Adolf von Harnack.* Berlin: W. de Gruyter.

Wüstenberg, R. (1998). *Theology of Life: Dietrich Bonhoeffer's Religionless Christianity.* Translated by D. Stott. Grand Rapids: Eerdmans.

Žižek, S. (1996). *The Indivisible Remainder: An Essay on Schelling and Related Matters.* London: Verso.

Žižek, S. (1999). *The Ticklish Subject: The Absent Centre of Political Ontology.* London: Verso.

Žižek, S. (2000). *The Fragile Absolute: Or, Why Is the Christian Legacy Worth Fighting for?* London and New York: Verso.

Žižek, S. (2001a). *On Belief.* London: Routledge.

Žižek, S. (2001b). *Did Somebody Say Totalitarianism? Five Interventions in the (Mis)use of a Notion.* London and New York: Verso.

Žižek, S. (2003). *The Puppet and the Dwarf: The Perverse Core of Christianity.* London: The MIT Press.

Žižek, S. (2006). *The Parallax View.* London: The MIT Press.

Žižek, S. (2008). *On Violence.* London: Picador.

Žižek, S. (2010). *Living in the End Times.* London: Verso.

Žižek, S. (2011). *The Parallax.* Available at http://www.youtube.com/watch?v=vdwF3j1F2pg. Accessed 20 September 2016.

Žižek, S. (2012a). *Less Than Nothing: Hegel and the Shadow of Dialectical Materialism.* London: Verso.

Žižek, S. (2012b). *The Year of Dreaming Dangerously.* New York and London: Verso.

Žižek, S. (2013). 'Neighbours and Other Monsters: A Plea For Ethical Violence', in Žižek, S., Santner, E., and Reinhardt, K. (eds.) *The Neighbour: Three Inquiries in Political Theology.* Chicago: The University of Chicago Press, pp. 134–190.

Žižek, S. (2014). *Absolute Recoil: Towards a New Foundation of Dialectical Materialism.* London: Verso.

Žižek, S. (2016). *Against the Double Blackmail: Refugees, Terror and Other Troubles with the Neighbours.* London: Allen Lane.

Žižek, S. (2018). 'Marx Reads Object-Oriented Ontology', in Žižek, S., Ruda, F., and Hamza, A. *Reading Marx.* Cambridge: Polity Press, pp. 17–61.

Žižek, S. and Milbank, J. (2009). *The Monstrosity of Christ: Paradox or Dialectic?* London: The MIT Press.

CHAPTER 4

Conclusion: Radical Critical Theology

This book set out in pursuit of a critical reflection on theological thought in the discipline's contemplative context without presuppositions. An open reflection on the content and implications of theological thought whose outcome is not predetermined and thus does not result only in affirmation of its existing views, but rather allows for overcoming of the erected boundaries or walls of theological 'knowledge'. A critical theological undertaking that not only speaks into its changing cultural context but allows it to challenge its own understanding is necessary in order to become aware of and examine theology's own assumptions and their implications.

To that end, I have entered in such a reflection on the social theology of the modern theologian Dietrich Bonhoeffer expressed in his first dissertation *Sanctorum Communio*, from the perspective of Slovenian post-Marxist philosopher Slavoj Žižek's theological materialism. The ground for such an undertaking was their shared conviction about not only the sociological potential of theology but its absolute necessity.

Equipped with a Hegelian conviction about the importance of contradictions for development of thought, Marxist understanding of our complicity in their obscuring, and Lacanian understanding of the psychological processes involved, Žižek examines accounts of knowledge for their contradictions in order to bring about change. In this revolutionary thought theology's subversive political potential is discerned in escaping the sempiternal ideological cycle. Its negativity, embodiment of excess or the excluded, detaches from and challenges the coordinates of the global capitalist order,

© The Author(s) 2019
B. Koltaj, *Žižek Reading Bonhoeffer*,
Radical Theologies and Philosophies,
https://doi.org/10.1007/978-3-030-26094-1_4

a sort of ontological subversion. That is why Christ dies to the Law, rather than fulfilling it. This is the Christian experience that Žižek refers to as necessary for change, rather than it being a reference to actually existing Christianity, which is of course rejected as having reinstated the Law and thus perverse. This experience, already observed with Job in the Old Testament but fully realised by Christ, is characterised by doubt and resistance to meaning and realisation of the abstruseness and ambiguity of reality. Thus Christ's realisation is that there is no God as the big Other maintaining and directing things. In other words, what dies on the Cross is God as the big Other. Indeed, it is not only that Job doubts God and Christ realises that where there is supposed to be God there is nothing, but rather that with Job, God doubts himself and himself dies on the Cross. Whenever meaning is no longer searched for, ideology collapses. That avoidance of meaning is theological, Žižek argues, the true subversive core of theology as challenging the imposition of meaning by pointing out the excluded and thus creating tension, the place where an alternative can emerge. The alternative is the struggling universality, where community is no longer reliant on any ethnic or political identity or order but directly confronted with each other and self-organising. This community is inherently fragile and thus far from stable, always more in need of emerging rather than existing. The question of whether community without the support of the big Other can persist should, from Žižek's perspective, be reformulated into whether the community relying upon it is authentic. Rather than maintaining a community form and thus assuming a position, materialist theology challenges it by recognising the excluded within it. For Žižek, theology is critical if we are to think of socio-political change.

Žižek's 'struggling universality' of abandonment and its ethic of indifference challenging any notion of identity was then applied in consideration of Bonhoeffer's own social theology. For Bonhoeffer, it was his liberal theological faculty in Berlin that introduced and, in a way, projected him into a reflection upon the social philosophical thinkers. This was observed in particular with regards to three figures: the systematic theologian Ernst Troeltsch and his interest in the sociological realities of theology; the historian of dogma and his dissertation supervisor Reinhold Seeberg and his philosophical openness in terms of the focus on the moral and social dimensions of theological reflection; and the church historian Adolf von Harnack and his ethical concern oriented towards action and the maturity of the world come-of-age and the place of faith within it. This setting provided the context for Bonhoeffer's argument about the sociological relevance of the theological concept of the church in *Sanctorum Communio*.

Reading the text alongside Žižek's community of the Holy Spirit in a way contextualised Bonhoeffer in his attempt to deal with sociological issues theologically as a theological search for an authentic community. The contrasting of his transcendental personalist community and ethic of universal love with Žižek's materialist ontological community and ethic of indifference revealed that while they both perceive their discipline to have a complex and interdisciplinary history and nature, and they agree that the essence of social concepts is theological and that theological concepts are social, they differ on the form that community takes. For Bonhoeffer an authentic form of community can only be grounded in and by God, while for Žižek it is grounded in the absence of God as the big Other. Thus, while the former sees a community without God as totalitarian, sinful, the latter sees the community with God as abstract. While the former employs theological concepts in order to ground his understanding as a sociality of separation, the latter employs them to reveal the cracks and fissures of that imposed understanding. While the former wishes to preserve the individuality rooted in God, the latter deems that as sacrificing the sociality enabled by God's absence. While the former holds that the community, individuality and their ethical claim are maintained and mediated by God, the latter argues that true engagement only occurs when these are left to their own devices. In summary, while Bonhoeffer and Žižek agree on the sociological import of theology, they differ on the resulting sociological form—a community reliant on God or one of his absence.

In the final part of the chapter, Bonhoeffer's thoughts on the social forms—society, mass and community—were applied to contemporary struggles for social change—*Occupy* and *Black Lives Matter*—and their analysis examined with Žižek. Bonhoeffer's description of society as selfish and perverse lends itself to Žižek's understanding of contemporary capitalist society, they also both recognise the responsive nature of the challenges and affirm the transcendent nature of the new form of community. Unfortunately, due to his maintenance of the distinction of church-community as created and sustained by God, Bonhoeffer does not recognise the dialectically tense relationship between these forms and thus reduces the struggles for social change to a reflex of mass-unity that is unable to bring about an alternative. With Žižek's help, this abstract understanding was challenged through Occupy and BLM to show instead that these forms embody a tense relationship where one emerges at the cracks of the other, thus accounting for the possibility of social change, rather than insisting upon total dependence on God in bringing it about.

By bringing Bonhoeffer's theological arguments into their contemporary context, his community, necessarily grounded in and by God due to humanity's sin and guilt, was challenged as abstracting and suspending identities only through the creation of a new one. Within this new reality no one is encountered in their existence directly but rather only because of their relation to God as the big Other. Not as who they are—the monstrous and mysterious other—but as a given from the perspective of deus superanus. Insofar as it does not originate in the constitutive exposure of the subject, Bonhoeffer's interpersonalism then is not one of direct ethical intersubjectivity. Furthermore, Bonhoeffer's insistence upon total depravity, prevents understanding of the reality of society's condition, unable to imagine an alternative or even less bring about change. This very much conforms to the conviction about the current socio-political setup of financial capitalism as the end of history and thus the only imaginable change to it is in the form of the apocalyptic and the current global visions of the End are always 'from the outside' rather than bringing about change. His understanding of the social forms of society, mass and community failed to grasp the dialectical connection between them and could not account for the possibility of social change. The question presents itself about the sociological potential that Bonhoeffer argues the church-community represents. Does its abstraction not represent a withdrawal from the Real conditions of the subject, community and their existence which has to be mediated through God? Does the presentation of God as their only hope for social change not result in alienation? A sort of retreat to a world that is not contingent but rather finished and stable as it is maintained by the transcendent. If, as Holsclaw argues, this understanding of the world as stable is the only means to freedom, then it negates the very possibility of change. The question emerges whether there is sufficient ground for such an understanding in the history of theological thought? While there are many elements that assert the control and stability of the world, there are also plenty of elements, starting with biblical texts, that testify to change not only of the world but also of our understanding of it and the role of the transcendent within it. After all, theological thinking cannot be carried out without reflecting critically on its content, presuppositions and their implications in the variety of its contexts, observing its manifestation through constant sublation. True, Bonhoeffer did attempt to overcome this problem later on through the concept of religionless Christianity that would represent engagement with a mature world where we must live without God. However, even this god-less living is mediated by God—'before and with God'—and insists on the concepts of transcendental God, sin and guilt. Those are the very grounding of his vicarious representation. Perhaps then, the challenge of how to repeat Bonhoeffer is to venture beyond the regulating of the big Other in pursuit of a community that is not marked by abstraction but understanding of and participation in an unfinished and contingent world where change is possible. Can we think theologically in such an engaged manner without constantly checking our sleeves for the trump card of transcendence and the duality of societies? A theological engagement that does not withdraw from the real conditions of the subject, community and their existence? A theological endeavour of this kind is above all critical. What form do theological concepts, such as God, church and sin, take in such an understanding? Exploration of this can only take place if we do not predetermine the outcome in any way.[1]

As proposed in the introduction and argued throughout, critical reflection on theological thought without presuppositions is not only possible but ontologically necessary for it is true to theology's critical character of challenging narratives and revealing exceptions in search of truth. Only in this way is the latter not reduced to a pitting of views or enforcing of position but constantly challenges its perceived dogma by pointing out its cracks, thus developing its own understanding. Does that mean that the only advantage of such a radical critical theology is negative, continually challenging a position and not providing one? I argue that this negativity becomes positive when we perceive that its accession to a position leads inevitably, not to an expansion and implementation but, a narrowing and diminishing of theology's potential, threatening to supplant entirely its radical character in the service of a position. Such an understanding of theology pursued in this book then is no doubt characteristically negative—a critique rather than a doctrine—but is for that reason functionally positive. Luke 17: 33 reads: 'Those who try to make their life secure will lose it, but those who lose their life will keep it'. This book has been an attempt at engaged reflection upon theological thought that does not retreat from the unfinished and contingent reality to a longed-for finished and definite one

---

[1] In my recent article 'Critical Theology: Why Hegel Now?' (2019), I have written about what such an imagined radical critical theology would look like in practice and, with the help of Hegel, outlined its envisaged reflection upon theological conceptions.

that is preordained by the big Other. Instead, it challenges any perception of stability and completeness, unmasks and deflates their temptation and topples their certitude, and is thereby an integral part of bringing about change. A radical critical theology.

Reference

Koltaj, B. (2019). 'Critical Theology: Why Hegel Now?' *International Journal of Philosophy and Theology*, https://doi.org/10.1080/21692327.2019.1581654.

CHAPTER 5

Afterword by Slavoj Žižek: The Fall That Makes Us Like God

After reading Koltaj's study with great admiration, I decided to focus in this brief afterword on a very specific topic: the challenge posed to the Christian theology by the vision (or, rather, hypothesis) of so-called Singularity. I am not dealing here with the technological feasibility of the project of Singularity (there are serious doubts about it), I just want to confront two different logics of the Fall and Redemption. The stakes of this difference are not only theological but also political: if one wants to preserve the emancipatory core of Christianity, it is crucial to remain faithful to the authentic Christian notion of Redemption. So let me begin by Michael Zimmerman's concise formulation of the project of Singularity which was elaborated in popular terms by Ray Kurzweil:

> the confluence of nanotechnology, artificial intelligence, robotics, and genetic engineering will soon produce posthuman beings that will far surpass us in power and intelligence. Just as black holes constitute a "singularity" from which no information can escape, posthumans will constitute a "singularity:" whose aims and capacities lie beyond our ken. Technological posthumanists, whether wittingly or unwittingly, draw upon the long-standing Christian discourse of "theosis," according to which humans are capable of being God or god-like. From St. Paul and Luther to Hegel and Kurzweil, the idea of human self-deification plays a prominent role. Hegel in particular emphasises that God becomes wholly actualized only in the process by which humanity achieves absolute consciousness. Kurzweil agrees that God becomes fully actual only through historical processes that illuminate and thus transform the

© The Author(s) 2019
B. Koltaj, *Žižek Reading Bonhoeffer*,
Radical Theologies and Philosophies,
https://doi.org/10.1007/978-3-030-26094-1_5

entire universe. The difference is that for Kurzweil and many other posthumanists, our offspring — the posthumans — will carry out this extraordinary process.[1]

Or, to quote Kurzweil himself from *The Singularity Is Near*: our civilization will 'expand outward, turning all the dumb matter and energy we encounter into sublimely intelligent—transcendent—matter and energy. So in a sense, we can say that the Singularity will ultimately infuse the universe with spirit'.[2] In short, Singularity is for Kurzweil 'a turning point in the evolutionary process that will give rise to extraordinary beings capable of awaking the entire material universe. Such an awakening may be viewed as actualizing a potential present from the very beginning. By capitalising "Singularity", posthumanists suggest that the event is not merely important, but numinous, that is, possessing what amounts to a sacred dimension. Posthumanists such as Kurzweil represent the future in ways consistent with at least some conceptions of God'. Therein resides the gnostic hypothesis of transhumanists:

> post-humans will eventually transform the entire universe into an all-powerful intelligence resembling in important respects the monotheistic God. Kurzweil's God does not transcend nature, but instead brings nature to the zenith of its intrinsic possibilities. /.../ only through humankind can such divine self-consciousness occur. After positing an Other to itself in the form of nature, which is Geist extended in space, Geist subsequently manifests itself as conscious humankind, which then sets about to know and thus to assimilate Otherness constituted by extended nature. Material things are "petrified intelligence" extended in space, whereas consciousness is liquefied intelligence unfolding through time (history). Estranged from the idea, nature is only the corpse of the understanding. Nature is, however, only implicitly the idea, and Schelling therefore called her a petrified intelligence, others even a frozen intelligence, but God does not remain petrified and dead, the very stones cry out and raise themselves to spirit [Geist].

The Hegelian (or, more broadly, German Idealist) references are clearly spelled out here, as well as the gap that separates the idea of Singularity from

---

[1] Michael E. Zimmerman, "The Singularity: A Crucial Phase in Divine Self-actualization?", Available at http://cosmosandhistory.org/index.php/journal/article/viewFile/107/213. Non-attributed quotes that follow are from this essay.

[2] Quoted from Zimmerman, op. cit.

the space of German Idealism. Inert material reality gets gradually spiritualized through the process of actualizing its spiritual immanent potentials. The first peak of this process is human intelligence in which Spirit becomes aware of itself, returns back to itself from its alienation/externalisation in material reality. But at this stage, Spirit remains opposed to reality, it becomes aware of itself as individual consciousness opposed to material reality. In order to fully actualize itself, Spirit has to overcome this opposition and become aware of itself as the spiritual dimension, the spiritual inner life, of the entire (material) reality itself. At this level, my self-consciousness overlaps with the self-consciousness of entire reality itself, or, in theological terms, my awareness of God is simultaneously the self-awareness of God himself. God is not an entity outside the process of reality which steers it from a safe distance; the process of reality is the process that takes place in God himself, it overlaps with the becoming of God himself. For theorists of Singularity, however, we, finite humans, cannot actualize the full unity of Spirit and reality—our separate individual awareness is a too strong obstacle. Reconciliation of reality with Spirit is achieved only when we renounce our separated individuality and become one with the Spirit which permeates reality itself, when our self-consciousness experiences itself as the self-awareness of reality itself… It is clear from, this short description, that the project of Singularity aims at nothing less than the overcoming of the Fall in the biblical sense of the term: hard work, bearing children… we all know the description from *Genesis* 3. Enough has been written about the paradoxes contained in it, especially about the most obvious one: why did God submit Adam and Eve to what is effectively a forced choice? Here is Stephen Greenblatt's version of this paradox which even mentions Elon Musk, one of the proponents of Singularity:

> Ancient commentators repeatedly asked why the God in the story, having commanded Adam and Eve not to eat of the tree of the knowledge of good and evil, did not do more to prevent them from the disastrous act of disobedience. To be sure, the Creator warned them that death would follow any violation of his prohibition, but how could the first humans have possibly understood what it meant to die? Why was the tree rooted in the very midst of the garden and not locked away, the way we lock away poison (or nuclear waste)? And how, before they had acquired knowledge of good and evil, could humans in their Edenic innocence have ever grasped the moral significance of what they were doing? Adam and Eve manifestly had insufficient knowledge of the long-term consequences of their actions, and God,

who could have implanted this knowledge in them far more easily than Elon Musk's proposed chip, evidently chose not to do so.[3]

More important for our purpose is the paradox of knowing: the serpent tells Eve that after eating the apple from the forbidden tree, 'you will be like God, knowing good and evil', and, as Hegel notices, the serpent doesn't lie – God immediately confirms it commenting that Adam and Eve are now 'like one of us' (let's ignore here the mysterious plural of gods). So how can eating the apple which brings knowledge and divinity throw the first humans into the misery of mortal life and ignorance? The standard explanation is, of course, that, by way of imposing on them a hard choice, biased as it is, God is bestowing on first humans their freedom, making them aware of their responsibility to choose between good and evil. Even the limitation of knowledge serves this purpose: if our knowledge is perfect, if all the details of the situation are clearly present in our mind, the choice is easy, but what makes a moral choice hard is precisely that we have to decide in a murky situation where the full burden of decision is upon us... In the continuation of the quoted passage, Greenblatt provides a succinct version of this argument:

> Virtually all the early interpreters agreed that the Creator did not want to compromise the essential nature of humans by taking away their freedom to choose, even though that freedom was the source of so much trouble and misery. If Adam and Eve knew everything that would follow from their actions – if they could make the inconceivably vast calculations that would give them, in Shakespeare's words, 'the future in the instant' – they might have avoided their catastrophic blunder, but it would, the Genesis story suggests, have been at the cost of their humanity. / This is not a celebration of ignorance or fecklessness. There was, after all, an explicit warning, however difficult it might have been for the first humans to interpret it correctly, and the consequences of the fateful choice were manifestly terrible. But the Bible represents humans neither as automata – the slaves of God – nor as miraculous sages, endowed with all the knowledge they need to make the inevitably correct decisions.[4]

---

[3] Quoted from https://www.theguardian.com/commentisfree/2018/dec/23/elon-musk-neuralink-chip-brain-implants-humanity.

[4] Quoted from op. cit.

However, the central enigma remains: in what precise way morality (knowing the difference between good and evil and acting upon it) implies ignorance (or, at least, a radical limitation of our knowledge)? The philosopher who confronted this issue and provided the only consequent answer was Kant. When Kant says that he reduced the domain of knowledge in order to make space for religious faith, he is to be taken quite literally, in a radically anti-Spinozist way: From the Kantian perspective, Spinoza's position appears as a nightmarish vision of subjects reduced to marionettes. What, exactly, does a marionette stand for as a subjective stance? In Kant, we find the term 'marionette' in a mysterious subchapter of his *Critique of Practical Reason* entitled 'Of the Wise Adaptation of Man's Cognitive Faculties to His Practical Vocation', in which he endeavours to answer the question of what would happen to us if we were to gain access to the noumenal domain, to the *Ding an sich*:

> Instead of the conflict which now the moral disposition has to wage with inclinations and in which, after some defeats, moral strength of mind may be gradually won, God and eternity in their awful majesty would stand unceasingly before our eyes. /…/ Thus most actions conforming to the law would be done from fear, few would be done from hope, none from duty. The moral worth of actions, on which alone the worth of the person and even of the world depends in the eyes of supreme wisdom, would not exist at all. The conduct of man, so long as his nature remained as it is now, would be changed into mere mechanism, where, as in a puppet show, everything would gesticulate well but no life would be found in the figures.[5]

So, for Kant, direct access to the noumenal domain would deprive us of the very 'spontaneity' which forms the kernel of transcendental freedom: it would turn us into lifeless automata, or, to put it in today's terms, into 'thinking machines'. And is this not ultimately presented as achievable in the prospect of Singularity? This prospect is not to be dismissed as yet another 'ontic' scientific research project of no authentic philosophical interest since it offers something effectively new and unheard-of which challenges our status of being-human: the prospect of actual (empirical) overcoming of our finitude/sexuality/embeddedness-in-the-symbolic. Entering this other dimension of Singularity becomes a simple positive fact, not a matter of sublime inner experience. What does this mean, for the status

---

[5]Immanuel Kant, *Critique of Practical Reason*, London: Macmillan 1956, pp. 152–153.

of our subjectivity and for our self-experience? Can we imagine a form of self-awareness that would be at the level of selfless floating in the space of Singularity?

Insofar as 'Fall' designates the wound (of separation, of the constitutive loss) which characterises our being-human as finite and sexed, proponents of Singularity want to heal the wound literally: to fill in the gap, to have man united with God by way of making him god-like, i.e. by way of providing him with properties and capacities which we (till now) experienced as 'divine'. What makes this option properly traumatic is that it turns around the gap that separates our ordinary daily experience from sublime speculations about our proximity to God. When someone talks about experiencing unity with God, a realist tells him to calm down: 'Don't get lost in your dreams, remember that you are still rooted in this miserable earthly reality!' But with the prospect of Singularity, the reply to this 'realist' view is easy: 'We are the true realists, we can provide divine immortality in our empirical reality, and it is you who still believes that the our material mortality is the ultimate horizon of our being that I effectively dreaming – you cling to the old notion of reality, ignoring the big breakthrough!'

As we have already seen, (some) proponents of Singularity read it in a Hegelian way, as the final reconciliation between Mind and Reality, as the healing of the wound of the Fall. However, such a reading is totally incompatible with Hegel's interpretation of the Fall. According to the standard reading of Paul, God gave Law to men in order to make them conscious of their sin, even to make them sin all the more, and thus make them aware of their need for salvation which can occur only through divine grace—however, does this reading not involve a strange perverse notion of God? The only way to avoid such a perverse reading is to insist on the absolute identity of the two gestures: God does not FIRST push us into Sin in order to create the need for Salvation, and THEN offer Himself as the Redeemer from the trouble into which He got us in the first place; it is not that the Fall is followed by Redemption: The Fall is identical to Redemption, it is 'in itself' already Redemption. That is to say, what IS 'redemption'? The explosion of freedom, the breaking out of the natural enchainment—and this, precisely, is what happens in the Fall. One should bear in mind here the central tension of the Christian notion of the Fall: the Fall ('regression' to the natural state, enslavement to passions) is stricto sensu identical with the dimension FROM WHICH we fall, i.e. it is the very movement of the Fall that creates, opens up, what is lost in it.

We all know the line '*die Wunde schliesst der Speer nur der Sie schlug*' from the finale of Wagner's *Parsifal*. Hegel says the same thing, although with the accent shifted in the opposite direction: the Spirit is itself the wound it tries to heal, i.e. the wound is self-inflicted. That is to say, what is 'Spirit' at its most elementary? The 'wound' of nature: subject is the immense—absolute—power of negativity, of introducing a gap/cut into the given-immediate substantial unity, the power of differentiating, of 'abstracting', of tearing apart and treating as self-standing what in reality is part of an organic unity. This is why the notion of the 'self-alienation' of Spirit (of Spirit losing itself in its otherness, in its objectivization, in its result) is more paradoxical than it may appear: it should be read together with Hegel's assertion of the thoroughly non-substantial character of Spirit: there is no *res cogitans*, no thing which (as its property) also thinks, spirit is nothing but the process of overcoming natural immediacy, of the cultivation of this immediacy, of withdrawing-into-itself or 'taking off' from it, of—why not—alienating itself from it. The paradox is thus that there is no Self that precedes the Spirit's 'self-alienation': the very process of alienation creates/generates the 'Self' from which Spirit is alienated and to which it then returns. (Hegel here turns around the standard notion that a failed version of X presupposes this X as their norm (measure): X is created, its space is outlined, only through repetitive failures to reach it.) Spirit's self-alienation is the same as, fully coincides with, its alienation from its Other (nature), because it constitutes itself through its 'return-to-itself' from its immersion into natural Otherness. In other words, Spirit's return-to-itself creates the very dimension to which it returns. (This holds for all 'returns to origins': when, from nineteenth century onwards, new Nation States were constituting themselves in Central and Eastern Europe, their discovery and return to 'old ethnic roots' generated these roots.)

What this means is that the 'negation of negation', the 'return-to-oneself' from alienation, does not occur where it seems to: in the 'negation of negation', Spirit's negativity is not relativized, subsumed under an encompassing positivity; it is, on the contrary, the 'simple negation' which remains attached to the presupposed positivity it negated, the presupposed Otherness from which it alienates itself, and the 'negation of negation' is nothing but the negation of the substantial character of this Otherness itself, the full acceptance of the abyss of Spirit's self-relating which retroactively posits all its presuppositions. In other words, once we are in negativity, we never quit it and regain the lost innocence of Origins; it is, on the contrary, only in 'negation of negation' that the Origins are truly lost, that their very loss is lost, that they are deprived of the substantial status of that which was lost. The Spirit heals its wound not by directly healing it, but by getting rid of the very full and sane Body into which the wound was cut. It is in this precise sense that, according to Hegel, 'the wounds of the Spirit heal, and leave no scars behind'[6]: Hegel's point is not that the Spirit heals its wounds so perfectly that, in a magic gesture of retroactive sublation, even their scars disappear; the point is rather that, in the course of a dialectical process, a shift of perspective occurs which makes the wound itself appear as its opposite—the wound itself is its own healing when perceived from another standpoint. At its sharpest, this coincidence of the opposites appears apropos self-consciousness, i.e. subject as thinking:

> Abstractly, being evil means singularizing myself in a way that cuts me off from the universal (which is the rational, the laws, the determinations of spirit). But along with this separation there arises being-for-itself and for the first time the universally spiritual, laws – what ought to be. So it is not the case that /rational/ consideration has an external relationship to evil: it is itself what is evil.[7]

And this brings us to *Genesis*: does the story of the Fall not say exactly the same thing? The serpent promises Adam and Eve that, by eating the fruit of the tree of knowledge, THEY will become like God; and after the two do it, God says: 'Behold, Adam has become like one of us'.(*Genesis* 3:22) Hegel's comment is: 'So the serpent did not lie, for God confirms what it said'. Then he goes on to reject the claim that what God says is meant with irony: 'Cognition is the principle of spirituality, and this /.../ is also the principle by which the injury of the separation is healed. It is in this principle of cognition that the principle of "divinity" is also posited'.[8] Subjective knowledge is not just the possibility to choose evil or good, 'it is the consideration or the cognition that makes people evil, so that consideration and cognition /themselves/ are what is evil, and that /therefore/ such cognition is what ought not to exist /because it/ is the source of evil'.[9] This is how one should understand Hegel's dictum from his

[6]G.W.F. Hegel, *Phenomenology of Spirit*, Oxford: Oxford University Press 1977, p. 129.

[7]G.W.F. Hegel, *Vorlesungen ueber die Philosophie der Religion II*, Frankfurt: Suhrkamp Verlag 1969, p. 206.

[8]Hegel, op. cit., p. 207.

[9]Op. cit., p. 205.

Phenomenology that Evil is the gaze itself which perceives Evil everywhere around it: the gaze which sees Evil excludes itself from the social Whole it criticises, and this exclusion is the formal characteristics of Evil. And Hegel's point is that the Good emerges as a possibility and duty only through this primordial/constitutive choice of Evil: we experience the Good when, after choosing Evil, we become aware of the utter inadequacy of our situation.

Pathbreaking as it is, one should say that this Hegel's reading of *Genesis* is too short at two (connected) topics, and the reason is not that Hegel a prisoner of his time to see the dimension he misses—much more paradoxically, in both cases, Hegel is here not Hegelian enough, he fails to make here a properly Hegelian twist. First, when he characterises an evil person, Hegel reduces evil to the moment of particularity in its opposition to universality (natural egotism, selfish behaviour…) This is why, as Hegel points out, every consistent figure of Evil has to display some features of Goodness—as one would expect, Hegel mentions Devil in Milton's Paradise Lost who is obviously a figure of great personal power, pursuing a project that he experiences as profoundly ethical… But was not at this point Schelling (in his On the Essence of Human Freedom) much more profound when he decoded in Evil a principled ('non-pathological' in Kant's sense) stance which is as such radically spiritual? True Evil has nothing to do with particular egotism and selfish interests but is a positive spiritual project for which people are ready even to sacrifice their lives (as Nazis did in order to exterminate Jews or dedicated Stalinist Communists did in order to crush the Trotskist or kulak resistance). If Hegel were to be fully consistent with the core of his own thought, he should even say that Good itself is nothing but universalized Evil, an Evil which wins over others and acquires the position of universality. Therein resides also Hegel's critique of abstract universality: for him, the French revolutionaries were evil in their terror precisely because they were thoroughly principled and ruthlessly pursued a universality which ultimately excluded all particular content. So when particular content is not reconciled with universality, the guilt is even more on the side of 'abstract' universality.

This brings us to the second of Hegel's limitations which is even more important for our concern. When Hegel characterizes Evil as *Entzweiung*, separation, self-division of the Absolute, he quietly ignores (in his reading if the Fall) the key fact that, when the Absolute is opposed to the 'fallen' particularity, the true guilt and responsibility are on the side of the Absolute itself. Back to the story of the Fall: What Hegel should have said (since it follows clearly from the inner logic of his thought) is that in all this affair the truly evil character is God Himself who pushes the first humans into the Fall, and what makes things even worse is that, instead of doing it openly, he as it were washes his hands and presents the Fall as the consequence of a 'free' human decision… This is why Christianity culminates in crucifixion, a scene in which the *Entzweiung* (which for Hegel formally defines Evil) is directly and explicitly transposed from the split between God and humans into God himself who (at the terrifying moment of 'Father, why have you abandoned me?') is split from himself? The category to be used apropos this displacement of the gap that separates us from God to a gap that separates God from himself is disparity, a term which occurs three times in a key passage from the Foreword to Hegel's Phenomenology of Spirit where he provides the most concise explanation of what it means to conceive Substance also as Subject:

> The disparity which exists in consciousness between the "I" and the substance which is its object is the distinction between them, the negative in general. This can be regarded as the defect of both, though it is their soul, or that which moves them. That is why some of the ancients conceived the void as the principle of motion, for they rightly saw the moving principle as the negative, though they did not as yet grasp that the negative is the self. Now, although this negative appears at first as a disparity between the "I" and its object, it is just as much the disparity of the substance with itself. Thus what seems to happen outside of it, to be an activity directed against it, is really its own doing, and Substance shows itself to be essentially Subject.[10]

Crucial is the final reversal: The disparity between subject and substance is simultaneously the disparity of the substance with itself—or, to put it in Lacan's terms, disparity means that the lack of the subject is simultaneously the lack in the Other: Subjectivity emerges when substance cannot achieve full identity with itself, when substance is in itself 'barred', traversed by an immanent impossibility or antagonism. In short, the subject's epistemological ignorance, its failure to fully grasp the opposed substantial content, simultaneously indicates a limitation/failure/lack of the substantial content itself.

Therein also resides the key dimension of the theological revolution of Christianity: the alienation of man from God has to be projected/transferred back into God itself, as the alienation of God from itself

---

[10]G.W.F. Hegel, *Phenomenology of Spirit*, p. 21.

(this is the speculative content of the notion of divine kenosis)—this is the Christian version of Hegel's insight into how the disparity of subject and substance implies the disparity of substance with regard to itself. This is why the unity of man and God is enacted in Christianity in a way which fundamentally differs from the way of pagan religions where man has to strive to overcome his fall from God through the effort to purify his being from material filth and elevate himself to rejoin God. In Christianity, on the contrary, God falls from itself, he becomes a finite mortal human abandoned by God (in the figure of Christ and his lament on the cross 'Father, why have you forsaken me?'), and man can only achieve unity with God by identifying with this God, God abandoned by itself.

Again, in his reading of *Genesis*, Hegel ignores this aspect: He only talks about the separation of man from God, and fails to mention that the reconciliation of God and man is also (primarily even) the reconciliation of God WITH HIMSELF—it is only through the reconciliation with humans that God truly becomes God (in the true concrete universality of this notion), so reconciliation between God and humanity is a key event in and for God himself... However, Hegel's main insight remains fully valid and pertinent: For Hegel, we, humans, reach immortality and infinity not by way of undoing the Fall, by way of somehow getting rid of the obstacle of our finite bodily existence and moving to another dimension of some higher reality, but by way of reconciling ourselves with (what appeared as) the obstacle and accepting that this 'obstacle' plays the positive role of sustaining the space of what it appears as the obstacle to.

God's greatest gift to us is our freedom, but we are free only insofar as God is alienated from Himself.

Bibliography

Agamben, G. (1998). *Homo Sacer: Sovereign Power and Bare Life*. Translated by D. Heller-Roazen. Stanford: Stanford University Press.

Agamben, G. (2002). *What Remains of Auschwitz: The Witness and the Archive*. Translated by D. Heller-Roazen. Stanford: Stanford University Press.

Agamben, G. (2005). *The Time That Remains: A Commentary on the Letter to the Romans*. Translated by P. Dailey. Stanford: Stanford University Press.

Althusser, L. (1971). *Lenin and Philosophy and Other Essays*. Translated by B. Brewster. London: New Left Books.

Althusser, L. (1972). *Politics and History: Montesquieu, Rousseau, Marx*. Translated by B. Brewster. London: New Left Books.

Althusser, L. (1997). *The Spectre of Hegel: Early Writings*. Translated by G.M. Goshgarian. London: Verso.

Anselm. (1898). *Cur Deus Homo?* London: Griffith Farrar.

Augustine. (1950–1954). *The City of God*. Washington, DC: The Catholic University of America Press.

Augustine. (1961). *The Confessions of St. Augustine*. Translated by R.S. Pine-Coffin. Middlesex: Penguin Books.

Badiou, A. (2003). *Saint Paul: The Foundation of Universalism*. Translated by R. Brassier. Stanford: Stanford University Press.

Badiou, A. (2006). *Being and Event*. Translated by O. Feltham. London: Continuum.

Badiou, A. and Balmès, F. (1976). *De l'ideology*. Paris: Francois Maspero.

Bady, A. and Konczal, M. (2012). 'From Master Plan to No Plan: The Slow Death of Public Higher Education', *Dissent Magazine* (Fall) [Online].

Available at http://www.dissentmagazine.org/article/from-master-plan-to-no-plan-the-slow-death-of-public-higher-education. Accessed 20 September 2016.

Barth, K. (1933). *The Epistle to the Romans*. Translated by E.C. Hoskins. London: Oxford University Press.

Barth, K. (1975). *Church Dogmatics I.1: Doctrine of the Word of God: Prolegomena to Church Dogmatics*. Edinburgh: T&T Clark.

Barth, K. (2003). *Church Dogmatics III.4: The Doctrine of Creation—The Command of God and the Creator*. Study edition. Translated by G.W. Bromiley. London and New York: T&T Clark.

Barth, K. (2010a). *Church Dogmatics IV.2: The Doctrine of Reconciliation*. Study edition. Translated by G.W. Bromiley. London and New York: T&T Clark.

Barth, K. (2010b). *Church Dogmatics IV.3.2: The Doctrine of Reconciliation*. Study edition. Translated by G.W. Bromiley. London and New York: T&T Clark.

Bayer, O. (1992). *Leibliches Wort: Reformation und Neuzeit im Konflikt*. Tübingen: J.C.B. Mohr.

Becker, B.W. (2019). 'From Psychoanalysis to Metamorphosis: The Lacanian Limits of Žižek's Theology', in Mitralexis, S. and Skliris, D. (eds.) *Slavoj Žižek and Christianity*. New York: Routledge, pp. 67–85.

Benjamin, W. (1920–1921). 'Zur Kritik der Gewalt', in Benjamin, W. *Walter Benjamin Gesammelte Schriften. Band II. 1*. Frankfurt am Main: Suhrkamp, pp. 179–204.

Benjamin, W. (1968). *Illuminations*. Translated by H. Zohn. New York: Schocken Books.

Benjamin, W. (author), Tiedemann, R. (ed.). (1972–1999). *Walter Benjamin Gesammelte Schriften. Sieben Bände*. Frankfurt am Main: Suhrkamp.

Bentley, J. (1982). *Between Marx and Christ: The Dialogue in German-Speaking Europe 1870–1970*. London: New Left Books.

Bethge, E. (1961). 'The Challenge of Dietrich Bonhoeffer's Life and Theology', *The Chicago Seminary Register*, 51(2), pp. 1–38.

Bethge, E. (1963). 'The Challenge of Dietrich Bonhoeffer's Life and Theology', in Smith, R.G. (ed.) *World Come of Age*. Philadelphia: Fortress Press, pp. 22–88.

Bethge, E. (1967). *Dietrich Bonhoeffer: Theologe – Christ – Zeitgenosse*. München: C. Kaiser Verlag.

Bethge, E. (1968). 'Bonhoeffer's Christology and His "Religionless Christianity"', *Union Seminary Quarterly Review*, 23(1), pp. 61–77.

Bethge, E. (1994). *Dietrich Bonhoeffer: Eine Biographie*. Gütersloh: C. Kaiser.

Bethge, E. (1999). *Dietrich Bonhoeffer mit Selbstbezeugnissen und Bilddokumenten*. Reinbek bei, Hamburg: Rowohlt.

Bethge, E., Bethge, R., and Gemmels, C. (eds.). (1986). *Dietrich Bonhoeffer: Sein Leben in Bildern und Texten*. München: C. Kaiser.

Blanton, W. (2013). 'Paul and the Philosophers: Return to a New Archive', in Blanton, W. and de Vries, H. (eds.) *Paul and the Philosophers*. New York: Fordham University Press, pp. 1–38.

Blanton, W. and de Vries, H. (eds.). (2013). *Paul and the Philosophers*. New York: Fordham University Press.

Boer, R. (2009). *Criticism of Heaven: On Marxism and Theology*. Chicago: Haymarket Books.

Bonhoeffer, D. (1996–2014). *Dietrich Bonhoeffer Works. 17 Volumes*. Minneapolis: Fortress Press.

Bonhoeffer, D. (1996). *Dietrich Bonhoeffer Works. Volume 2: Act and Being—Transcendental Philosophy and Ontology in Systematic Theology*. Translated by M. Rumscheidt. Minneapolis: Fortress Press.

Bonhoeffer, D. (2003). *Dietrich Bonhoeffer Works. Volume 4: Discipleship*. Translated by B. Green and R. Krauss. Minneapolis: Fortress Press.

Bonhoeffer, D. (2004). *Dietrich Bonhoeffer Works. Volume 5: Life Together and Prayerbook of the Bible*. Translated by J.H. Burtness. Minneapolis: Fortress Press.

Bonhoeffer, D. (2006). *Dietrich Bonhoeffer Works. Volume 16: Conspiracy and Imprisonment 1940–1945*. Translated by L.E. Dahill. Minneapolis: Fortress Press.

Bonhoeffer, D. (2006). *Dietrich Bonhoeffer Works. Volume 6: Ethics*. Translated by K. Krauss, C.C. West, and D.W. Stott. Minneapolis: Fortress Press.

Bonhoeffer, D. (2007a). *Dietrich Bonhoeffer Works. Volume 13: London 1933–1935*. Translated by I. Best. Minneapolis: Fortress Press.

Bonhoeffer, D. (2007b). *Dietrich Bonhoeffer Works. Volume 3: Creation and Fall—A Theological Exposition of Genesis 1–3*. Translated by D.S. Bax. Minneapolis: Fortress Press.

Bonhoeffer, D. (2008) *Dietrich Bonhoeffer Works. Volume 10: Barcelona, Berlin, New York: 1928–1931*. Translated by D.W. Stott. Minneapolis: Fortress Press.

Bonhoeffer, D. (2009a). *Dietrich Bonhoeffer Works. Volume 1: Sanctorum Communio—A Theological Study of the Sociology of the Church*. Translated by R. Krauss and N. Lukens. Minneapolis: Fortress Press.

Bonhoeffer, D. (2009b). *Dietrich Bonhoeffer Works. Volume 12: Berlin: 1932–1933*. Translated by D.W. Stott, I. Best, and D. Higgins. Minneapolis: Fortress Press.

Bonhoeffer, D. (2010). *Dietrich Bonhoeffer Works. Volume 8: Letters and Papers from Prison*. Translated by I. Best, L.E. Dahill, R. Krauss, and N. Lukens. Minneapolis: Fortress Press.

Boucher, G. (2005). 'The Law as Thing: Žižek and the Graph of Desire', in Boucher, G. Glynos, J., and Sharpe, M. (eds.) *Traversing the Fantasy: Critical Responses to Slavoj Žižek*. Aldershot: Ashgate, pp. 23–46.

Boucher, G., Glynos, J., and Sharpe, M. (eds.). (2005). *Traversing the Fantasy: Critical Responses to Slavoj Žižek*. Aldershot: Ashgate.

Bowie M. (1979). 'Jacques Lacan', in Sturrock, J. (ed.) *Structuralism and Since*. Oxford: Oxford University Press, pp. 116–153.

Boyton, R. (2001). 'Enjoy Your Žižek: An Excitable Slovenian Philosopher Examines the Obscene Practices of Everyday Life, Including His Own,' *Linguafranca*, 26 (March 2001). Available at http://linguafranca.mirror.theinfo.org/9810/zizek.html. Accessed 20 September 2016.

Bultmann, R. (1933). 'Die Aufgabe der Theologie in der gegenwärtigen situation', *Theologische Blätter* XII, pp. 161–166.

Busch Nielsen, K., Nissen, U., and Tietz, C. (eds.). (2007). *Mysteries in the Theology of Dietrich Bonhoeffer*. Göttingen: Vandenhoeck & Ruprecht.

Butler, J., Laclau, E., and Žižek, S. (2000). *Contingency, Hegemony, Universality: Contemporary Dialogues on the Left*. London and New York: Verso.

Caputo, J.D. (2009). 'The Monstrosity of Christ: Paradox or Dialectic?'. Review of *Monstrosity of Christ*, by S. Žižek and J. Milbank. *Notre Dame Philosophical Reviews* [Online]. Available at http://ndpr.nd.edu/review.cfm?id=17605 Accessed 20 September 2016.

Chesterton, G.K. (1916). *The Book of Job*. London: C. Palmer & Hayword.

Chesterton, G.K. (1996). *Orthodoxy*. New York: Doubleday.

Chesterton, G.K. (2006). *The Complete Father Brown Stories*. Ware: Wordsworth Editions.

Chieza, L. (2006). 'Pasolini, Badiou, Žižek und das Erbe der christlichen Liebe', in de Kessel, M., and Hoens, D. (eds.) *Wieder Religion? Christentum in zeitgenössischen kritischen Denken*. Wien: Turia & Kant, pp. 107–126.

Clar, A.C. and Mawson, M. (eds.). *Ontology and Ethics: Bonhoeffer and Contemporary Scholarship*. Eugene: Pickwick Publications.

Collier, A. (2001). *Christianity and Marxism: A Philosophical Contribution to Their Reconciliation*. London: Routledge.

Cremer, A.H. (1903). *Die Grundwahrheiten der christlichen Religion nach Dr. R. Seeberg*. Gütersloh: Bertelsmann.

Dahill, L.E. (2009). *Reading from the Underside of Selfhood: Bonhoeffer and the Spiritual Formation*. Eugene, OR: Pickwick Publications.

Dahill, L.E. (2013). '"There's Some Contradiction Here": Gender and the Relation of *Above* and *Below* in Bonhoeffer', in Frick, P. (ed.) *Bonhoeffer and Interpretive Theory: Essays on Method and Understanding*. Frankfurt am Main: Peter Lang, pp. 53–84.

Davis, C., Milbank, J., and Žižek, S. (eds.). (2005). *Theology and the Political: The New Debate*. Durham: Duke University Press.

Davis, C., Milbank, J., and Žižek, S. (eds.). (2010). *Paul's New Moment: Continental Philosophy and the Future of Christian Theology*. Grand Rapids: Brazos Press.

de Gruchy, J. (1999). *The Cambridge Companion to Dietrich Bonhoeffer*. Cambridge: Cambridge University Press.

DeJonge, M.P. (2012). *Bonhoeffer's Theological Formation: Berlin, Barth, and Protestant Theology*. Oxford: Oxford University Press.

de Kessel, M. and Hoens, D. (eds.). (2006). *Wieder Religion? Christentum in zeitgenössischen kritischen Denken*. Wien: Turia & Kant.

Delpech-Ramey, J. (2010). 'Supernatural Capital: A Note on the Žižek-Milbank Debate', *Political Theology*, 11(1), pp. 122–123.

de Lubac, H. (2007). *Corpus Mysticum: The Eucharist and the Church in the Middle Ages*. Translated by G.C.J. Simmonds, R. Price, and C. Stephens. Notre Dame: University of Notre Dame Press.

Depoortere, F. (2008). *Christ in Postmodern Philosophy: Gianni Vattimo, René Girard and Slavoj Žižek*. London and New York: T&T Clark.

de Vries, H. and Sullivan, L.E. (eds.). (2006). *Political Theologies: Public Religions in a Post-Secular World*. New York: Fordham University Press.

D'Isanto, L. (1992). 'Bonhoeffer's Hermeneutical Model of Community', *Union Theological Seminary Quarterly Review*, 46, pp. 135–148.

Dramm, S. (2001). *Dietrich Bonhoeffer: Eine Einführung in sein Denken*. Gütersloh: C. Kaiser and Gütersloher Verlag. English: (2007) *Dietrich Bonhoeffer: An Introduction to His Thought*. Translated by T. Rice. Peabody: Hendrickson Publishers.

Dumas A. (1971). *Dietrich Bonhoeffer: Theologian of Reality*. London: SCM Press.

Eagleton, T. (2004). *After Theory*. London: Penguin Books.

Eagleton, T. (2005). *Holy Terror*. Oxford: Oxford University Press.

Eagleton, T. (2008). *Trouble with Strangers: A Study of Ethics*. Oxford: Wiley-Blackwell.

Eagleton, T. (2009). *Reason, Faith, and Revolution: Reflections on the God Debate*. New Haven and London: Yale University Press.

Esposito, R. (2008). *Bios: Biopolitics and Philosophy*. Minneapolis: University of Minnesota Press.

Feil, E. (1991). *Die Theologie Dietrich Bonhoeffers: Hermeneutik, Christologie, Weltverständnis*. München: C. Kaiser.

Feldmann, C. (1998). *'Wir hätten schreien müssen': Das Leben des Dietrich Bonhoeffer*. Freiburg im Breisgau: Herder.

Feuerbach, L. (1989). *The Essence of Christianity*. Translated by G. Elliot. New York: Prometheus Books.

Fichte, J.G. (1956). *Grundlage der gesammten Wissenschaftslehre, 1974*. Hamburg: Meiner.

Fink, B. (1995). *The Lacanian Subject: Between Language and Jouissance*. Princeton: Princeton University Press.

Floyd, W.W. (1988). *Theology and Dialectics of Otherness: Bonhoeffer and Adorno*. Lanham: University Press of America.

Floyd, W.W. (1991). 'The Search for an Ethical Sacrament: From Bonhoeffer to Critical Social Theory', *Modern Theology*, 7(2), pp. 175–193.

Floyd, W.W. (2008). 'Kant, Hegel and Bonhoeffer', in Frick, P. (ed.) *Bonhoeffer's Intellectual Formation*. Tübingen: Mohr Siebeck, pp. 83–119.

Franz, M. (2013). 'Inside and Beyond the 'Bonhoeffer Archive'—Foucaultian Reflections on the Discourse of Bonhoeffer's Life in Theology', in Frick, P. (ed.) *Bonhoeffer and Interpretive Theory: Essays on Method and Understanding*. Frankfurt am Main: Peter Lang, pp. 27–51.

Freud, S. (1939). *Der Mann Moses und die monotheistische Religion*. Amsterdam: A. de Lange.

Freyer, H. (1923). *Theorie des objektiven Geistes*. Leipzig and Berlin: B.G. Teubner.

Frick, P. (ed.). (2008). *Bonhoeffer's Intellectual Formation*. Tübingen: Mohr Siebeck.

Frick, P. (ed.). (2013). *Bonhoeffer and Interpretive Theory: Essays on Method and Understanding*. Frankfurt am Main: Peter Lang.

Frick, P. (2017). *Understanding Bonhoeffer*. Tübingen: Mohr Siebeck.

Fromm, E. (1941). *Escape from Freedom*. New York: Farrar & Rinehart.

Goodchild, P. and Phelps H. (eds.). (2017). *Religion and European Philosophy: Key Thinkers from Kant to Žižek*. Oxford: Routledge.

Gray, J. (2012). 'The Violent Visions of Slavoj Žižek', *New York Review of Books*, 59(12). Available at http://www.nybooks.com/articles/archives/2012/jul/12/violent-visions-slavoj-zizek/. Accessed 20 September 2016.

Green, C.J. (1999). *Bonhoeffer: A Theology of Sociality*. Cambridge: Eerdmans.

Gregor, B. and Zimmermann, J. (eds.). (2009). *Bonhoeffer and Continental Thought*. Bloomington: Indiana University Press.

Grimshaw, M. (2019). 'Žižek and the Dwarf: A Short-Circuit Radical Theology', in Mitralexis, S. and Skliris, D. (eds.) *Slavoj Žižek and Christianity*. New York: Routledge, pp. 199–218.

Gutierrez, G. (1974). *A Theology of Liberation: History, Politics and Salvation*. Translated by I. Caridad and J. Eagleson. London: SCM Press.

Hamilton, W. (1962). 'A Secular Theology for a World Come of Age', *Theology Today*, 18, pp. 435–459.

Hamilton, W. (1966) *The New Essence of Christianity*. New York: Association Press.

Hamza, A. (2016). 'Going to One's Ground: Žižek's Dialectical Materialism', in Hamza, A. and Ruda, F. (eds.) *Slavoj Žižek and Dialectical Materialism*. New York: Palgrave Macmillan, pp. 163–175.

Hamza, A. and Ruda, F. (eds.). (2016). *Slavoj Žižek and Dialectical Materialism*. New York: Palgrave Macmillan.

Hardt, M. and Negri, A. (2000). *Empire*. Cambridge: Harvard University Press.

Hardt, M. and Negri, A. (2005). *Multitude: War and Democracy in the Age of Empire*. London: Hamish Hamilton.

Harris, M.M. (2011). 'The Meaning of Christ and the Meaning of Hegel: Slavoj Žižek and John Milbank's (A)symmetrical Response to Capitalist Nihilism', *Reviews in Cultural Theory*, 2(2), pp. 35–41.

Hart, W.D. (2002), 'Slavoj Žižek and the Imperial/Colonial Model of Religion', *Nepantla: Views from South*, 3(3), pp. 553–578.

Hegel, G.W.F. (1977a). *Faith and Knowledge*. Translated by W. Cerf and H.S. Harris. Albany: SUNY Press.

Hegel, G.W.F. (1977b). *Phenomenology of Spirit*. Translated by A.V. Miller. Oxford: Oxford University Press.

Hegel, G.W.F. (1983). *Hegel and the Human Spirit*. Translated by L. Rauch. Detroit: Wayne State University Press. Available at https://www.marxists.org/reference/archive/hegel/works/jl/ch01a.htm. Accessed 20 September 2016.

Hegel, G.W.F. (1991). *Elements of the Philosophy of Right*. Translated by H.B. Nisbet. Cambridge: Cambridge University Press.

Hegel, G.W.F. (1998). *Lectures on the Philosophy of World History*. Translated by H.B. Nisbet. Cambridge: Cambridge University Press.

Hegel, G.W.F. (2006). *Lectures on the Philosophy of Religion*. Translated by R.F. Brown, P.C. Hodgson, and J.M. Stewart. Oxford: Clarendon Press.

Hegel, G.W.F. (2010a). *The Science of Logic*. Translated by G. di Giovanni. Cambridge: Cambridge University Press.

Hegel, G.W.F. (2010b). *Encyclopedia of the Philosophical Sciences in Basic Outline*. Translated by K. Brinkmann and D.O. Dahlstrom. Cambridge: Cambridge University Press.

Heidegger, M. (1962). *Being and Time*. Translated by J. Macquarrie and E.S. Robinson. New York: Harper.

Hirsch, E. (1926). *Die idealistische Philosophie und das Christentum: Gesammelte Aufsätze*. Gütersloh: C. Bertelsmann.

Hobbes, T. (1949). *De Cive or The Citizen*. New York: Appleton-Century-Crofts.

Hobbes, T. (2002). *Leviathan*. Project Gutenberg [Online]. Available at https://www.gutenberg.org/ebooks/3207. Accessed 7 October 2016.

Holl, K. (1959). *The Cultural Significance of the Reformation*. New York: Meridian.

Holm, J. (2002). 'G.W.F. Hegel's Impact on Dietrich Bonhoeffer's Early Theology', *Studia Theologica*, 56(1), pp. 64–75.

Holsclaw, G. (2014). *Transcending Subjects: Augustine, Hegel, and Theology*. Chirchester: Wiley-Blackwell.

Horkheimer M. (2002). 'Traditional and Critical Theory', in *Critical Theory: Selected Essays*. Translated by W.J. Greenstreet. New York: Continuum, pp. 188–243.

Houlgate, S. (1991). *Freedom, Truth and History: An Introduction to Hegel's Philosophy*. London: Routledge.

Jones, G. (1990). *Bultmann: Towards Critical Theology*. Cambridge: Polity Press.

Jones, G. (1995). *Critical Theology: Questions of Truth and Method*. Cambridge: Polity Press.

Jüngel, E. (1972). *Unterwegs zur Sache: Theologische Bemerkungen*. München: Chr. Kaiser Verlag.

Jüngel, E. (1983). *God as the Mystery of the World*. Grand Rapids: Eerdmans.

Kaltenborn, C.J. (1973). *Adolf von Harnack als Lehrer Dietrich Bonhoeffers*. Berlin: Evangelische Verl. Anst.

Kaltenborn, C.J. (1981). 'Adolf von Harnack and Bonhoeffer', in Klassen, A.J. (ed.) *A Bonhoeffer Legacy: Essays in Understanding*. Grand Rapids: Eerdmans, pp. 48–57.

Kant, I. (1998). *The Critique of Pure Reason*. Translated by P. Guyer. Cambridge: Cambridge University Press.

Keller, C. (2005). *God and Power: Counter-Apocalyptic Journeys*. Minneapolis: Augsburg Fortress Press.

Kierkegaard, S. (1962). *Works of Love*. Translated by H.V. Hong and E.H. Hong. New York: Harper & Row.

Kierkegaard, S. (1968). *Concluding Unscientific Postscript*. Translated by D.F. Swenson and W. Lowrie. Princeton: Princeton University Press.

Kierkegaard, S. (1970). *Tagebücher. Band 4*. Düsseldorf and Köln: Diedrichs.

Kierkegaard, S. (1991). *Practice in Christianity*. Translated by H.V. Hong and E.H. Hong. Princeton: Princeton University Press.

Kierkegaard, S. (2005). *Fear and Trembling*. Translated by A. Hannay. London: Penguin Books.

Klassen, A.J. (ed.). (1981). *A Bonhoeffer Legacy: Essays in Understanding*. Grand Rapids: Eerdmans.

Kojève, A. (1969). *Introduction to the Reading of Hegel*. New York: Basic Books.

Koltaj, B. (2019). 'Critical Theology: Why Hegel Now?' *International Journal of Philosophy and Theology*, https://doi.org/10.1080/21692327.2019.1581654.

Kotsko, A. (2005). 'Objective Spirit and Continuity in the Theology of Dietrich Bonhoeffer', *Philosophy & Theology*, 17(1 & 2), pp. 17–31.

Kotsko, A. (2008). *Žižek and Theology*. London and New York: T&T Clark.

Kotsko, A. (2009). 'That They Might Have Ontology', *Political Theology*, 10(1), pp. 115–124.

Kristof, A. (1997). *The Notebook: The Proof—The Third Lie*. Translated by A Sheridan, D. Watson, and M. Romano. New York: Grove Press.

Lacan, J. (1991). *The Seminar of Jacques Lacan: Book II: The Ego in Freud's Theory and in the Technique of Psychoanalysis 1954–1955*. Translated by S.W.W. Tomaselli. New York: W.W. Norton.

Lacan, J. (1992). *The Seminar of Jacques Lacan Book VII: Ethics of Psychoanalysis*. Translated by D. Porter. New York: W.W. Norton.

Lacan, J. (1997). *The Seminar of Jacques Lacan: The Ethics of Psychoanalysis*. Translated by D. Porter. London: W.W. Norton.

Lacan, J. (1998). *The Seminar of Jacques Lacan: The Four Fundamental Concepts of Psychoanalysis*. Translated by A. Sheridan. London: W.W. Norton.

Lacan, J. (2000). *The Seminar of Jacques Lacan: On Feminine Sexuality, the Limits of Love and Knowledge*. Translated by B. Fink. London: W.W. Norton.

Lacan, J. (2006). 'The Function and Field of Speech in Language in Psychoanalysis', in *Écrits: The First Complete Edition in English*. Translated by B. and H. Fink. London: W.W. Norton, pp. 197–268.

Laclau, E. (2001). 'Hegemony: The Genealogy of a Concept', in Laclau, E. and Mouffe, C. *Hegemony and Socialist Strategy*. London and New York: Verso, pp. 7–46.

Laclau, E. and Mouffe, C. (2001). *Hegemony and Socialist Strategy*. London and New York: Verso.

Løland, O.J. (2018). *The Reception of Paul the Apostle in the Works of Slavoj Žižek*. New York: Palgrave Macmillan.

Macherey, P. (1978). *A Theory of Literary Production*. Translated by G. Wall. London: Routledge & Kegan Paul.

Mackintosh, H.R. (1937). *Types of Modern Theology: Schleiermacher to Barth*. London: Nisbet & Co Ltd.

Marcuse, H. (1955). *Reason and Revolution: Hegel and the Rise of Social Theory*. London: Routledge & Kegan Paul.

Marion, J-.L. (1991). *God Without Being*. Translated by T.A. Carlson. Chicago: University of Chicago Press.

Marsh, C. (1992). 'Human Community and Divine Presence: Dietrich Bonhoeffer's Critique of Hegel', *Scottish Journal of Theology*, 45(4), pp. 427–428.

Marsh, C. (1994). *Reclaiming Dietrich Bonhoeffer: The Promise of His Theology*. New York and Oxford: Oxford University Press.

Mawson, M. (2018). *Christ Existing as Community: Bonhoeffer's Ecclesiology*. Oxford: Oxford University Press.

McGowan, T. (2016). 'The Necessity of an Absolute Misunderstanding', in Hamza, A. and Ruda, F. (eds.) *Slavoj Žižek and Dialectical Materialism*. New York: Palgrave Macmillan, pp. 43–56.

Melville, H. (2009). *Bartleby the Scrivener: A Story of Wall Street*. New York: Melville House Publishing.

Milbank, J. (2005). 'Materialism and Transcendence', in Davis, C., Milbank, J., and Žižek, S. (eds.) *Theology and the Political: The New Debate*. Durham: Duke University Press, pp. 393–428.

Milbank, J., Pickstock, C., and Ward, G. (eds.). (1999). *Radical Orthodoxy: A New Theology*. New York: Routledge.

Mitralexis, S. and Skliris, D. (eds.). (2019). *Slavoj Žižek and Christianity*. New York: Routledge.

Mitralexis, S. and Skliris, D. (2019). 'The Slovenian and the Cross: Transcending Christianity's Perverse Core with Slavoj Žižek', in Mitralexis, S. and Skliris, D. (eds.) *Slavoj Žižek and Christianity*. New York: Routledge, pp. 1–45.

Moltmann, J. (1967). *Theology of Hope*. Translated by J.W. Leitch. New York and Evanston: Harper & Row.

Moltmann, J. (1974). *The Crucified God*. Translated by R.A. Wilson and J. Bowden. New York: Harper & Row.

Moltmann, J. (1981). *The Trinity and the Kingdom: The Doctrine of God*. New York: Harper & Row.

Moltmann, J. (1984). 'The crucified God', *Theology Today*, 31(1), pp. 6–12.

Myers, T. (2003). *Slavoj Žižek*. London: Routledge.

Nietzsche, F. (1964). *Morgenröte, Gedanken über die moralischen Vorurteile*. Stuttgart: Kröner.

Nowers, J. (2013). 'Hegel, Bonhoeffer and Objective Geist: An Architectonic Exegesis', in Clar, A.C. and Mawson, M. (eds.) *Ontology and Ethics: Bonhoeffer and Contemporary Scholarship*. Eugene: Pickwick Publications.

Occupy London. (2011). 'Help Us Draft the Global Statement for the Occupy Movement', *The Guardian*, 15 November. Available at http://www.guardian.co.uk/commentisfree/2011/nov/15/draft-statement-occupy-london. Accessed 20 September 2016.

O'Neill, J.C. (1970). 'Bultmann and Hegel', *The Journal of Theological Studies*, 21(2), pp. 388–400.

Onfray, M. (2007). *Atheist Manifesto: The Case Against Christianity, Judaism and Islam*. New York: Arcade Publishing.

Ott, H. (1972). *Reality and Faith: The Theological legacy of Dietrich Bonhoeffer*. Translated by A.A. Morrison. Philadelphia: Fortress Press.

Padusniak, C. (2019). '"No Wonder, Then, That Love Itself Disappears': Neighbour Love in Žižek and Meister Eckhart', in Mitralexis, S. and Skliris, D. (eds.) *Slavoj Žižek and Christianity*. New York: Routledge, pp. 86–103.

Pangritz, A. (2000). *Karl Barth in the Theology of Dietrich Bonhoeffer*. Grand Rapids: Eerdmans.

Pangritz, A. (2008). 'Dietrich Bonhoeffer: "Within, Not Outside, the Barthian Movement"', in Frick, P. (ed.) *Bonhoeffer's Intellectual Formation: Theology and Philosophy in His Thought*. Tübingen: Mohr Siebeck, pp. 245–282.

Pannenberg, W. (ed.). (1963). *Offenbarung als Geschichte*. Göttingen: Vandenhoeck und Ruprecht. English: (1968) *Revelation as History*. Translated by E. Quinn. New York: Macmillan.

Pappas, J.L. (2019). 'Rethinking Universality: Badiou and Žižek on Pauline Theology', in Mitralexis, S. and Skliris, D. (eds.) *Slavoj Žižek and Christianity*. New York: Routledge, pp. 154–166.

Pfeifer, G. (2016). *The New Materialism: Althusser, Badiou and Žižek*. New York: Routledge.

Phillips, J.A. (1967). *Christ for Us in the Theology of Dietrich Bonhoeffer*. New York: Harper & Row.

Plant, S. (2004). *Bonhoeffer*. London and New York: Continuum.

Pound, M. (2008). *Žižek: A (Very) Critical Introduction*. Grand Rapids and Cambridge: Eerdmans.

Pound, M. (2017). 'Slavoj Žižek (1949–)', in Goodchild P. and Phelps H. (eds.) *Religion and European Philosophy: Key Thinkers from Kant to Žižek* (Oxford: Routledge), pp. 479–491.

Prenter, R. (1967). 'Dietrich Bonhoeffer and Karl Barth's Positivism of Revelation', in Smith, R.G. (ed.) *World Come of Age*. London: Collins, pp. 93–130.

Pugh, J.C. (2008). *Religionless Christianity: Dietrich Bonhoeffer in Troubled Times*. London: T&T Clark.

Rahner, K. (1970). *The Trinity*. Translated by J. Donceel. New York: Herder and Herder.

Rahner, K. (1976). *Grundkurs des Glaubens: Einführung in den Begriff des Christentums*. Freiburg: Herder.

Rasch, W. (2004). *Sovereignty and Its Discontents: On the Pimacy of Conflict and the Structure of the Political*. London: Birkbeck Law Press, 2004.

Raschke, C. (2014). 'The New Hegelian Moment—Why Postmodernism Needs to Retrace Its Own Radically Real, Rational, and (Of Course) Rhizomic Roots', *The Other Journal*, May 23. https://theotherjournal.com/2014/05/23/the-new-hegelian-moment-why-postmodernism-needs-to-retrace-its-own-radically-real-rational-and-of-course-rhizomic-roots/.

Raschke, C. (2015). *Force of God: Political Theology and the Crisis of Liberal Democracy*. New York: Columbia University Press.

Raschke, C. (2016). *Critical Theology: Introducing an Agenda for an Age of Global Crisis*. Downers Grove: IVP Academic.

Rasmussen, L. (1972). *Dietrich Bonhoeffer: Reality and Resistance*. Nashville: Abingdon Press.

Ritschl, A. (1882). *Die Christliche Lehre von der Rechtfertigung und Versöhnung: Vol. 1*. Bonn: A. Marcus.

Robbins, J.W. (2003). *Between Faith and Thought: An Essay on the Ontotheological Condition*. Charlottesville: University of Virginia Press.

Robbins, J.W. (2016). *Radical Theology: A Vision for Change*. Bloomington: Indiana University Press.

Robinson, D.S. (2018). *Christ and Revelatory Community in Bonhoeffer's Reception of Hegel*. Tübingen: Mohr Siebeck.

Roberts, R.H. (2005). 'Theology and Social Sciences', in Ford, D.F. and Muers, R. (eds.) *The Modern Theologians*. Oxford: Blackwell, pp. 375–377.

Rose, G. (1981). *Hegel Contra Sociology*. London: Athlone Press.

Rumscheidt, M. (ed.). (1988). *Adolf von Harnack: Liberal Theology at Its Height*. London: Collins.

Rumscheidt, M. (1999). 'The Formation of Bonhoeffer's Theology', in de Gruchy. J.W. (ed.) *The Cambridge Companion to Dietrich Bonhoeffer*. Cambridge: Cambridge University Press, pp. 50–70.

Safatle, V. (2016). 'Politics of Negativity in Slavoj Žižek: Actualizing Some Hegelian Themes', in Hamza, A. and Ruda, F. (eds.) *Slavoj Žižek and Dialectical Materialism*. New York: Palgrave Macmillan, pp. 69–84.

Samuels, R. (1997). *Between Philosophy and Psychoanalysis*. New York: Routledge.

Scheler, M. (author), Frings, M.S. (ed.). (2005a). *Gesammelte Werke II: Der Formalismus in der Ethik und die materiale Wertethik: Neuer Versuch der Grundlegung eines ethischen Personalismus*. Bern: Francke Verlag.

Scheler, M. (author), Frings, M.S. (ed.). (2005b). *Gesammelte Werke VII: Wesen und Formen der Sympathie – Die deutsche Philosophie der Gegenwart*. Bern: Francke Verlag.

Schelling, F.W.J. (1946). *Die Weltalter: Fragmente in den Urfassungen von 1811 und 1813*. München: Biederstein & Leibniz.

Schelling, F.W.J. (1994). *On the History of Modern Philosophy*. Translated by A. Bowie. Cambridge: Cambridge University Press.

Schneider, N. (2010). 'Orthodox Paradox: An Interview with John Milbank', *The Immanent Frame*, 17 March. Available at http://blogs.ssrc.org/tif/2010/03/17/orthodox-paradox-an-interview-with-john-milbank/. Accessed 20 September 2016.

Seeberg, R. (1908). *The Fundamental Truths of the Christian Religion*. Translated by G.E. Thompson and C. Wallentin. London: Williams & Norgate.

Seeberg, R. (1927a). *Die Christliche Dogmatik: Band 1*. Erlangen: Deichert.

Seeberg, R. (1927b). *Die Christliche Dogmatik: Band 2*. Erlangen: Deichert.

Seeberg, R. (1953). *Lehrbuch der Dogmengeschichte*. Darmstadt: Wissenschaftliche Buchgesellschaft.

Sharp, G. (2011). 'Q&A: Gene Sharp', *Al Jazeera*, 6 December. Available at http://www.aljazeera.com/indepth/opinion/2011/12/201112113179492201.html. Accessed 20 September 2016.

Sharpe, M. (2004). *Slavoj Žižek: A Little Piece of the Real*. Aldershot: Ashgate.

Sharpe, M. and Boucher, G. (2010). *Žižek and Politics: A Critical Introduction*. Edinburgh: Edinburgh University Press.

Sigurdson, O. (2010). 'Beyond Secularism? Towards a Postsecular Political Theology', *Modern Theology*, 26(2), pp. 177–196.

Sigurdson, O. (2012). *Theology and Marxism in Eagleton and Žižek: A Conspiracy of Hope*. New York: Palgrave Macmillan.

Sigurdson, O. (2013). 'Slavoj Žižek, the Death of God, and Zombies: A Theological Account', *Modern Theology*, 29(3), pp. 361–380.

Singer, P. (1983). *Hegel*. Oxford and New York: Oxford University Press.

Staats, R. (1981). 'Adolf von Harnack im Leben Dietrich Bonhoeffers', *Theologische Zeitschrift*, 37, pp. 94–122.

Stavrakakis, Y. (1999). *Lacan and the Political*. London: Routledge.

Strauss, D.F. (1864). *Das Leben Jesu*. Leipzig: F.A. Brockhaus.

Taubes, J. (1993). *Die politische Theologie des Paulus: Vorträge, gehalten an der Forschungsstätte der evangelischen Studiengemeinschaft in Heidelberg, 23–27. February 1987*. München: Wilhelm Fink.

Taylor, K-Y. (2016). *From #BlackLivesMatter to Black Liberation*. Chicago: Haymarket Books.

Taylor, M.C. (1984). *Erring: A Postmodern A/theology*. Chicago: University of Chicago Press.

Taylor, M.C. (1987). *Altarity*. Chicago: University of Chicago Press.

Taylor, M.C. (2000). *Journeys to Selfhood*. New York: Fordham University Press.

The Pervert's Guide to Cinema. (2006). Directed by S. Fiennes [DVD]. Charlottesville and Wien: Amoeba Films and Mischief Films.

The Pervert's Guide to Ideology. (2013). Directed by S. Fiennes [DVD]. New York: Zeitgeist Films.

Tödt, I. (ed.). (1988). *Dietrich Bonhoeffers Hegel-Seminar 1933: Nach den Aufzeichnungen von Ferenc Lehel*. München: Chr. Kaiser.

Troeltsch, E. (1911). *Die Bedeutung der Geschichtlichkeit Jesus für den Glauben*. Tübingen: J.C.B. Mohr.

Troeltsch, E. (1912). *Protestantism and Progress: A Historical Study of the Relation of Protestantism to the Modern World*. Translated by W. Montgomery. London: Williams & Norgate.

Troeltsch, E. (1923). *Die Soziallehren der christlichen Kirchen und Gruppen*. Tübingen: J.C.B. Mohr.

Tupinamba, G. (2019). 'Concrete Universality: Only That Which Is Non-All Is for All', in Mitralexis, S. and Skliris, D. (eds.) *Slavoj Žižek and Christianity*. New York: Routledge, pp. 104–116.

Vattimo, G. (2002). *After Christianity*. Translated by L. D'Isanto. New York: Columbia University Press.

Ventis, H. (2019). 'Pacifist Pluralism Versus Militant Truth: Christianity at the Service of Revolution in the Work of Slavoj Žižek', in Mitralexis, S. and Skliris, D. (eds.) *Slavoj Žižek and Christianity*. New York: Routledge, pp. 117–153.

von Harnack, A. (1890). *Lehrbuch der Dogmengeschichte*. Freiburg: J.C.B. Mohr.

von Harnack, A. (1900). *Geschichte der Königlich Preussischen Akademie der Wissenschaften zu Berlin*. Berlin: Reichsdruckerei.

von Harnack, A. (1902). *What Is Christianity*. Translated by T.B. Saunders. London: Williams & Norgate.

von Harnack, A. (1906a). *Reden und Aufsätze: Band 1*. Giessen: Alfred Töpelmann.

von Harnack, A. (1906b). *Reden und Aufsätze: Band 2*. Giessen: Alfred Töpelmann.

von Harnack, A. (1906c). *Reden und Aufsätze: Band 3*. Giessen: Alfred Töpelmann.

von Zahn-Harnack, A. (1951). *Adolf von Harnack*. Berlin: W. de Gruyter.

Ward, G. (1995). *Barth, Derrida and the Language of Theology*. Cambridge: Cambridge University Press.

Ward, G. (1997). (ed). *The Postmodern God: A Theological Reader*. Oxford: Blackwell.

Ward, G. (2000a). *Cities of God*. New York: Routledge.

Ward, G. (2000b). *Theology and the Contemporary Critical Theory*. London: Macmillan.

Ward, G. (2005). *Christ and Culture*. Malden: Blackwell.

Ward, G. (2013). 'How Hegel Became a Philosopher: Logos and the Economy of Logic', *Critical Research on Religion*, 1(3), pp. 270–292.

Ward, G. (2016). *How the Light Gets in: Ethical Life 1*. Oxford: Oxford University Press.

Warlick, I. (2012). 'Postsecularity, Hegel and Friendship: An Interview with Graham Ward', *Radical Orthodoxy: Theology, Philosophy, Politics*, 1(1 & 2), pp. 333–348.

Wright, E. and Wright, E. (eds.). (1999). *The Žižek Reader*. Oxford: Blackwell.

Wüstenberg, R. (1998) *Theology of Life: Dietrich Bonhoeffer's Religionless Christianity*. Translated by D. Stott. Grand Rapids: Eerdmans.

Yerkes, J. (1978). *The Christology of Hegel*. Albany: SUNY Press.

Žižek! (2005). Directed by A. Taylor [DVD]. New York: Zeitgeist Films.

Žižek, S. (1972). *Bolečina razlike*. Maribor: Obzorja.

Žižek, S. (1976). *Znak, Označitelj, Pismo*. Beograd: Mladost.

Žižek, S. (1982). *Zgodovina in Nezavedno*. Ljubljana: Cankarjeva Založba.

Žižek, S. (1984). *Birokratija I Uživanje*. Beograd: Studentski Izdavački Centar.

Žižek, S. (1989). *The Sublime Object of Ideology*. London: Verso.

Žižek, S. (1991a). *For They Know Not What They Do: Enjoyment as a Political Factor*. London: Verso.

Žižek, S. (1991b). *Looking Awry: An Introduction to Jacques Lacan Through Popular Culture*. Cambridge: The MIT Press.

Žižek, S. (1992). *Enjoy Your Symptom! Jacques Lacan in Hollywood and Out*. New York and London: Routledge.

Žižek, S. (1993). *Tarrying with the Negative: Kant, Hegel and the Critique of Ideology*. Durham: Duke University Press.

Žižek, S. (1994). *The Metastases of Enjoyment: Six Essays on Women and Causality*. London: Verso.

Žižek, S. (ed.). (1995). *Mapping Ideology*. London and New York: Verso.

Žižek, S. (1996). *The Indivisible Remainder: An Essay on Schelling and Related Matters*. London: Verso.

Žižek, S. (1997). *The Plague of Fantasies*. London and New York: Verso.

Žižek, S. (1999a). *The Ticklish Subject: The Absent Centre of Political Ontology*. London: Verso.

Žižek, S. (1999b). *Human Rights and Its Discontents*. [Lecture delivered at Bard College]. 15 November. Available at http://www.lacan.com/zizek-human.htm. Accessed 20 September 2016.

Žižek, S. (2000a). *The Art of the Ridiculous Sublime: On David Lynch's Lost High-way*. Seattle: The Walter Chapin Simpson Centre for the Humanities, University of Washington Press.

Žižek, S. (2000b). *The Fragile Absolute: Or, Why Is the Christian Legacy Worth Fighting for?* London and New York: Verso.

Žižek, S. (2001a). *The Fright of Real Tears: Krzysztof Kieslowski Between Theory and Post-theory*. Bloomington: Indiana University Press.

Žižek, S. (2001b). *On Belief*. London: Routledge.

Žižek, S. (2001c). 'The Rhetorics of Power', *Diacritics*, 31(1), pp. 91–104.

Žižek, S. (2001d). *Did Somebody Say Totalitarianism? Five Interventions in the (Mis)use of a Notion*. London and New York: Verso.

Žižek, S. (2002a). *Welcome to the Desert of the Real! Five Essays on September 11 and Related Dates*. London: Verso.

Žižek, S. (2002b). *Revolution at the Gates: Selected Writings of Lenin from 1917*. London and New York: Verso.

Žižek, S. (2002c). 'I Plead Guilty—But Where Is the Judgment?', *Nepantla: Views from South*, 3(3), pp. 579–583.

Žižek, S. (2003). *The Puppet and the Dwarf: The Perverse Core of Christianity*. London: The MIT Press.

Žižek, S. (2006a). *How to Read Lacan*. New York and London: W.W. Norton.

Žižek, S. (2006b). *The Parallax View*. London: The MIT Press.

Žižek, S. (2007). *In Defence of Lost Causes*. London: Verso.

Žižek, S. (2008a). 'Between Fear and Trembling: On Why Only Atheists Can Believe,' 8 November, mp3 file, 2:11:58, Stevenson Centre Lecture Hall, Vanderbilt University. Available at http://discoverarchive.vanderbilt.edu/handle/1803/501. Accessed 20 September 2016.

Žižek, S. (2008b). *On Violence*. London: Picador.

Žižek, S. (2009a). 'From Job to Christ: A Paulinian Reading of Chesterton', in Caputo, J.D. and Alcoff, L.M. (eds.) *Paul Among the Philosophers*. Bloomington: Indiana University Press, pp. 39–58.

Žižek, S. (2009b). *First as Tragedy, Then as Far as Farce*. London and New York: Verso.

Žižek, S. (2010a). 'A Meditation on Michelangelo's Christ on the Cross', in Davis, C., Milbank, J., and Žižek, S. (eds.) *Paul's New Moment: Continental Philosophy and the Future of Christian Theology*. Grand Rapids: Brazos Press, pp. 176–179.

Žižek, S. (2010b). 'Paul and the Truth Event', in Davis, C., Milbank, J., and Žižek, S. (eds.) *Paul's New Moment: Continental Philosophy and the Future of Christian Theology*. Grand Rapids: Brazos Press, pp. 92–99.

Žižek, S. (2010c). *Living in the End Times*. London: Verso.

Žižek, S. (2011). *The Parallax*. Available at http://www.youtube.com/watch?v=vdwF3j1F2pg. Accessed 20 September 2016.

Žižek, S. (2010d). 'How to Begin From the Beginning', in Žižek, S. and Douzinas, C. (eds.) *The Idea of Communism: Vol. 1*. London: Verso, pp. 209–226.

Žižek, S. (2012a). *Less Than Nothing: Hegel and the Shadow of Dialectical Materialism*. London: Verso.

Žižek, S. (2012b). *The Year of Dreaming Dangerously*. New York and London: Verso.

Žižek, S. (2012c). *The Heart of the People of Europe Beats in Greece*. Available at http://www.youtube.com/watch?v=SWtn7iECkyY. Accessed 20 September 2016.

Žižek, S. (2013a). 'Neighbours and Other Monsters: A Plea For Ethical Violence', in Žižek, S., Santner, E., and Reinhardt, K. (eds.) *The Neighbour: Three Inquiries in Political Theology*. Chicago: The University of Chicago Press, pp. 134–190.

Žižek, S. (2013b). 'The Necessity of a Dead Bird', in Blanton, W. and de Vries, H. (eds.) *Paul and the Philosophers*. New York: Fordham University Press, pp. 175–185.

Žižek, S. (2014). *Absolute Recoil: Towards a New Foundation of Dialectical Materialism*. London: Verso.

Žižek, S. (2016). *Against the Double Blackmail: Refugees, Terror and Other Troubles with the Neighbours*. London: Allen Lane.

Žižek, S. (2018). 'Marx Reads Object-Oriented Ontology', in Žižek, S., Ruda, F., and Hamza, A. *Reading Marx*. Cambridge: Polity Press, pp. 17–61.

Žižek, S. (2019). 'Afterword: the Antinomies That Keep Christianity Alive', in Mitralexis, S. and Skliris, D. (eds.) *Slavoj Žižek and Christianity*. New York: Routledge, pp. 219–227.

Žižek, S. (n.d.) 'Repeating Lenin'. Available at http://www.lacan.com/replenin.htm. Accessed 20 September 2014.

Žižek, S. and Daly, G. (2004). *Conversations with Žižek*. Cambridge: Polity Press.

Žižek, S. and Douzinas, C. (eds.). (2010). *The Idea of Communism: Vol. 1*. London: Verso.

Žižek, S. and Dupuy, J-P. (2014). *Žižek and Dupuy: Religion, Secularism, and Political Belonging*. Available at https://www.youtube.com/watch?v=NEEBYNNpX9o. Accessed 20 September 2016.

Žižek, S. and Gunjević, B. (2012). *God in Pain: Inversions of Apocalypse*. New York: Seven Stories Press.

Žižek, S. and Milbank, J. (2009). *The Monstrosity of Christ: Paradox or Dialectic?* London: The MIT Press.

Žižek, S., Ruda, F., and Hamza, A. (2018). *Reading Marx*. Cambridge: Polity Press.

Žižek, S., Santner, E., and Reinhardt, K. (2013). *The Neighbour: Three Inquiries in Political Theology*. Chicago: The University of Chicago Press.

Žižek, S. and Schelling, F.W.J. (1997). *The Abyss of Freedom—Ages of the World*. Ann Arbor: University of Michigan Press.

INDEX

Printed by Printforce, the Netherlands